STUDIES IN TUDOR HISTORY

STUDIES IN
TUDOR HISTORY

BY

W. P. M. KENNEDY

KENNIKAT PRESS
Port Washington, N. Y./London

STUDIES IN TUDOR HISTORY

First published in 1916
Reissued in 1971 by Kennikat Press
Library of Congress Catalog Card No: 73-118480
ISBN 0-8046-1229-3

Manufactured by Taylor Publishing Company   Dallas, Texas

TO

A. F. POLLARD

Professor of English History in the University of London

AS A TOKEN OF FRIENDSHIP AND

REGARD

PREFACE

My object in publishing this collection of studies in Tudor history is to present to the general student and reader some material connected with subjects which must be treated very briefly in the general histories of the period. The specialist will find little new in this volume, but I venture to hope that those for whom it is written will get a better insight into some of the complicated aims and intricate problems of sixteenth-century life. There is a general unity in the studies, which I may call the ideal of Tudor government. This ideal can be traced through the entire age, and it will serve to connect the studies.

In many cases I have ventured to differ from other writers on sixteenth-century history, and even from my own previous work. In all cases, however, I have conscientiously re-worked the materials, and my conclusions have been arrived at independently, as an outcome of this re-working. In addition, I have done my utmost to lift the book out of the atmosphere of controversy which has unfortunately gathered round Tudor history. I know, from experience, how difficult it is to do this, and I am conscious that I have at times failed in my ideal. But I would ask my critics and readers to accept my intentions in good faith, and to believe that I have approached the various subjects with no desire to prove any case, or to bolster up any controversial position.

The materials on which I have worked will be quite evident to the student, and I have not thought it necessary to burden such a book as this with footnotes or lists of authorities. The general reader must accept in good faith my statements of facts, and I have done my utmost, while writing far from the larger libraries and collections of originals, to see that the references, etc., in my notebooks on the period are as accurate as possible. I have, of course, used the writings of almost every previous historian, and I have also incorporated some of my previous work on various subjects; but in no case have I deliberately stated a position at which I have not myself arrived.

It would be impossible for me to acknowledge in detail all my obligations. I would, however, record my thanks to the keepers of the various collections of manuscripts and to the authorities at the various libraries for all their courtesy and kindness to me. My special gratitude must be given to Professor Pollard and Dr. Walter Frere. Professor Pollard has kindly added to his friendship by accepting the dedication of the book, and I cannot let it go to press without stating that I am indebted to him in almost every chapter. I would specially thank him for permission to use his analysis of the reign of Henry VII., and for his generous and friendly advice. To Dr. Walter Frere I owe the sincerest thanks. I began the intimate study of the Edwardine and Elizabethan literature, referred to in this volume, with his elaborate chronological manuscript catalogue of it in my hand, and if I have succeeded at all in acquiring a contemporary outlook on Tudor history, it is due to the ideals which he laid before me many years ago. I would ask him, then, to accept my sincerest thanks for kindnesses which survive in spite of changes. Finally, I would thank my colleague, Professor H. Carr, for his encouragement as the book was written.

St. Michael's College,
   Toronto,
      May 7, 1915.

CONTENTS

STUDIES IN TUDOR HISTORY

I

THE POLICY OF HENRY VII.

THE reign of Henry VII. has suffered at the hands of historians and students of English history. It has either been overlooked as of little moment, or phases of it—such as the rebellions—have received consideration out of all proportion to their importance. There are several reasons for all this. The materials for the history, though by no means small, do not present such a wide or rich field for research as those generally connected with Tudor reigns, and the intimate student of the century has been drawn aside to the abundant harvest of research elsewhere. In addition, Henry VII.'s reign lies between two periods with a more fascinating history—the Wars of the Roses and the break with Rome. It is filled with little romance, little national excitement, and is apparently dull and drab compared with the years which preceded and followed it. There is no insane but kaleidoscopic civil war. There is no exciting game in politics and religion.   There are no big men and no big methods.   It is a back-water of national life when placed beside the fluctuating hopes of York and Lancaster or the pregnant policies of Henry VIII., Wolsey, and Thomas Cromwell.   It stands between two worlds.   It is a period of transition and national uncertainty, and such periods do not usually attract as much attention as those in which home and foreign politics, and commercial and industrial progress are secure and prominent.   But for all that, it is a reign of extreme importance. Beneath its somewhat dull and commonplace life, movements were going on of real value. Behind its prosaic monotony there lay great purposes and persevering aims, which left a permanent mark on Tudor life.   In addition, perhaps no English Sovereign succeeded as well as Henry VII. in carrying out the policy emphatically necessary for England at the moment. He grasped the national needs, and his reign became the successful reply to them.   From this point of view, then, his rule and statecraft deserve more than a record of his descent, of his struggle for the crown, of the revolts, of his parsimony, or of his grim humour.   They take their place—and it is one of no mean importance —among the records of real statesmanship, which sees not only the present but the past and the future.   Henry VII., as King, was neither national hero nor brilliant conqueror, but he was something far more valuable, when the

national circumstances are considered—he was
a wise, practical, and successful statesman.

Before considering him in this connection, we
must take a broad survey of the age and of
England's needs, and then consider the man himself as he entered on his work.   This general
survey will serve to gather up the contemporary
conditions, the new movements, the national
changes, and the difficult problems which needed
immediate solution.   An estimate of Henry's
character, as he ascended the throne, will place
him in relationship to all these, and bring to the
front the qualities with which he was going to
meet his task.   There lay before him not merely
a country which his sword had given him, and
requiring only careful dealings after a civil war,
but a country breaking away from many of the
old national traditions and quite inexperienced
in the new conditions which must inevitably
touch it, if it were to remain a nation.   It was
a difficult and doubtful outlook, and it required
a statesman, not a politician or a soldier.

Bosworth Field, from one point of view, was
the death-blow to many of the mediæval ideals.
The feudal system for better or worse was broken,
and with it must disappear those theories of
communal life, which placed the village, town,
estate or realm above the mere caprice or whim
of the individual.   From the moment that life
in England became consciously national down to
the end of the fifteenth century, there is evident,
in civil and religious life, a clearly defined prin-

ciple at work—the good of the corporate body, rising up in varied grades to the throne. It is true that it is not a uniformly harmonious prin-ciple, but on it everyone, in spite of fluctuations and modifications, based his life and actions. The Church lent her undisputed authority to emphasize and inculcate the ideal. It was an inherent part of the national life. It was an unconscious, not a reasoned position. We may state it in crude form : before the sixteenth century it was considered that the nation reaped greater advantages as a whole from a restraint of individualism than from allowing the individual free scope. This ideal permeated every detail of national life, from the Church down to the petty details of dress and hunting. And it must be remembered this ideal was no mere tyrannical imposition of Kings or nobles—it was part and parcel of the people's corporate mind, which as often as not brought rulers into line with it. This conception was rudely shaken in the Wars of the Roses, which thinned the ranks of the nobility, who to an almost inconceivable extent had accepted the responsibilities which the theory imposed on them. They recognized their obliga-tions far more than most of us are usually prepared to allow ; and as yet the fascination of money-making had not come to build up such a barrier between classes as to obscure moral obligations. Almost suddenly all this changed. When a New World awoke ambitions and aroused the spirit of adventure, when the com-

mercial outlook became wider and more alluring,
it suddenly dawned on the nation that money
was the great means for advancement, and money
soon became an end in itself.   It was not hard,
when the mediæval ideal had been completely
broken in the Civil War, to argue that the old
outlets for wealth were too numerous and unpractical, when the nation was called to take
her place in a competitive age.   In addition,
such excuses were in many respects easily
justified.   There had settled down on the
Western World a spirit of religious indifference
not unlike that in our own time.   The Church
had failed in the administration of her wealth,
and it soon became evident that men would
argue that money was better employed as capital
for new adventures, while they would view with
disapproval bodies within the Church which held
land or were the recipients of bequests which by
the very nature of the case could not benefit the
community by passing through individual hands
in speculation.   Henry VII.'s reign stands at
the beginning of the period which saw the
national ideals, as revered in the Middle Ages,
abandoned for what we may broadly call individualism.   This new spirit, then, must not be
forgotten.   A nation was beginning to burn its
boats.   There was restlessness abroad, and men
were waiting in a transition period.   The old
had gone, which—in theory at least, and to a
large degree in practice—had made responsibility
its keynote ; the new was unformed, undefined, un-

tried. In addition, the Renaissance emphasized the disappearance of this mediæval ideal. The old learning was in its last throes. It had been concerned with the best that was possible for mankind as a body, and had paid little or no attention to form for the sake of form alone. Now the call of the Renaissance was a call to form, and therefore a call to the individual— *le style c'est l'homme.* Thought is common to a school, style is peculiar to the individual. The Renaissance message was rather a call to perfection in the vehicle of thought, and literature passed slowly but surely from the broad, communal outlook to the personal. This rise of individualism is common to the age, and it necessarily presented problems, because it created a new national outlook. In addition, there were other problems presented to Henry from the condition of England owing to the Civil Wars. The country was entirely out of hand, and social evils were rampant. Murder and sudden death followed battle. Administration had broken down in the atmosphere of factious and rival dynasties. There was no security in any sphere of national life. What the nation needed was not more laws or more government. It needed justice and peace. It needed continuity of rule and of organization. The new individualism had run wild. On every side men wanted to carry out their own ideas, to have their own way. The question to be settled by Henry VII. was whether he could control indi-

viduals and restrain personal ends—whether he
could discipline the strong individualism of the
age in the interests of the State.   This in reality
was the great problem which he had to face.
His holding of the throne was purely a personal
matter, and depended on himself.   His future
marriage to Elizabeth of York, while it was
essential to his sovereignty, was merely a part
of his personal policy in this connection, and it
reduced the possibilities of a civil war to a
minimum.   Henry had to try to create a communal will to which individuals must bow down.
Not only must law and order be kept, but such
a nationality created as would fit England to
take her place among the new nations.   If he
did not succeed in this undertaking, England
could not take share in the new age, in which
consolidation was to be the feature, however
strong she might be in individuals.   When
France, Spain, Sweden, and even the Empire,
were coming under this new influence, Henry
could not afford to be a weak-willed King or a
mere figure-head if England was to remain even
independent.   Much of this consolidation
depended on himself.   Could he make his people
loyal to the throne?   If he could, half the battle
would be won, for there still remained in the
mind of Europe a wonderful complicated ideal
of the royal-man as worked out by the Church
and elaborated in intricate detail by the
mediæval lawyers.   Loyalty to the throne would
create a respect for law, and respect for law

would subordinate excessive individualism to the common good of the State. Of course, this loyalty could reach absurd and destructive positions. Many wept over Richard II. and canonized Henry VI. But in principle it would, if secured, almost solve the gravest of his difficulties.

Henry Tudor had been prepared for his hazardous and ambiguous kingship in an excellent school. His boyhood was surrounded by complications owing to his mother's descent from John of Gaunt. At one time he was a semi-prisoner, at another he was in London and presented to Henry VI., whose death with that of his son made him the representative of the House of Lancaster. Years of exile followed, during which he was pursued by the jealousy of Edward IV. The disappearance of the Princes in the Tower further complicated his life. He became more than ever the centre of Lancastrian hopes, and of course the natural leader against Richard III., who did his utmost to make his residence in any country abroad impossible. The issue lay indeed between him and Richard. It was hardly a national question. The world could not hold both men, and while Richard reigned Henry would have no likelihood of personal safety. Sooner or later, unless Henry preferred death in another way, he was bound to risk his life in battle against Richard. Stanley decided Bosworth Field in Henry's favour, and the decision of one man gave him his life and his

throne.   Henry was twenty-eight years of age
at the moment, and he could look back on an
excellent schooling for the work which lay ahead.
He had been brought up amid plots and counter-
plots.   He had had adventures by sea and by
land, and had learned caution and wary foresight.   He had lived among outlaws and exiles,
and among them he had acquired the balance of
character which comes from alternating hopes
and fears.   He had seen much of political
jealousies, of fickle characters, and of ambitious
schemes, and had thus acquired a shrewd insight
into the vagaries of men and their ways.   He
was not the man to give his confidence lightly or
to trust others with any grave concern.   He had
seen too much of the motives which changed
friends into foes to depend implicitly on anyone.
His keen mind had been developed in a world of
insecurity, and he had added to it, through
experience, self - control, patience, tact, and
shrewdness—the very qualities which England
needed at the moment, and they characterize
almost uniformly his rule.

Parliament confirmed the decision of battle,
and we are thus saved the unnecessary and
laborious task of considering Henry's claim to
the throne, which is a fit subject only for school-
books.   Nor need we delay over the threadbare
problem as to which parts of England were
Lancastrian or Yorkist.   It is enough to know
that where mediæval ideals lingered there were
possibilities of revolt, and where commerce and

trade were developing the possibilities were small. It seems to me that it has been an entire mistake to class the revolts against Henry as those of a party. They were revolts which foreign enemies and difficulties in home government fostered. Behind each one of them lie taxation, discontent, and European jealousies. From the beginning Henry had a national policy of progressive consolidation, and this required money. It was fortunate for him that old ideas had died out so widely, as he could never have held his throne had the nation as a whole been as feudal as those parts which lent aid to Lovell, Simnel, and Warbeck. But he grasped the new currents abroad, and he saw how far they had influenced England. Most men welcomed the peace which he brought with him, and were prepared to help him against any breaches of it. The continuance of it lent security to their new adventures. Henry saw the trend of the national mind, and most of his subjects were ready to pay his taxes, because they knew that his government meant security and development. The King's wisdom lay in his insight. He determined to advance his country along lines of prosperity, while he strengthened his own position by amassing wealth. He found out that England would in the long run pay for prosperity, and this fact helped him to base deeper the foundations of his throne. Fines flowed in from every revolt. Even the most serious of them—Perkin Warbeck's—did not hurt the new King. Out of

it he made money and gained foreign credit.
At first he was merely considered a lucky soldier
to whom chance had given a crown which he
would fail to hold.   To the surprise of all, he
not only maintained his position, but consoli-
dated his kingdom.   This was Henry's first
aim, and it brought him respect in Europe.   A
less shrewd man might have attempted at once
to gain national support by a successful foreign
war, and European regard by a series of
triumphs over some Continental nation.   Henry
saw that a throne founded on military glory was
at the best insecure, and that the loyalty of a
people would in future depend more on peace and
national prosperity than on the precarious excitement of battle.   He gained the loyalty of his
people, he unified his Government, and he showed
Europe that he was a man of stern purpose and
shrewd outlook.   From every foreign embassy
in England reports were sent praising the
English monarch's success, and in due course
Ferdinand and Isabella of Spain agreed to the
marriage of their daughter with Prince Arthur,
while the Spanish Ambassador acted for Henry
in arranging a peace between England and
Scotland.   We are not concerned as yet with
the problems which arose out of the Spanish
alliance, but it was a triumph for Henry's statesmanship that his heir should wed into the royal
family of the most successful country in Europe.
Doubtless the transactions connected with it give
us the impression that Catherine was bought and

sold like a parcel of merchandise. But Henry took the Spanish monarchs as he found them, and, while the whole thing seems to us intolerably mean, there is much insight in the negotiations, and Henry knew to the finest detail what he was doing. Indeed, when Arthur died, and Catherine was betrothed to her brother-in-law, there can be little doubt that Henry's diplomacy more than his scruples lay behind the delay in carrying out the new marriage. The Spanish monarchs urged it, because they required English aid against Louis XII. of France, but Henry was seeking other friendships abroad, and he was not prepared to hazard them by a tie with Spain, which would have injured them. The closing years of his reign do not contain much in connection with our subject. There were the well-known executions, and these serve to illustrate the fact that the King had secured his throne, but they also prove that the shrewdness of the earlier years was declining into suspicion. The work of Empson and Dudley also witnesses alike to strength and weakness. Henry knew the value of money and its necessity for a monarch at the time, but he resorted to a means which turned his foresight into refined extortion.

In surveying the constitutional aspects of the reign, Henry's statesmanship is seen almost at every point. It must be remembered that as yet there was really no such thing as the Constitution, and it is almost absurd to speak of a Tudor monarch as acting unconstitutionally.

On the other hand, the development of England
and the growth of new ideas brought to the front
the question of the King's authority and power,
but there is little evidence that much change was
made.   Henry held tenaciously to as much of
the old as he could.   Doubtless personal motives
urged him to do so, as his hold on the throne
was a personal matter ; but there can be little
doubt, when the entire constitutional aspects of
the reign are considered, that he found this
method best suited for the purposes in hand.
There was not much new legislation, and legislation of all kinds came from the King and his
advisers.   This is an important point, which is
liable to be forgotten.   Ample evidence exists to
prove that laws were settled by the King's judges
before they reached Parliament.   Behind the
legislation there stood the King.   With it we
have no concern here, as it is known to every
student of the period, but it is important to note
that it all tended to strengthen the Crown, and,
however we may view such a result to-day, there
can be no doubt that this was an untold blessing
to England at the moment.   England had plenty
of laws and abundance of legal machinery ; what
was required was a power which would see that
the machinery worked in carrying out the laws.
The student can read elsewhere academic discussions in connection with Henry's legislation.
It makes little difference whether this was new
or a reform of the old.   One thing remains clear
—Henry personally restored law and order, by

making the monarchy stronger than it had ever been since the time of William the Conqueror.

When we turn from politics and constitutional questions to those of an economic and social character, we shall find the same strong will and the same far-seeing purpose at work. There was a new commercialism abroad, and foreign markets were necessary if the enterprise of Englishmen at home was to become of national value. The records of Henry's reign are as a consequence full of commercial treaties. In this connection a wise diplomacy was necessary. Englishmen demanded much and were prepared to concede little. In addition, individuals had as yet little chance, and English foreign trade was largely controlled by such corporations as the English Staple at Calais, who lived on terms of rivalry with the English Merchant Adventurers at Antwerp. Indeed, Henry made little headway against such companies, and the individual trader had to wait many years for opportunities. In dealing with foreign corporations, however, he was more successful. The foreign companies in England, such as the merchants of the Hanse and the Venetians, had established many privileges which placed their English rivals at a disadvantage. To remedy this Henry placed foreign companies under double taxation, though reserving to himself the right of controlling the levy on them. In addition, he made heroic efforts to open up the Baltic trade, and for this purpose commercial

arrangements were made with Riga and
Denmark. To the far-off Mediterranean he sent
English ships, where English officials guarded
their interests. But Henry knew that he could
not overthrow the Hanseatic control of trade
unless his commercial relations with the Netherlands were improved, and, through the various
political complications with the Emperor, he
kept this object in view until finally his relationship was placed on a satisfactory basis. Commercial treaties, however, needed support, and
Henry saw that they got it. Acts of Parliament
helped to strengthen them, and English ships
and English sailors carried English goods.
With Henry, too, began that spirit of adventure
which has characterized England ever since. It
may well be considered in connection with the
economic history. In 1484 Cabot came in
Venetian galleys to England and settled in
London. In course of time he came in touch
with the ambitious merchants of Bristol. Henry
had been interested in the plans of Christopher
Columbus, and had only been prevented from
seeing him, and perhaps helping him, by a storm
which prevented his visit to England to ask
Henry's aid. When it became known in 1493 that
Columbus had found a new world, Henry's
interest in Cabot and his projects increased.
This interest took practical form after a royal
visit to Bristol in 1495-96, when letters patent
were issued by Henry " to our well-beloved John
Cabot, citizen of Venice, to Lewis, Sebastian,

and Santius, sons of the said John, full and free authority, leave and power to sail to all parts, countries and seas of the East, of the West, and of the North under our banners and ensigns, with five ships, of what burden soever they be, and as many mariners or men as they will have with them in the said ships, upon their own proper costs and charges, to set out, discover and find whatsoever isles, countries, regions or provinces of the heathen and infidels in what part of the world soever they be, which before this time have been unknown to all Christians." New lands discovered by the Cabot family must come under the English flag. The King was to receive a fifth of the profits of successful voyages, after necessary expenses had been deducted. All imports from these new lands were to come in duty free, and the right of visiting them could only be granted to others by the licence of Cabot and his sons. On May 2, 1497, Cabot set sail, and on June 24 he sighted Cape Breton. Cabot returned in high spirits, was called to Court, and received a present and a pension. In the following February further letters patent were issued, English ships were provided, and Henry financed several members of the new expedition. The details have been obscured, but it is only necessary to point out that John Cabot deserves a much larger credit in these early foundations of empire than has been given to him. Our main interest lies in the fact that Henry's successful policy at home and abroad had not only

made them possible, but had advanced England
into the company of those who were destined to
build empires beyond the seas.   We have considered his policy at home, and seen its wisdom
and success; we now turn to consider the same
wisdom at work in foreign affairs, with results
equally fortunate.

In foreign politics Henry was always an
Englishman.   He had seen enough of the caprice
and jealousies of European monarchs to convince
him that if he could build up an England strong
enough to do without them, he had no reason
either to attack or to court them.   All his
diplomacy in dealing with Continental Powers
aimed at developing and benefiting his country.
He had no military ambitions, no thirst for
conquests, and above all no desire to spend
money.   He knew the history of the Hundred
Years' War, and the glory of Henry V. had not
protected his successor nor guaranteed his
success.   War, too, brought with it uncertainty,
probably factions, certainly differences of opinion
and an increased burden of taxation—all of
which would be detrimental to the national consolidation.   On the other hand, he turned his
attempts at war into profits.   His people paid
war taxes, and his enemies paid peace taxes.
To the superficial student this may appear an
obvious triumph, and such it undoubtedly was,
but the success of the policy lies deeper than the
surface.   When Brittany appealed to Henry for
aid against being absorbed into France, English

traditions and apparently advantages to England
were on the side of the appeal. France was the
traditional enemy, and many would have been
ready to take up arms to carry on even a senti-
mental campaign, in the hope of reversing the
disasters which attended English arms under
Henry VI. In addition, if France became con-
solidated, it would at once make her the only
serious maritime rival of England in Northern
Europe. A victorious campaign would enhance
England's greatness and would cripple France.
Thus the national feelings and the possible
national benefits backed up the diplomacy of
Spain and the Empire in favour of a war with
France. Henry gave a characteristic answer.
He prepared for war, crossed into France, and
concluded an advantageous treaty, while at the
same time he learned beyond all shadow of doubt
that Ferdinand and Maximilian were not to be
relied on. In addition, he had lived in Brittany,
and he knew that anti-French sentiment would
not rally the Bretons to a struggle which might
have lasted for a generation. He took the field
knowing all the time that his action was merely
surface play. Charles VIII. gave him an ample
reward for peace, abandoned the claims of Perkin
Warbeck, and recognized Henry as rightful King
of England. We have already spoken of his
dealings with Spain, but as the issue showed,
his French policy was by far the more important.
Henry succeeded in turning the traditional
enemy of England into a friend. He had now

little to gain from Spanish support.   His throne
was secure, which was by no means the case when
he arranged Prince Arthur's marriage.   Henry
was determined to have no war with France.
He was content to watch France and Spain
campaign in Italy, even ready to play off one
against the other, but war never seriously
entered his mind.   His desire for the friendship
of the Netherlands was based on a similar policy
of benefiting his country.   Perhaps the personal
element entered in, as he hoped through friendship with Philip to get hold of Edmund, Earl of
Suffolk, grandson of Richard, Duke of York; but
his main object all along seems to have been his
desire to assist English commerce.   In addition,
he sought the friendship of Philip when
Ferdinand of Spain, weakened by the death of
Isabella, had made a *modus vivendi* with France.
The Netherlands, indeed, served him as an
offset against both Ferdinand and Maximilian,
once he had, by a lucky storm, secured Philip's
friendship, the Intercursus Magnus, and the
person of the Earl of Suffolk.   The marriage of
his daughter Margaret to James IV. of Scotland
bears witness also to his policy of consolidation.
Too much foresight, however, has been attributed
to it.   Men have been apt, after the union of the
two Crowns which sprang from it, to credit Henry
with an almost superhuman insight into human
mortality.   But as part of his policy it served
its purpose during the reign.   Wisdom, too,
marked his dealings with Ireland.   His Irish

policy was not brilliant, but what policy ever
has been?   It was at any rate the best and
wisest which he could give.   The Poynings
régime was in reality an effort to save England
from her own rulers in Ireland, but finally
Henry found it better and certainly cheaper to
let the representative of the paramount faction
govern Ireland.   Kildare had all the honours
and responsibilities, while he paid for the
administrative outlay.   In all this foreign policy
—and Ireland may be included in it—there is
little that stirs enthusiasm.   Dreams of empire
never entered Henry's head; he knew nothing of
fanciful ambition.   He was, however, something
far greater than a visionary or a lucky soldier.
He knew his limitations, he knew his mission,
he understood his purpose.   Recognizing to the
full how far he could go and how much he could
do, he carried out with success his home and
foreign policies.

Something may be said of ecclesiastical affairs
in so far as they illustrate our subject.   Henry
was a devout and pious Churchman.   In
ecclesiastical polity, however, there are obvious
traces of Henry's statecraft.   Dogma and
religion were never in question, but in other
matters Henry and Rome were united by purely
business ties.   Henry used Churchmen for his
purposes, and preferred them because of their
advantages to him; on the other hand, there were
Papal provisions.   It was quite to his mind that
his ministers should be rewarded by ecclesiastical

promotions.   Indeed, it was the only reward which he intended to give them if they wanted to serve him.   One other point deserves mention. Perhaps the gravest dangers to law and order had arisen from the benefit of clergy and the right of sanctuary, and Henry made efforts to see that the terrible abuses connected with both were curtailed.   These efforts were indeed part of his home policy.   His other relations with the Church were almost uniformly amicable.   If his policy failed, it failed chiefly in connection with these ecclesiastical privileges, which were stretched to cover cases which the Church should never have countenanced.

Thus, then, the sixteenth century in England begins with a strong and purposeful Sovereign. He gained the throne at a moment of national peril, when a false step would have meant years of further misrule and perhaps of national ruin. Affairs outside emphasized the difficulties within, and personal ambition needed a severe hand if the kingdom were to be guided through one of the most difficult periods in her history.   Henry entered on his task with grim determination, patient statesmanship, and exceptional wisdom, and he carried it through by an unswerving adherence to an ideal.   Determination, patience, and wisdom are not the stuff of which popularity in Kings is made, and Henry cannot be called a popular monarch, but he did for England the one thing which she needed : he welded her together as a nation, he gave her law and order, and he prepared her to go out into the future as the gates of history closed on the ideals and nationalism of the Middle Ages. He laid permanent foundations, when a weaker policy would have built up a temporary success on the shifting sands of personal fame.

II

HENRY VIII. AND CLEMENT VII.

By an arrangement made on June 23, 1503, between Henry VII. and the Sovereigns of Spain, Catherine of Aragon, widow of Prince Arthur, was destined to become the wife of Henry, the second son of the English King, provided that the necessary dispensation was obtained from Rome. The treaty appears to have been of Spanish origin, as it speaks of Catherine's marriage to Prince Arthur as not only solemnized, but afterwards consummated. In England, however, it was generally believed that the marriage had not been consummated, and Catherine herself later confirmed this general belief, while Henry VIII. did not consistently deny that he had once admitted the truth of Catherine's statement. However that may be, the Spanish monarchs urged their representative at Rome to obtain a dispensation in the exact words of the marriage treaty, in order to obviate any difficulties with the English. Two Popes died in quick succession—Alexander VI. and Pius III.—and the matter came before Julius II., who was elected in November, 1503. There was further delay.   Julius II. doubted if he could *prima facie* grant a dispensation in such a case, but he promised that, if he could, he would satisfy both monarchs.   Finally a dispensation was granted in two forms.   A brief was sent to Catherine's mother on her death-bed, and this was followed by a Bull of dispensation.   The two documents cover all debatable matter in connection with the case at this point.   If the marriage had been consummated, the impediment set up by affinity was removed.   If the marriage had not been consummated, yet there was an *impedimentum publicæ honestatis* as it had been solemnized *in facie ecclesiæ*.   This impediment was also removed.   After various delays, due to the political craft of the time, Henry was married as King of England to Catherine on June 11, 1509.   Archbishop Warham solemnized the marriage.   Between January, 1510, and the end of 1514, Catherine gave birth to four sons and a daughter, all of whom were either stillborn or died shortly after their birth.   The Princess Mary was not born till February, 1516.   To these family troubles—and the death up to this point of all his sons was a serious matter to Henry—political troubles were added.   Catherine's father, whose ambassador she was in England, began to play false with the English King, who in return prepared to make an offensive alliance with Louis XII.   Nor was this his only reply. He threatened Catherine personally with a divorce, on account of her father's double deal-

ings.   Common talk in England during the late
summer of 1514 said that the King intended to
repudiate his wife, because he was unable to
have children by her, by annulling his marriage
and obtaining what he wanted from the Pope.
Time brought further disappointments.   In 1525
Catherine became forty years of age, and all
hope of an heir through her disappeared.
Henry's anxieties about the succession grew.
Grave possibilities lay before England if Mary
succeeded; and even if she succeeded, her
marriage would present subtle difficulties.   These
anxieties are no mere creation of the partisan
historian.   In 1519 the foreign ambassadors
reported to their governments the names of
different nobles who hoped to obtain the Crown
of England.   In 1525 Henry was making
arrangements to ensure the succession of his
bastard son, Henry Fitzroy, whom he created
Duke of Richmond and Somerset.   Rumours
were circulated that he would seek in marriage
for his bastard some princess nearly related to
the Emperor.   It was suggested, to make the
succession secure, that he should marry him to
his half-sister Mary—a suggestion which came
to the mind of Campeggio, when he arrived in
England in 1528, as a means for avoiding the
divorce.   Now these anxieties and dealings fully
warrant us in saying that Henry's difficulties
about the succession were not invented to justify
himself after the actual divorce proceedings
began.   I think they do more.   They enable us

to say that his desire to get rid of Catherine did not originate in a passion for Anne Boleyn. Henry did not want for illicit love. He had never been a faithful husband, as Elizabeth Blount and Mary Boleyn at least could testify, if others were not forthcoming. He wanted an heir who could sit on the throne of England with some degree of legality and legitimacy. A bastard could not hold the throne securely, even though the outrageous suggestion already mentioned were carried out. It is true that Anne Boleyn complicated the business, especially when she became pregnant, as Henry was then determined to hurry on some sort of divorce from Catherine, which would enable him to make Anne's child legitimate in some way. The point, however, to insist on at this stage is that two years at least before Anne is heard of in the history Henry is getting anxious about the succession; and that as early as 1514, when Anne was not ten years old, Henry was threatening to divorce Catherine because she was unfortunate with her children, and the public were saying that her marriage would not secure her against divorce.

Anne Boleyn returned to the English Court from France in 1522. It is impossible to determine the exact date when Henry became fascinated with her. In April, 1525, Warham evidently referred to the King's determination to obtain a divorce, but it is not clear whether this reference is to be assigned to the general

causes already referred to as influencing the
King, or to the influence of Anne. The royal
love-letters afford us no help, as they are undated.
For a while the King's purpose remained merely
a purpose, and no efforts were made to carry it
out. The next point in the history is connected
with the mission of the Bishop of Tarbes to
England in February, 1527, to strengthen the
English alliance by arranging a marriage between
Mary and Francis I. In May, 1527, Mary was
betrothed to the Dauphin. Within three months
Henry and Wolsey stated that Tarbes, during
the negotiations, had thrown doubt on the King's
marriage to Catherine. No one knows whether
this happened or not. It is quite possible that
Tarbes did mention the question of Mary's
legitimacy; but what is at least clear is that
neither Wolsey nor the King claimed that Tarbes
was the first to suggest doubts as to the validity
of Henry's marriage. Wolsey said that the
French Ambassador raised the question in connection with his mission. Henry said that the
doubts which Tarbes had suggested confirmed the
suspicions which he had long before entertained.
It was about this time, however, that Anne and
Henry began to have an understanding. It
seems reasonable to suppose that Henry would
not have begun actual proceedings for a divorce
until he was sure of Anne, and from the May of
1527, when the French alliance was celebrated,
negotiations were urged on with uniform zeal.
Passion had now come to fan the vague deter-

minations of years before. It was only reasonable, according to the King, that his mind should be set at rest, and that his marriage should be enquired into. I believe that a secret understanding with Anne at this time accelerated the enquiry held by Wolsey and Warham on May 17, 1527; I do not believe that it originated it. That the understanding was secret is quite clear, for Wolsey believed that Henry had in view a French Princess, Renée, daughter of Louis XII. This private enquiry, to which Wolsey consented, may have received his support simply because he hoped that it might show the King how tedious, if not hopeless, his object was. On the other hand, Wolsey and Henry may have entered into a collusive suit to obtain the King's divorce in England, and then to have it confirmed in Rome. Whatever the reason may be, Wolsey summoned Henry to explain why he lived with his brother's widow. Pleas on both sides were entered, and the Court was adjourned on May 31. It is well to remember that Warham had originally objected to the marriage. Catherine had already taken alarm. In the previous March she warned the Imperial Ambassador that she would need his protection. Indeed, the Ambassador wrote to Charles on May 18 that Wolsey was scheming to bring about the Queen's divorce. Her fears were confirmed on June 22, when the King told her that he could no longer live with her as his wife, as his spiritual advisers had told him that they had been living in sin

for eighteen years.   Tears and remonstrances
followed, and Catherine solemnly declared that
the marriage could not be invalid on the plea
of affinity, as her marriage with Prince Arthur
had never been consummated.   The King urged
secrecy on her, stating that he only desired to
satisfy his conscience and to protect her good
name.

While Wolsey and the King were carrying out
their subtle plans in England, the army of
Charles V., on May 6, 1527, sacked Rome, and
Clement VII. became a prisoner in the hands
of Catherine's nephew.   If the English plans
were to reach a satisfactory issue, Clement must
be freed, as he would never confirm a divorce
granted in England against the aunt of his
captor.   Wolsey set out in the following July
for France ostensibly to cement the French
alliance, but in reality to attempt a huge plot
to further the divorce, on which both he and his
Sovereign were determined, although Wolsey had
Renée in view, and Henry Anne.   This French
mission disclosed to Wolsey that he had not the
King's entire confidence.   His plans to secure
the control of the Church during Clement's
captivity failed.   If the contemporary surmise
that he intended to separate the Church in
England from the Apostolic See was true, evidence of the project has not survived.   Whatever
the attempts may have been, they all turned out
futile.   Clement must become the final court of
appeal, and he must be approached at once, as it

was said that Charles already knew something of Henry's plans. Indeed, unknown to Henry or Wolsey, Catherine's case had been laid before her nephew, who informed the Imperial Ambassador in England on July 29 that he had sent Cardinal Quignon to Rome to protect his aunt's interests and to request the Pope to withdraw Wolsey's powers as *legatus a latere*.

Meanwhile Wolsey urged Henry to send the Bishop of Worcester, Ghinucci, to Rome, to ask for a council in France during the Pope's captivity, but Henry's plans were different, and he and Wolsey began, at this point, to act apart. Wolsey wanted Henry to marry Renée as a buttress for his own policy. His aim was to secure the French alliance and to erect a strong bulwark in Europe against the Emperor. In addition, he did not want to declare Catherine's marriage invalid apart from the Pope, for that would erect barriers against his own designs on the Papal chair, would curtail his honours, as his legative powers would disappear, and would effectively make Clement the ally of Charles V., whereas Wolsey hoped to unite him with England and France against the Emperor. On the other hand, Henry had determined that Anne should be his new wife. He knew that Anne and Wolsey would be hostile, as Anne belonged to the strong anti-clerical party, and he feared if he told Wolsey that Wolsey might back out of the divorce proceedings entirely. Instead, therefore, of sending Ghinucci to Rome as an Italian

skilled in the legal methods of the Papal Court,
Henry determined to act apart from Wolsey,
who found in September that he did not enjoy
the King's entire confidence, when William
Knight, the King's secretary, met him at
Compiègne with royal letters desiring the
Cardinal to forward him to Rome.   Anne was
demanding a position or a promise which a
married man could not give, and Henry hoped
that he would, without difficulty, obtain either
a licence for bigamy, or a decree that his
marriage with Catherine was null owing to some
flaw in the dispensation, and thus satisfy Anne's
determination to secure herself against the ruin
which had been the lot of her sister Mary.   When
Wolsey came back to England he found out two
important things—that Anne was the object of
the King's desire, and that Knight had been sent
to Rome to obtain a licence for Henry to marry
another wife without divorcing Catherine, the
children of both marriages to be legitimate.
Wolsey remonstrated on the folly of such a
mission, and Knight's instructions were recalled ;
but the King determined once more to act apart
from Wolsey, and instructed Knight to obtain
the Pope's sanction to a draft Bull, in which
Henry declared that he was under excommunication by marrying Catherine, from which he hoped
soon to be released by a competent judge, and
giving him permission, when thus relieved, to
take any woman as his wife, even though related
to her in the first degree of affinity, contracted

by either lawful or unlawful connection.   This dispensation would be necessary for the King's marriage to Anne, even supposing his marriage to Catherine were declared null and void, as he had contracted affinity with her by immoral relations with her sister Mary.   Knight easily obtained this dispensation.   The document was passed with a few unimportant corrections, and Knight started home full of pride in his success. The document in reality was worthless until Henry's marriage with Catherine was decided. Wolsey knew this, and messengers from the King met Knight on his homeward journey, with instructions that he should return to Clement to obtain some further documents.   It is not possible to determine the exact terms of Knight's new demands, but it is generally believed that Wolsey desired for the King a commission that someone should examine the dispensation under which Henry had married Catherine, and if it were found invalid, this someone—obviously Wolsey—should pronounce the marriage null and void.   Knight arrived in Rome at the beginning of December, while letters from England urged the Pope to act if he did not wish to lose England and endanger Wolsey's life. Knight pressed into his service Sir Gregory Casale, the King's Italian agent, and, interview- ing the Pope at Orvieto, whither he had escaped, he at length obtained the commission, but in an altered form.   Cardinal Pucci had read the original, and told the Pope that " it could not pass without perpetual dishonour to the Pope, the King, and Cardinal Wolsey." The draft was altered in such a way as to render it useless for practical purposes. Knight started homewards once again convinced of his skill, but when Wolsey saw the altered document he said that it was " as good as none at all." At the beginning of 1528 a new embassy was discussed, and in February Edward Foxe and Stephen Gardiner started for Orvieto to obtain a decretal commission for Wolsey and some others—a commission laying down the law by which such a case should be determined. Those to whom this decretal commission was addressed should try and decide without appeal the question as to whether the facts were really such as to render the dispensation of Julius II. invalid. Gardiner and Foxe plied the Pope with mighty arguments and undignified threats, but the Pope yielded only a general commission, with which Foxe set off to England. He persuaded Henry and Anne that it would be quite easy to win over the Pope to give a private promise that he would confirm the sentence and not revoke the case to Rome. Wolsey, however, was far from satisfied. The commission was as valueless for the object which he had in view as the document obtained by Knight a few months previously. Gardiner was informed of Wolsey's dissatisfaction, and urged to obtain the decretal commission by pointing out that if it were not forthcoming the King would proceed to desperate measures. Wolsey

himself wrote to the Pope urging him to grant
the decretal commission, which he would keep
secret, if he wished to hold England, to preserve
the dignity of the Apostolic See, and to preserve
Wolsey's life.   Gardiner was also instructed to
take a most solemn oath that it would be shown
only to the King.   Finally the Pope agreed to
send Campeggio to England to try the case with
Wolsey, and the Italian Cardinal took with him
a decretal commission, but under strict injunctions not to use it in the trial, but to show it to
the King and his colleague and then to destroy
it.   The exact terms of this secret decretal
commission are unknown, as no record of it has
survived.   It must have been an important
document, as we shall see later.   Gregory Casale
appears to have known nothing of its terms in
the February of 1529, though the Pope, in spite
of protests on Catherine's behalf, made by
Muxetula, the Spanish Ambassador, gave a
written promise on July 23, 1528, that he would
not revoke or interfere with the commission, but
would confirm the Cardinal's decision.   The
Emperor's cause was not now so strong in Italy.
The French had won numerous successes.
Clement had said, when he had granted the document given to Knight, that he could excuse
himself to Charles, if the French came near
Rome and threatened it, by saying that he acted
under pressure.

Campeggio started for England on July 25,
1528.   Within a few weeks the Emperor's cause

was strengthened in Italy. Lautrec, the French commander, died, and the Genoese Admiral Doria deserted the French for Charles. When Campeggio arrived in Paris in September the effects of the political changes in Italy were at once apparent. Sanga, the Papal Secretary, wrote him that, as the Emperor was victorious, the Pope must not give him any pretext for a fresh rupture, lest the Church should be utterly annihilated. Campeggio must do his best to restore affection between Henry and Catherine, and he must on no account pronounce any opinion without a new and express commission from the Pope. This advice was repeated in stronger terms a few days later. The Emperor's power over the Church was great enough to involve its ruin, and Campeggio was told not to be surprised when once more, and within such a short time, he was ordered not to proceed, under any pretext, to sentence without express commission, but to prolong the matter as long as possible. Indeed, it is quite clear that these letters only confirmed what had already been arranged. From the evidence of two men, Contarini and Navagero, who interviewed Campeggio on his journey, it is evident that there was never any real intention of having sentence pronounced in England. The Pope himself assured Charles, who in his turn assured Catherine, that nothing would be done to her detriment, and that the whole case would be referred to Rome. Campeggio arrived in

England in October. His attempts at a settlement proved futile. Henry would not take back Catherine, Catherine would not retire to a convent. Henry's will was fixed, and the piety with which he had lived during the plague of the summer included no repentance with regard to Catherine. Catherine confessed to Campeggio that her marriage with Arthur had never been consummated. The King and Wolsey demanded that the secret decretal should be shown to the council. Campeggio refused, and determined to burn it. Wolsey applied to Rome for permission for Campeggio to hand over the decretal. To Clement the move was obvious. Once Henry and Wolsey had in their possession a decretal stating what the law was, it only remained for them to prove that Julius II. had been deceived, and they would see that that was accomplished. Clement detected Wolsey's craft, and despatched Francesco Campana to Campeggio, ordering him to destroy the document. On his arrival he found that Clement was reported to be dying. For the moment the decretal survived, as it would have been rash to destroy it at such a time. With Clement's recovery, however, dangers in this connection disappeared, and Campeggio destroyed the document. Meanwhile, from an unexpected quarter, an opportunity for delay came to the help of Campeggio. Catherine produced a copy of the brief sent to her mother on her death-bed. Henry and Wolsey knew nothing of this brief, and months were spent in trying

to obtain the original from the Emperor.   Every
effort was in vain.   Charles was far too careful,
and Wolsey was damaging his case by various
letters to the Pope.   He offered to give up his
commission and leave the decision to Clement,
if he would guarantee that the sentence would
be favourable to Henry.   He asked, if Henry
agreed to take monastic vows as a means for
persuading the Queen to enter a convent, would
the Pope dispense him and permit him then to
marry the woman whom he wished; or would
the Pope give Henry permission to have two
wives.   Some of these suggestions may not have
reached Clement, but Wolsey had undoubtedly
damaged Henry's case from the points of view
of reason and justice.   In addition, Charles was
gaining ground with Clement, and Spanish
influence was added to Wolsey's folly.
Campeggio opened Court on May 31, 1529, and
in due course Catherine appealed to Rome.   On
July 23 Campeggio adjourned the Court till
October.   The Court never met again.   Before
the vacation was ended Henry knew that the case
had been transferred from England, and Clement
and Charles were united as never before.   Wolsey
had begun to see that all his political moves to
play France off against the Empire and *vice
versa* had failed.   His demands that the Pope
should declare the brief a forgery without having
seen it added to the obvious lack of faith in
friendships and treaties.   Indeed, Clement could
not but see that, quite apart from his obvious

obligations to the Emperor, Wolsey was no just judge for Catherine, and that the case must go to Rome. As a matter of fact, he merely held back the decision at which he had arrived almost a month before Campeggio's Court opened, in order not to rile Henry and until his treaty with the Emperor was fully ratified. Henry hastened matters. The revocation of the commission had been further delayed when Clement promised the Imperialists that nothing further should be done in England, but Henry continued to urge on the trial there, and on every side justice seemed to call on Clement to procure an honourable trial in Rome. Even the English agents there confessed that there was no other course open for Clement, who, however, pleaded for delay. Indeed, a year later, Charles feared that Clement would yield to a trial and sentence in England. Campeggio left England, but only after Henry's officials had unsuccessfully searched his luggage for the decretal commission. Early in August, 1529, Henry knew that Charles and Clement had completed their alliance, and that his suit against the Emperor's aunt had been revoked to Rome.

On November 3 one of the most famous Parliaments ever summoned in England assembled. It was the boldest bid for luck which Henry ever tried. Henry had been summoned to Rome to plead before a foreign Court. The nation, however opposed to the divorce, would never endure such an insult. Henry took good care that that side of the business should be kept well to the front. Wolsey's fall was assured after the failure of the trial in England. Henry proceeded with great foresight. He began by seeing that Parliament was strengthened in its anti-clericalism by the introduction of measures dealing with fees, pluralities, and such like. Doctrine was, of course, not in question. When Parliament was prorogued on December 17 it was in no very good temper with the clergy, and that was Henry's desire. It did not meet again until January 16, 1531, and much happened inside the year. Clement saw that there were storms ahead, but the Imperial influence was entirely against concessions. In March, 1531, Tarbes told Francis I. that Clement was so upset that he wished Henry and Anne were married " by dispensation of the English legate or otherwise, provided it was not done by his authority, or in diminution of his power as to dispensation and limitation of Divine law." Later on in September he suggested that Henry should have two wives. The latter suggestion was undoubtedly a ruse on the part of Clement to get Henry to acknowledge his dispensing power, about which the English King had first begun to entertain doubts in the summer of 1529. Both suggestions, however, show how desperate Clement was. But Henry was determined to marry Anne by listening to neither suggestion. His marriage to her must be carried out by the highest ecclesiastical authority recognized in England. Clement held that position, but

Henry knew a way to get rid of Clement and erect another authority if Clement would not fall in with the royal wishes.   Clement forced Henry's hand.   On March 7, 1530, by a Bull fixed on the church doors of Dunkirk, Bruges, and Tournay, the King of England was ordered to desist from a second marriage on the pain of excommunication.   It was a strange position, and could not be reconciled with the Bishop of Tarbes's announcement to Francis I.   A few days later he prohibited all writings against Henry's marriage with Catherine, but no prohibition extended to those who defended it.   Immediately before Parliament reopened Clement prohibited the Archbishop of Canterbury from hearing the suit, and every assembly of laity, clergy, Universities, Parliaments, etc., from judging or pronouncing on the case.   Henry replied by a proclamation based on the Statute of Provisors prohibiting the importation of anything from Rome prejudicial to England or the King's purposes, and he bribed as far as he could the Universities of Europe to declare in his favour.   He forwarded to Rome a memorial signed by the noblemen round the Court and by the country gentry, in favour of his case.   When Parliament assembled Henry gave the Pope stronger replies.   The clergy acknowledged him Supreme Head of the Church as far as the law of Christ allowed.   Henry pardoned their breach of *præmunire,* which Parliament confirmed, passing at the same time an Act embodying their own pardon from the guilt of a like offence. Parliament was prorogued on March 31.

On May 31 a large deputation of Bishops and lords visited Catherine, after Henry had had a long consultation with his Council. The deputation complained that the King was grievously offended by the scandal which she had caused by having him cited publicly to plead in Rome. They asked that she should agree that the trial should be held at some place and by judges above suspicion. Disasters personal and national were foretold, and Catherine was reminded that the King had lately been declared head of the spirituality and temporality in England. Catherine answered with dignity, but remained unmoved. Henry had begun the case with the Pope, and with the Pope she was determined that it should remain. In October another deputation visited her. The Queen was asked to allow the case to be decided by the English bishops. Another refusal followed. These interviews confirmed her in believing what was undoubtedly true, that there could be no justice for her before any English court. Within a few weeks the King separated from Catherine, whom he never saw again after the close of 1531, and Anne Boleyn occupied the Queen's apartments, being attended in royal state.

When Parliament assembled in January, 1532, Henry strengthened his position. The famous Supplication against the Clergy was approved by the Commons and presented to the King. Whatever its origin, it showed Henry's determination to accentuate the divergencies between the Church and the laity. In addition, an Act was passed restraining the payment of Annates to Rome. It makes little difference to the fact that this Bill had a difficult passage, and that the King was present at the voting. An important clause leaving the execution of the Bill to Henry's discretion gave him a valuable lever against the Pope. The French Envoy at the time noticed Henry's skill—" he has caused the nobles and people to remit all to his will, so that the Pope may know that if he does nothing for him the King has the means of punishing him." Finally, the provisions that Bishops could be confirmed and consecrated without the Pope were left at Henry's disposal. Nor did the prorogation of Convocation take place without the submission of the clergy. They handed over their legislative power to the King, promising to draw up no new canons without the King's licence, and they agreed to a revision of the canon law by a committee of thirty-two appointed by the King.

In Rome the case dragged its slow length along. In spite of repeated requests on the part of the Imperialists to settle the matter once for all, Clement was compelled to watch Henry's " excusator," Edward Carne, occupy two whole years striving to prove that Henry could not with dignity plead at Rome. But Clement was not idle. On January 25, 1532, he sent Henry

a letter of admonition, in which he said that he
had heard that Catherine had been banished
from the Court, and that Henry " had taken in
her stead a certain Anne," with whom he was
living publicly as his wife.   He called on him
to restore Catherine to her place as wife and
Queen, and " to send away Anne " until sentence
was   given.   Henry   paid   no   attention.
Catherine was removed further from the Court,
and Anne was created Marquis of Pembroke—a
marquis in her own right.   In October he made
further plans to get the venue of the trial
changed.   He met Francis I. at Boulogne, and
the two monarchs agreed to bring pressure on
Clement against the Emperor; but very little
came of these political moves.   Francis I. was
anxious to marry his second son to the Pope's
niece, and was not likely to be dictatorial.
Indeed, Clement issued another brief to Henry
on November 15, 1532, which repeated the
admonitions of the previous January, and
forbade him to divorce himself from Catherine
by his own authority, or to marry Anne or any
other woman, adding that any such marriage
would be invalid.   This brief was not made
public until the nuncio had informed Henry,
which he did before January 27, 1533.   The brief,
however, was published at Dunkirk on the 21st
and at Bruges on the 23rd of January.

For the moment Henry changed his policy, but
not because of Papal briefs or threats from Rome.
In the middle of January, 1533, he knew that

Anne was pregnant, and her child must be made
legitimate. He saw that there was no hope from
Rome in this connection, but he was determined
to use Rome in such a way as would enable him
to obtain an adequate place in law for Anne's
offspring. Could not the Archbishop of Canterbury pronounce his divorce, and could not the
Archbishop's Court be made the final court of
appeal? Warham had died in the previous
August, and Henry resolved to have Thomas
Cranmer as his successor. Cranmer's connection
with the King was well known at Rome, and
Henry's aim now was to get the customary briefs,
etc., for Cranmer's consecration without arous-
ing the Pope's suspicions. Anne and the King
were privately married, while in public the King
received the Spanish Ambassador more cordially
than he had done for years. At Rome, his
agents were treating Clement with greater
courtesy, and Henry himself opened up a generous correspondence with the Pope. He declared
himself willing to oppose a general Council, and
he let it be known that he might reconsider his
attacks on the Apostolic See. Indeed, at that
moment he was actually helping the Pope by
withholding his consent to the Act of Annates,
and in return he hoped that Clement would
grant him the necessary documents for Cranmer's
consecration, without the usual payment. It
was a bold stroke of diplomacy. Henry had
played his hand with consummate skill.
Consistory granted Henry's request, and the
Bulls arrived in England in March. When

Parliament assembled Henry kept up the appearance of friendship with the Papacy. The Papal
nuncio came with him in state to Parliament,
and everyone was saying that there was a secret
arrangement between the King and the Pope.
In such an atmosphere anything might be done.
Convocation decided that the Pope had no dispensing power in a case such as Henry's.' The
famous Act of Appeals was passed, which
abolished appeals to Rome, and rendered anyone
who brought in any Bulls of excommunication
liable to *præmunire*. Henry's game was won.
On April 11 Cranmer, of course acting on advice,
wrote to the King asking for permission to
decide the King's case in a court of his own.
The commission was naturally issued, and on
May 23, 1533, he pronounced Henry's marriage
to Catherine of Aragon invalid. On the 28th he
enquired into Anne's marriage with the King,
and found it lawful, although he did not publish
his reasons. She was crowned on June 1 Queen
of England. On July 11 the Pope excommunicated Henry and pronounced his divorce and his
re-marriage null. He was allowed till the end
of September to give up Anne and to make his
peace with the Pope before open sentence was
given. On September 7 Elizabeth was born.
In March, 1534, sentence was given at Rome that
Henry's marriage to Catherine was valid.
Within a year every tie that bound England to
Rome was broken. The Royal Supremacy,
which had taken five years to build, was fully
completed by legislation.

III

THE LITERATURE OF THE EDWARDINE REFORMATION

DURING the reign of Henry VIII. no important change had been made in the public services of the Church, if we except the order authorizing the English Litany and the Episcopal Injunctions, which in two dioceses at least required the Epistle and Gospel to be read in English on Sundays and holy days. The Act of the Six Articles, which was passed in 1539, was definitely Catholic. Recantations of heresy and burnings for maintaining it characterized the last year of Henry's rule. A Royal Proclamation a few months before his death had ordered the burning of heretical books. Any possibility of a *modus vivendi* with Lutheranism had gradually disappeared. Generally speaking, there was little evidence that the new reign should begin with an extreme reaction. On the other hand, when the history is more closely examined, there emerge valuable indications which go to show that this reaction was not entirely accidental or unexpected.

Henry, according to Cranmer, had under

consideration a few months before his death drastic changes in the Mass. The foreign ambassadors noticed signs of change just before the reign closed, while Chapuys was assured that the reforming party had gained the upper hand. In addition, when we examine Henry's last actions, it would seem clear that he had advanced in the direction of reform. Reformers had been chosen as tutors for his son, and some of the conservative councillors had been removed. When the new Government was formed, it is significant that, with Gardiner and Thirlby excluded, Tunstall infirm, and the rest of the Catholics who remained weak and inconsistent, the rule passed into the hands of a majority sufficiently strong to override any opposition among themselves. The problem which presented itself to the Government in connection with religious affairs was hardly that of how to hold itself together in carrying out its policy, but rather that of how the nation could be carried with it, and how national approval could be secured. Indeed, any possibility of internal weakness was almost at once removed. Lord Chancellor Wriothesley gave the reformers an opportunity to proceed against him on a technical point, and forfeited his office, but not before he had been compelled to strengthen the Council by drawing up fresh commissions for the Bishops, who in future were to hold office *durante bene placito* and *quamdiu se bene gesserint*. With regard to educating the nation towards the pro-

posed reforms, a method was resorted to which
is worthy of the student's attention, since it has
not been sufficiently emphasized by historians.
It would seem certain that the Press was utilized
to a very large extent, and while the Council may
not have given explicit approval to much of the
literature, there can be little doubt that this
approval was implicitly given.   Tudor governments did not tolerate publications which were
detrimental to them.   I think, too, that this
literature was not merely haphazard.   The
gradual advance in reforming principles which it
shows would almost seem to prove that it was
directed from some authoritative source, and
that the Edwardine policy was not a mere series
of accidents, but that *The Second Prayer Book*
was the logical outcome of a considered plan,
which began as soon as Edward VI. ascended
the throne.   It is true that this view is not the
one generally accepted.   It has been customary
to say that the final Edwardine reform was the
outcome of exceptional circumstances which
occurred between 1550 and 1552.   It is possible,
however, to show that 1552 is the lineal
descendant of 1547, and that *The First Prayer
Book* was merely a stop-gap, while the literature
of education went on without a break.   Indeed,
as events proved, *The First Prayer Book* was
premature, as the work of educating the nation
had not gone far enough.   On the other hand,
it is possible to consider it as either *ballon
d'essai* or as a temporary concession, since the

Ordo Communionis had not been a success. Whatever its actual place in the Edwardine Reformation may be, it seems impossible to conclude, in view of the literature which we shall examine, that the Government ever meant it to be permanent.

Any real progress which Reformation principles had made among the people during the reign of Henry VIII. must be traced to various editions of the New Testament and Bible in English, as these were full of mistranslations, and, in addition, voluminous notes were added of a decidedly Protestant character. The most important volume is undoubtedly Tyndale's *New Testament,* which was surreptitiously imported into England in 1526. From that year down to July, 1546, it was included among the lists of prohibited books issued either by episcopal or royal authority. The earliest of these prohibitions speaks of it as " craftily translated " and as having in it " many heretical articles and erroneous opinions pernicious and offensive." We are not concerned with the history of the English Bible under Henry VIII. further than to point out that this *New Testament* passed through several editions in less than twelve years, and that from the passing of the Act of Six Articles till Henry's death only one edition appeared. From the accession of Edward VI. to 1553 seventeen editions were issued. Now, as we shall see, the evidence is entirely against the supposition that there was a popular demand for the book, and we can only conclude that there lay behind its frequent publication the approval and authority of the Government. In addition, Tyndale's *New Testament* was supplemented by various editions of the complete Bible, which contained notes and comments of a distinctly Reformation character, especially against the Sacrifice of the Mass and the Real Presence, while the words of institution were uniformly explained as being used in a figurative sense. It is unnecessary to examine in detail the character of either Tyndale's volume or of these English Bibles, as they are well known to students of Reformation history, but it is necessary to emphasize the fact that the new Government immediately countenanced their circulation, and that at a time when they had no reason to believe that there would be a demand for them.   This toleration is also interesting in view of the fact that during the Royal Visitation of 1547 orders were issued that only those who had been licensed and authorized were to be permitted to read the Bibles which were provided in the parish churches.   It would thus seem that while a plausible effort was being made to control the reading of Scripture by the laity in volumes which contained no virulent notes or comments, every opportunity was given them to read editions which were not only full of wilful mis-translations, but were also provided with the extremest expositions of foreign reform.   Nor can the issuing of these editions be considered as either accidental or as a business speculation on the part of the publishers. The Edwardine Government was not slow in destroying and in prohibiting any books with which it was not in sympathy. There can be little doubt that the whole affair was part of a deliberate policy, from which there was no deviation throughout the reign. The other official literature of 1547, in addition to the Bible provided in churches already referred to, consisted of Cranmer's *Book of Homilies,* Udall's edition of Erasmus' *Book of Paraphrases,* and King Henry VIII.'s *Primer* in Latin and English. The *Paraphrases* were utterly opposed to the popular versions which we have considered, while the *Homilies*—if we except that on Salvation—and the *Primer* were not violent and extreme in comparison with the various pamphlets encouraged and countenanced by authority. It would thus appear that at the beginning of the reign open sanction was given to a moderate position, but that this was discounted by popular literature, which, with the approval of the Government, attacked Catholicism in the most offensive language, and disseminated the theories and teachings of the most radical Protestantism. The policy was at once bold and cautious. It was possible to point to the official publications as evidence of moderation if the country grew restless; and it was equally possible to call the unofficial but approved publications as witnesses of sound reforming zeal, if the people demanded an advance along the line of extreme Continental reform. Later on, when the Government felt secure, it disclosed its aims in full; but for the moment it established for itself a means of escape, if such a dilemma should immediately arise.

We have seen that the various versions of the Scriptures which were permitted based their chief attack on the Mass and Real Presence. In the literature which we must now consider the weight of attack also fell on these two subjects, and the earliest important official change in the services came in connection with the administration of Communion. Popular preachers had got out of hand, and " in their sermons, preachings, lectures, communications," called the Sacrament " by such vile and infamous words as Christian ears abhor to hear rehearsed." Thus Parliament complained, and a penal statute was passed in the first session of the reign " against such as shall speak unreverently of the Sacrament of the Altar." The Government did not intend that its caution should be nullified; but the same Act notably omitted the use of the word Mass and spoke of " the Supper and Table of the Lord," and, in addition, ordered that in future Communion should be given in both kinds. On March 8, 1548, this Act bore fruit in a publication known as *The Order of the Communion,* which provided in English a rite to be inserted by the priest in the Latin Mass, when administering Communion in both kinds to the laity. The

most interesting part of the pamphlet in connection with our subject is undoubtedly the
proclamation which formed the preface.   In this
the King is made to say that he was able
to discern in what directions the further reform
which the document promised was necessary.
This proclamation is of great importance, as it
is the first official pronouncement of the new
policy.   The next publication belongs to the
summer of the same year, and is entitled *The
Psalter, or Book of the Psalms, whereunto is
added the Litany and certain other devout
prayers set forth with the King's most gracious
licence of July, 1548.*   This volume is of interest
from two points of view.   Not only did it contain
for the first time the petition in the Litany for
deliverance from " the tyranny of the Bishop of
Rome and all his detestable enormities," but the
Eucharist was definitely stated to be only a
memorial, and the Real Presence was implicitly
denied.   This clear statement regarding the Mass
is remarkable considering that it was made with
official sanction while the Latin Mass was still
in use.   However, it was quite in keeping with
the aims of the Government, and these can be
followed in detail by an examination of some of
the literature which appeared between *The Order
of the Communion* and *The First Prayer Book.*
As this literature is of considerable volume, it
will only be possible to select the most clear-cut
statements, and for the sake of convenience to
divide it into new books and reprints or importa-

tions and translations.   It has not been thought necessary to refer to the better known books dealing with ceremonial and church furniture, as this has been minutely examined during the Anglican controversies of the last century. Indeed, much of the literature which is here referred to deals with the Mass, and incidentally with Baptism.   With regard to the general style of these books, it is well to point out that for the most part it is almost impossible to quote them in detail, and almost equally impossible to read them with patience, as they are full of the greatest blasphemy.   Beginning, then, with the second division, the positions taken up will, as a rule, be referred to in general terms.   And it is well to remember that, side by side with all these pamphlets, the circulation of Tyndale's *New Testament* never ceased, with notes and comments regularly changed to suit the wishes of the Government.

The years 1547 and 1548 saw the translation of Marcourt's *Declaration of the Mass,* of Luther's *Disclosures of the Canon of the Popish Mass,* and of a numerous and miscellaneous crowd of books by the foreign reformers, including Melanchthon, Calvin, Zwingli, and Bullinger. Cranmer himself translated a Lutheran Catechism and bowdlerized the original.   These books are better known than some of those to which we shall refer later, but one and all contained attacks on the Mass.   There is no evidence to prove that the Government made any attempt

to suppress them, and, as is well known, England
now became the harbour of refuge for many
Continental reformers, whose various opinions
were represented by the various translations.
Books and refugees were, however, one in their
attacks against the Mass and in the desire to
educate the people against it.   Of the lesser
known books in this division it is well to refer
to *The Disclosing of the Canon of the Popish
Mass,* which consisted of a translation of one of
Luther's sermons, with a preface by the translator.   The sermon is in Luther's characteristic
style.   The priest " plays the fool with bread
and wine."   The devil is the author of the canon,
and the Mass is a blasphemy unequalled among
the heathen.   The editor almost surpasses
Luther in the vehemence of his abuse.   He rings
the changes on the Devil's authorship, and calls
on the civil power to rescue England from
the " bloody kingdom of Antichrist."   This
language is mild compared with that of *The
Reckoning and Declaration of the Faith,* which
had been written in 1543 and was now imported.
Quotations from this work would only show the
extremes of language which belong to the literary
movement.   In *The Lamentation of a Christian
against the City of London,* which had originally
appeared in 1545 and was now reprinted, a
defence of the Chantries Act was made the
occasion for an attack, in no very decent style,
on the Mass in general, and for the expression
of an assurance that in due time the King and

his counsellors would carry reform in England
to the successful issue which it had reached in
many German cities.   The author, however, is
careful in dealing with the Sacrifice of the Mass
and the Real Presence.   He denounces emphatically any idea of sacrifice—there is but a memorial
of Christ spiritually present with two or three
gathered together in His name.   On the other
hand, those who believe in the Real Presence can
do so, as it is immaterial to salvation, but there
must be no worship of Christ as present.   In
addition, the bishops come in for some severe
treatment, and various ceremonies are denounced.   In dealing with clerical celibacy and
penance, the writer almost surpasses any of his
contemporaries in the sordid filth of his
language.   It is important to remember the
attitude taken up here towards the Real
Presence, as it will reappear in some of the
original publications to which reference will be
made later.   Among other less known reprints
are those of William Turner and Richard Tracy,
which had been included among the prohibited
books in the reign of Henry VIII.   Tracy's
Brief and Short Declaration took up a definite
Zwinglian position, to which was added a new
excuse for the vernacular—that the understanding and hearing of the words of institution was
necessary to the validity of the Sacrament.   The
Government is relied on to further the reformation of all abuses in the Mass, which only served
" to encourage the covetous appetite, drunken-

ness, whoredom, and lusts of the wicked priests." Another work by the same author which now appeared was entitled *A most Godly Instruction,* which was merely a preface to Tyndale's *A Brief Declaration of the Sacraments,* in which the Sacraments were defined as " bodies of stories only, and there is none other virtue in them than to testify and exhibit to the senses and understanding the covenants and promises made in Christ's blood." All sacrificial doctrine was denied : " the cause of the institution was to be a memorial, to testify that Christ's body was given and His blood shed for us." Turner's *New Dialogue, wherein is contained the Examination of the Mass,* is too blasphemous to be referred to, and, if for nothing else, it deserved the condemnation given to it in the preceding reign. Another of his reprints, however, deserves attention. It was a translation of a tract by Regius, and was entitled *A Comparison between the Old Learning and the New.* The tone of the book is Calvinistic. There ought to be no distinction between priests and Bishops. General Councils and Canon Law ought to give place to the powers of the local congregation and its rulings over its members.

A much more voluminous literature meets us when we turn to consider the original works which were tolerated by the Edwardine Government. They are also more interesting than reprints or translations, many of which are full of statements which either did not apply to con-

ditions under Edward VI. or did not go far
enough to suit the purposes of the new régime.
It is in the latter connection that they are
specially valuable, as they throw a very clear
light on the Edwardine policy, which, without
them, would be almost inexplicable. That this
was their purpose seems quite clear. They were
openly sold throughout the country at the local
markets. No effort is made in them to follow
serious controversy. Their main object was to
bring into disrepute everything Catholic—
especially the Mass—and thus to prepare the way
for further measures by the Government. Nor
must it be forgotten that the circulation of such
blasphemy was countenanced at a time when the
Mass was still the worship of England. It is
impossible to believe that the scurrilous literature of the reign was purely the outcome of
individual fanaticism or the excessive zeal of a
few extremists. Indeed, we shall see that when
the Government found that its reforms had
outrun discretion it was not slow to restrain the
Press. Had these early books been of no value
to it, there were not wanting means to prevent
them from being circulated broadcast among the
people.

The most famous of the original new books is
undoubtedly Gilby's *Answer to the Devilish
Detection of Stephen Gardiner,* which was published at the beginning of 1548. Gilby's
language is the refinement of abuse. The Sacrament is the " Popish idol," " the poetical

changeling." " A piece of paste is carnally worshipped with fond gestures." " A vile cake to be made God and man." Gilby's efforts were nobly seconded. *The True Judgment and Declaration of a Faithful Christian* defended the extremest form of sixteenth-century Sacramental theology, and concluded with a pious prayer for the young Josias that "he may purge the English Church from all abominations." *The Old Faith of Great Britain and the New Learning of England* included an inaccurate and somewhat imaginary account of Christianity in England before the arrival of St. Augustine, and a description of his reception, which is naturally much to his disadvantage. The writer proves, much to his satisfaction, that " the Popish priesthood is a damnable sect." He exhorts his readers to let the Mass return to Rome with Augustine's other trinkets. The second part of the work is a justification of reform, an explicit denial of the Real Presence, and an appeal to Scripture as interpreted by the author. From *The News from Rome* might be culled some choice flowers of language and logic, but the real value of the pamphlet in this connection is its call on the faithful to have patience, knowing that further reform would come, and exhorting them to be earnest in the declaration of their religion. *The Treatise against the Privy Mass* belongs to the same tribe. Violence excels itself to prove that the " Privy Mass " is not only temporal but eternal death. The sacrificial aspect of the

Eucharist is denied.   The distinction between clergy and laity is obscured, and the Real Presence is compared to the presence of Christ with the Father and Holy Ghost at the baptism of faithful infants.   *The New Dialogue* is without equal in its blasphemy.   The King and Government are congratulated on their efforts so far, but are urged to take away the Mass, " the one abomination that sitteth sore on man's conscience."   There are many other little books of the same class, all characterized by their blasphemous style and by their exhortations to the King and his advisers to proceed to further reform.   Among the State Papers and documents of the period I have not found any order before *The First Prayer Book* was issued prohibiting their circulation.

There is a special class of books among these original publications which deserves attention. It may be called the astute class.   A book entitled *A Christian Sentence and True Judgment of the Most Honourable Sacrament* took up a position somewhat similar to that already noticed in *The Lamentation of a Christian*.   The writer explains himself as holding that the words of institution were merely figurative, but he seems careful to point out that there is room for many opinions about the Real Presence, and that mutual forbearance in connection with them is necessary.   Similarly, while his own sympathies are in favour of Communion in both kinds, he does not go as far as to blame those who receive in one. After all, according to the writer, it is of little matter, as consecration produces no effects. Equally remarkable is the position advanced in *A Compendious Treatise of Slander*. It is almost impossible not to believe that the respect asked in this book for older customs and traditions, provided they were not enforced as *de fide,* was not part of a deliberately prepared plan. This surmise is fully supported by the tract known as *Unwritten Verities,* which Strype—on slender evidence however—ascribes to Cranmer. I have not seen the original, which may be among the Parker MSS. at Cambridge. Emphasis is laid on the authority of kings and princes over the clergy, that they are bound to condemn things not written in Scripture, but that many things may be tolerated until such times as the civil authorities are prepared to forbid them. As far as the writer's mind can be seen, the tract aims at preparing the country, at the expense of the clergy, for further reform, while it disarms the reader by its moderate and conciliatory tone.

It is rather difficult to explain why there should be even the appearance of moderation in a few books and so much vehemence and outrageous language in the majority. The books themselves and the contemporary letters of the period seem, however, to provide the best answer. In spite of all the efforts made by what must be called an organized Press, there still remained in the country an overwhelming number of people who adhered to Catholic faith and practice. Almost every book to which we have referred deplores the fact that the country was still joined to its idols, while the original letters of these years show that little or no advance had been made in making the rank and file of the nation ready to receive and welcome any extreme reform. We shall see later that this suggested explanation is supported by almost convincing evidence. The Government appears, even before *The First Prayer Book* was issued, to have taken alarm at the failure of the extreme literature to produce the desired effect, and to have decided that an element of judicious moderation should be introduced into some of the books in order to hide their real policy, and to obscure their aims. They appear to have thought that, while the Sacrifice of the Mass and the Real Presence must go, it would prepare the way for these reforms if the people were led to believe that other things might be tolerated. Thus vital and immaterial things were mixed up in the hope, as I think, of encouraging the people to remain quiet and to accept a reform which might not be complete or sweeping. That they were ready to produce a new service book was well known throughout the country. The debate on the Sacrament in December, 1548, clearly shows the direction which theological thought was taking. In addition, it was preceded by a translation of one of Martyr's tracts, entitled *Of the Sacrament of Thanksgiving, a Short Treatise of Peter Martyr's*

Making. This was dedicated to Somerset, praising his zeal in calling the learned and well-minded together for such a debate, and providing him with a concise analysis of Martyr's position. Transubstantiation was denied. There was no intermixture of the natures or substances of bread and wine and the body and blood. The presence of Christ belonged to the receivers. All reservation and worship were condemned. It is not merely a coincidence that Martyr's tract provided the main positions taken up by the reforming party at the subsequent debate. When *The First Prayer Book* was issued, it was apparently moderate in theological reform, while certain things were retained on the principle outlined in *Unwritten Verities*. Nor was *The First Prayer Book* given to the people without a certain amount of deliberate equivocation. A concession was made from *The Order of the Communion* and the act for Communion in both kinds by bringing back the word "Mass," in connection, however, with "the Lord's Supper"; but the First Act of Uniformity led the public to believe that the book came forth "with one uniform agreement" of the "Archbishop of Canterbury and certain of the most learned and discreet bishops and other learned men of this realm" selected by the King. This "uniform agreement" cannot be supported as an historical position. In addition, from the preparatory debates certain important facts emerge. Tunstall objected to the omission of adoration. Those

who drew up the book believed there was nothing
to adore. Cranmer declared that our faith is
not to believe Him to be in the bread and wine,
but that He is in heaven. Thirlby, Bishop of
Westminster, upset calculations when he drew
attention to the fact that the Lords must not
think that the book had been agreed on by the
Bishops, but must remember that it was presented for discussion. Bonner declared the book
heretical. Cranmer and Ridley passed quite over
to the anti-Catholic side. When the final voting
took place it would seem, as far as it is possible
to arrive at figures, that out of twenty-seven
bishops, ten opposed the Government, four
cannot be accounted for, and thirteen favoured
the measure now passed. However patient *The
First Prayer Book* may have been of a Catholic
interpretation, we cannot overlook this debate.
It shows that in the minds of its compilers there
was no belief which in any just use of the term
could be called a belief in the Real Presence.

When the book was enforced it was at once
evident that the fears which I have suggested
as existing in the minds of the authorities were
far from groundless. The policy of education
had signally failed. It is impossible here to
consider in detail the reception which was
extended throughout the country to *The First
Prayer Book,* and the subject has been dealt
with by other writers more or less adequately.
The Western Revolt, however, needs closer consideration. The demands which the rebels

made showed how deeply they felt the change. They demanded, among other things, the restoration of the Act of Six Articles, of the Mass, of the reserved Sacrament, Communion in one kind, opportunities for Baptism at any time. They made an explicit statement of their faith in the Real Presence—" there is very really the body and blood of our Saviour Jesus Christ, God and man, and that no substance of bread and wine remaineth after, but the very same body that was born of the Virgin Mary and was given upon the Cross for our redemption." A mild answer was returned in the King's name, but it contained the strange statement, " As for the service . . . it seemeth to you a new service, and indeed is none other than the old, the self-same words in English which were in Latin, saving a few things taken out so fond that it had been a shame to have heard them in English." Such a sentence comes dangerously near lying. Cranmer, however, threw mildness to the winds in his personal reply. The rebels had advanced on a tender place when they pointed out that the changes had not been carried out by the Bishops and other ministers of the Church. This home-thrust evidently angered the Archbishop, whose reply is full of irritation and scorn. The rebels are " ignorant men " of Devon and Cornwall. The skill with which obedience to the Pope was mixed up with disloyalty to the throne is one of Cranmer's finest pieces of composition, and it set the example for many a future Elizabethan defence of the English Reformation. The whole composition needs careful reading, especially his excuse for the use of English, and his reply to the insurgents when they said that they knew no English, that neither did they know Latin. Cranmer was doubtless out of temper, and his display of learning is largely discounted by this fact. It is unnecessary to follow the military history. Peter Martyr soon lashed Oxfordshire into a similar revolt. Only the presence of foreign mercenaries, lack of some plan on the part of the rebels, and ignorance of the Government's unpreparedness, saved the situation. A small element of good fortune would have given the rebels London and left the kingdom at their mercy. What chiefly concerns us has been to show that *The First Prayer Book* was not received with anything which could be called a welcome. When the literature which we have considered has been taken into consideration I think that it is almost impossible to doubt that even at the time when the new service book appeared it was never meant to be permanent. The generally accepted position that *The Second Prayer Book* was purely the outcome of the accidental presence of foreign reformers in England and of their growing influence cannot be maintained, at least dogmatically. It is impossible to explain the literature which the Government's policy fostered before the publication of *The First Prayer Book* if this usual position be adhered to. Only one theory seems to satisfy the situation, and that is that *The First Prayer Book* was either issued as a mere effort to beat time, or that it was meant to test public opinion. Whatever the real purpose, it certainly showed the Government that it had as yet failed to educate the people sufficiently, and this was immediately recognized. In August, 1549, an order from the Council prohibited the publication of all books except those licensed and approved by a Government Committee. We shall see how that approval worked, and the kind of books to which it was given. Even before the day arrived for the compulsory use of *The First Prayer Book,* Bucer and Fagius wrote from Lambeth to the ministers at Strasburgh that concessions had been made in it only for a time. It will be recalled that they were the guests of Archbishop Cranmer. When this is considered in connection with the fact that the literature which we shall now consider as the means adopted for further national education in religious matters bore the imprimatur of the Council, it will materially strengthen the theory advanced in relation to *The First Prayer Book*— that it did not represent the real beliefs and wishes of those who drew it up.

Before considering the literature which preceded and surrounded *The Second Prayer Book,* there are several matters which must be mentioned if the history is to be understood. Firstly, Somerset's fall, wrongly interpreted by the

people as the herald of a reaction, prepared the
way for further reform. Bonner of London,
Gardiner of Winchester, Heath of Worcester,
and Day of Chichester, were deprived. Secondly,
the old service books were destroyed with ruth-
less vandalism. Thirdly, every effort was made,
both by royal letters to the Bishops and by the
zeal of the new licensed preachers, to see that
The First Prayer Book was forced into national
use. And, finally, the foreigners resident in
England, while deploring that there was still a
wide field for the propagation of Reformation
principles owing to the stubbornness of the
people in receiving the new religion, were not
slow to see that the Government had for the
moment merely stopped to take breath, and that
they fully realized the extent of their mission.
In addition, it is well to recall the various interpretations put on the teaching of *The First
Prayer Book,* as consideration of them is
necessary to understand the official version. It
is well known that, in connection with the
Eucharist, men of such opposing principles as
Bishop Gardiner and Bucer found that it fitted
in with their beliefs. Gardiner maintained that
the Prayer Book was patient of a Catholic meaning, and Bucer appears to have been satisfied,
or at least conservative, when reviewing *The
First Prayer Book* in relation to further reform.
It is interesting to note that two such men
were moderately pleased, because it has been
customary to bring Gardiner forward by himself

as a witness on behalf of the new service book.
However that may be, Cranmer issued in 1550
his *Defence of the True and Catholic Doctrine
of the Sacrament,* which can obviously be considered as the official interpretation of *The First
Prayer Book.* This treatise is of immense
importance in connection with the subject under
consideration, as it supports in a remarkable
way the contention that there was never any
intention on the part of the Edwardine
Reformers to make *The First Prayer Book* final.
In answer to his opponents, Cranmer says :
" And as concerning the form of doctrine used
in this Church of England in the Holy Communion, that the body and blood of Christ be
under the forms of bread and wine . . . I take
to be a plain untruth." " We say that Christ
is not there, neither corporally nor spiritually,
but in them that worthily eat and drink the
bread and wine; He is spiritually and corporally
in heaven." " The bread and wine be made
unto us the Body and Blood of Christ (as it is
in the Book of Common Prayer), but not by
changing the substance of bread and wine
into the substance of Christ's natural Body
and Blood, but that, in the godly using of them,
they be unto the receivers Christ's Body and
Blood. . . . So is the water in Baptism, and
the bread and wine in the Lord's Supper, to the
worthy receivers, Christ Himself and eternal life,
and to the unworthy receivers everlasting death
and damnation, not by conversion of one

substance into another, but by godly or ungodly use thereof." We need not follow Cranmer's controversy further, nor make any attempt to balance the various passages of his writings which belong to this period of his life. His work is merely referred to for the purpose of showing what he, as the chief compiler of *The First Prayer Book,* considered that it meant. His interpretation must also be looked on as representing the minds of those who helped him in his work. He published it with the royal licence and approval. Had we not possessed as much literature as we do preceding *The First Prayer Book,* we might have been excused for thinking that Cranmer's interpretation merely represented one of his many intellectual changes, and that it was an effort on his part to fit in the apparently Catholic teaching of the new service book with his own position. It cannot be thus isolated, considering the literature to which we have referred. Cranmer's explanation is part and parcel of a clearly defined plan. His work fits into its place in the literary policy, and, indeed, serves to bring into clearer relief the fact that he and his associates deliberately drew up an ambiguous book, the meaning of which would be made officially apparent within a short time after its publication. It is true that Cranmer is not definitely at this stage a Zwinglian. But a spiritual presence in the godly using of the elements is sufficiently vague to leave room for any explanation.

Before continuing to discuss the literature, something must be said in connection with Baptism, as it is surprising to find that on the whole the Edwardine Reformers were more moderate in connection with it than with Eucharistic teaching. There can be little doubt that the presence of numerous Anabaptists from the Continent accounted for this moderation. It is hardly too much to say that they saved the situation in the Baptismal Office of 1552; for that office, weakened though it was from the Catholic point of view by the changes deliberately introduced, is comparatively orthodox when read in connection with contemporary literature. The general teaching running through this literature is distinctly uniform. Children are already Christians by virtue of their parents' faith, and Baptism but seals and confirms them as Christians. A book written in 1551 by John Vernon, entitled *A Most Sure and Strong Defence of the Baptism of Children,* may be taken as typical. " The infant is not baptized for the intent that by Baptism, that is to say, by the outward washing of water, he should be made the child of God; but he is therefore baptized because he was afore the child of God, through grace and promise. . . . Spiritual things . . . be not attributed unto the outward washing, but to the whole action, which containeth the faith of the minister, of the Church, and of him that is baptized, also the grace, election, and promise of God. It is, then, chiefly attributed to that which is signified by the pouring on of the water." The whole position is built up round the analogy of circumcision. The children of the faithful receive Baptism as an assurance of the promises made to them and their seed. This publication, of course, carried with it the Government's approval. The theory can be read more clearly elaborated in contemporary letters, which, however, lie outside our survey. One reference must therefore suffice. Peter Martyr, in writing to his friend Bullinger after *The Second Prayer Book* appeared, noticed the various difficulties which had arisen in connection with baptismal teaching, and deplored the fact that it was not made sufficiently clear that Baptism did not confer grace. In Bullinger's *Decades,* which belong to an earlier date, Baptism is also looked on as similar to circumcision. The general teaching of this work is strongly in favour of the theory that it was merely a sign of grace, and is sufficient to outweigh any expressions which might be patient of a Catholic meaning. Bullinger's writings, as is well known, enjoyed the greatest popularity, and were among the books which the Edwardine Bishops ordered to be provided in cathedral and parish libraries.

Between the publication of *The First Prayer Book* and *The Second Prayer Book* it is rather significant that the greater part of the pamphlet literature that has survived belongs to the years 1549 and 1550. From August, 1549, all books

were published with the approval of the Council,
and it would appear that more diligent efforts
were made in the months immediately succeeding
the abolition of Catholic worship to promulgate
extreme Reformation teaching than at any other
time during these years.   It is justifiable at
least to suppose that this fact was not accidental.
The aim was to discount any feeling of relief
which *The First Prayer Book* might have produced in the minds of a conservative nation, by
flooding the country at the same time with such
literature as would serve both as a commentary
on it and as forerunner of further reform.   It
is also remarkable that while the new book might
be explained in a Catholic sense, the literature
which accompanied it, with the approval and
sanction of the same Government as issued the
Prayer Book contained Sacramental teaching
such as would satisfy the most zealous reformer.
The new service book could hardly have reached
the country districts when Thomas Lancaster's
*The Right and True Understanding of the Supper
of the Lord* was published, which clearly abandoned any possible double dealing.   The Sacraments were signs and nothing more.   The " daily
sacrifice " came in for some severe and characteristic treatment.   Only " beastly heretics "
received the " abominable doctrine " of the Real
Presence.   The minister merely required a
" call " from the congregation.   This was followed by Ochino's *A Tragedy of the Unjust
Usurped Primacy of the Bishop of Rome,* duly

dedicated to the young Supreme Head of the
Church.   Ochino's work, if somewhat less
obvious in its historical setting than those of his
contemporaries, is worthy of attention, as it is
full of violent fancy.   The author reconstructs,
through nine lively dialogues, the whole of
Church history, much to the disadvantage of the
Popes and the Church of Rome.   The devil
figures prominently throughout, as in all Reformation literature—here as the author of the
original scheme of founding the Church to defeat
God's purposes and to prevent the spread of
religion.   As the plot progresses the destruction
of the devil's ingenuity is graphically described.
Henry VIII. and Cranmer receive or take due
credit, and Edward VI. and his advisers come
in for their share in the work.   No one can read
the concluding pages of this work without being
convinced that from the very beginning the aim
of the Edwardine Government was to set up and,
indeed, to go beyond the theological and ceremonial position laid down in *The Second Prayer
Book* of 1552.   The policy reached in that year
is thus distinctly outlined in 1549.   Dedicated to
the King, and issued under the Council's letters
of approval, the book cannot be passed over
lightly.   Edward is made to utter words telling
of extreme measures about to be taken, while
his councillors join in approval of his godly
intentions.   During the next year—1550—the
publications were much more numerous.   At the
head of this year's writers stands the notorious

John Bale, who is without rival for blasphemy, violence, and scurrility. His *Examinations of Mistress Anne Askewe* had been scattered broadcast at the beginning of the reign. In 1550 he received the Government's permission to issue a work entitled *The Image of Both Churches, being an Exposition of the Most Wonderful Book of Revelation of St. John the Evangelist*. This consisted of a commentary, verse by verse, on *The Apocalypse,* and on all possible occasions attacks are made on " the Romish Pope sitting in the most pestilent seat of errors," " the great Antichrist of Europe . . . king of faces, the prince of hypocrisy, the man of sin, the father of errors, and the master of lies." The sacrifice of the Mass and the Real Presence are denied in blasphemous terms. Bishops and priests are " consecrate whoremongers, the defilers of all honesty . . . under the title of vows maintaining Sodom and Gomorre." Bale's language renders detailed quotation impossible. Yet the book was considered worthy of an honoured place among the approved literature, on the principle that the end justified the means. That the Council was now ready to press every possible writer into their service is clear. As early as 1548 some of John Vernon's works were evidently not suitable, as the way had not then been sufficiently prepared for them. However, in 1550 his *Five Abominable Blasphemies contained in the Mass* and his *Godly Sayings of the Old Ancient Fathers upon the*

Sacrament were considered sufficiently valuable for authoritative publication. Vernon proceeds in a business-like manner to reduce all patristic teaching on the Eucharist to the lowest Reformation level. Most interesting of all, with *The First Prayer Book* in front of him, he clearly states that his position is that taken up by the Government, and he exhorts his readers to follow his Sacramental teaching as that " which our most Sovereign Lord the King and his honourable Council have set forth." What is this official teaching which Vernon recommends ? There is no Sacrifice of the Altar, there is merely a remembrance of the death of Christ; baptized children are partakers of the body of Christ, though they do not receive the Sacrament; believing in Christ is to eat His body, and the faithful feed on Him daily in reading or listening to the Scriptures. Vernon's tracts, taken in connection with the fact that an edition of the Scriptures which came forth almost at the same time contained a clear reference to the King's teaching and intentions, are of material value in attempting to secure some light on the methods of reform. Another work belonging to the same year and entitled *The Battery of the Pope's . . . High Altar* attacked all the ancient teaching by an attempt to overthrow the Old Testament idea of sacrifice through quotations and arguments drawn from the New Testament. It was dedicated in fulsome terms to the Lord Chancellor, and it contains almost the earliest reference to sitting at the reception of Communion. The author seems quite satisfied that the Pope, his baggage and teaching, have been weeded out of English religion, and his book, issued with the Council's licence, reads like a song of satisfied triumph. Contemporary with this book were some violent publications by Thomas Becon, the personal friend of Cranmer and Somerset. Becon ran Bale a close second in blasphemy and abuse, but, acting on the principle that any language was suitable for attacking the ancient faith, his works were approved and circulated. Somewhat later appeared Hooper's *Godly Confession*. His difficulties with the Government were almost entirely over ceremonial, but this work can be considered in relation to our present subject. In the year following the introduction of *The First Prayer Book* Hooper wrote of his dissatisfaction with it, but in a tone pointing to reform. His *Godly Confession* was issued with the official approval, and dedicated in an introductory epistle to the King and Privy Council. Although Hooper submitted his confession and faith in this letter to the judgment of the King, Council, and Parliament, yet the fact that his book was licensed for publication is sufficient to show that the Government was not opposed to his teaching. The *Godly Confession* is sober and dignified in style, and begins with a detailed confession of faith along the lines of the Apostles' Creed. Care is taken to uphold the authority of the King

and civil magistrates, and to magnify the office
of preaching.   Hooper then gives his idea of the
visible Church and of the Sacraments and
ministry.   In place of circumcision and the
paschal lamb the Church has Baptism and the
Lord's Supper, which declare the grace of God.
Thus Christ's coming has only changed the
elements of the Sacraments and not the Sacraments themselves.   They have their peculiar
promises and peculiar elements and peculiar
ceremonies, but they are only visible signs of
grace.   In dealing with the Sacraments in closer
detail, Hooper denied forgiveness of sins through
Baptism, which is but a " sign, seal, and confirmation of redemption by faith."   He defends
infant Baptism along the usual lines.   With
regard to the Eucharist, he says : " As for the
Supper of the Lord . . . I believe it is a
remembrance of Christ's death, a seal and confirmation of His precious body given unto death,
wherewith we are redeemed.   It is a visible word
that preacheth peace between man and man,
teacheth to condemn the world for the hope of
the life to come."   In connection with the
ministry, Hooper's teaching is extreme.   " I
believe that the Church is bound to no sort of
people, or any ordinary succession of Bishops,
Cardinals, or such like, but unto the only Word
of God. . . .   I am sorry with all my heart
to see the Church of Christ degenerate into a
civil policy . . . so that the Holy Ghost must
be captive and bondman to Bishops' sees and
palaces."   In the following year a work of an

advanced character was issued under the Council's licence and dedicated to the Duchess of Somerset. It is in the form of a dialogue, and entitled *The True Belief in Christ and His Sacraments*. The tone throughout is Calvinistic. Salvation by faith alone and election to eternal life and eternal damnation are insisted on. With regard to the Eucharist, it is merely a commemoration of Christ's death for the redemption of those whom God has predestined to salvation. This publication may have had little influence, as Calvinism did not spread to any large extent in England during the reign; but it is interesting because it shows how the Government welcomed and approved of anything which might turn the public from the old faith.

Before concluding this survey of the literature of the Edwardine Reformation, and before referring to *The Second Prayer Book*, reference must be made to the official edition of Tyndale's *New Testament*, which appeared immediately before the publication of *The Second Prayer Book*. It has already been pointed out that Tyndale's translation was consistently circulated throughout the reign. Five or six editions were issued, with the usual class of notes, in the year immediately succeeding *The First Prayer Book*, but on June 10, 1552, a special licence was issued to Richard Jugge to publish a new edition, which had been " overseen by persons meet for that purpose " and fully approved by them. All other editions were also forbidden. With regard to the text of this edition nothing need be said, as it has no relation to our subject; but the notes are of the greatest value, illustrating as they must do the beliefs of the Edwardine Government and Reformers. They also mark the culminating point of Reformation teaching during the reign. It may be said with safety that in no other publication of the period was the influence of Calvinistic theology more marked. This influence cannot easily be accounted for. It may have been due to the publication of foreign confessions of faith, or to Cranmer's desire to form a confederation of Protestant nations against Rome. The doctrine of election is explicitly maintained. Salvation is granted by God's pleasure to whom He will, independent of all human works or merits. The Gospel may be preached to all the world, but only in order that the predestined may learn to know Him. No repentance can renew those who fall away from grace. The notes on the Sacraments are typical of the age. Those on Baptism are somewhat confusing, and it is rather difficult to arrive at any clear teaching in connection with it, but the weight of evidence would seem to be in favour of the theory that it did not confer grace. On the other hand, in connection with the Eucharist there is no ambiguity. " The corporal presence of Christ is not necessary and needful for us; for it is His Word only, received through faith, that healeth us. . . . As the cup is the New Testament, so the bread is the body of Christ; by the New Testament he understandeth the forgiveness of sins. But the cup doth only represent unto us the New Testament, that is to say, the forgiveness of sins which we have in the blood of Christ." Three editions of this New Testament preceded *The Second Prayer Book* and one, in 1553, followed it.

With this service book we have no immediate concern. On November 1, 1552, it deposed its parliamentary predecessor and became the official Prayer Book of the nation. The Second Act of Uniformity, however, must be considered. Firstly, it declared that *The First Prayer Book* was " agreeable to the Word of God and to the primitive Church." Secondly, it noticed that in different parts of the country a considerable number of people did " wilfully and damnably before Almighty God abstain and refuse to come to their parish churches " to take part in this worship " agreeable to the Word of God and to the primitive Church." It then proceeded to note that there were many differences in the use of the service book, and that the new edition was issued to amplify the previous work, to take away doubts, and to provide " a plain and manifest explanation thereof." *The First Prayer Book* " had been faithfully and godly perused, explained, and made fully perfect," and in this form was annexed to the Act of Parliament. Thus the process was : *The Second Prayer Book* explained *The First Prayer Book; The First Prayer Book* was merely a translation, purged of excessive ceremonial, of the older rites, but it was also agreeable to the primitive Church. It all reads like an attempt to hide wilful lying.

It is difficult to believe Tudor Acts of Parliament in every detail, but if we must do so the interpretation given to *The First Prayer Book* by the Second Act of Uniformity fits in with the idea that it was merely a stop-gap, and did not represent the real opinions or aims of those who drew it up—a contention for which I think I may claim a certain justification when considered in connection with the literature to which we have referred. This literature has by no means been examined completely. There are extant a considerable number of pamphlets to which reference has not been made, but as they are along lines similar to those which I have mentioned I have not thought it necessary to deal with the literature in full. The questions which lie before the student are : Was *The First Prayer Book*—no matter in what sense it may be interpreted—sincere ? Was *The Second Prayer Book* merely a base surrender to the influence of the foreign divines and reformers resident in England? It is usually held that *The First Prayer Book* represented the English position, and that its successor was forced on the Government, and in turn on the people, by the presence of Continental zealots in the country. This statement of the case is, I think, unhistorical. Had *The First Prayer Book* been an honest effort to stereotype the Anglican form of worship, it is impossible to believe that the Government would have tolerated the literature, already considered, which appeared before Midsummer Day, 1549, and would have licensed the literature, already considered, which appeared after August, 1549. The two positions cannot be reconciled except on the theory that *The First Prayer Book* was a stop-gap and a *ballon d'essai,* and that it was in no sense of the word honest or sincere. It seems to me that it takes its place logically and historically in the literature of the period only by accepting the contention suggested. However deplorable the history, it is at least better to attempt to fit it into its proper place than to formulate a theory out of modern Anglican controversy. Nor, on the other hand, can the meaning of *The First Prayer Book* be considered apart from the official literature which surrounded it. Theological questions must yield to historical methods, and it must be explained, just as any other book, according to the known opinions of those who drew it up. At any rate, if our theory is not dogmatically proved, it has, I think, on its side a considerable weight of evidence which cannot be dismissed either with contempt or scorn. Of course, it may be suggested that *The First Prayer Book* was quite sincere, and that the Government meant to conciliate the Conservatives through it, and to please the Liberals by the official literature. Such a suggestion only needs to be mentioned in order to be dismissed. The Edwardine Government could hardly afford to provide such a voluminous literature when the nation was almost entirely against reform.

IV

SOME ASPECTS OF EDWARDINE LIFE

THE history of the reign of Edward VI. has suffered from the controversies of modern time. A literature has gathered round *The First* and *Second Prayer Books* out of all proportion to their value, and the smallest details of ceremonial in Edwardine churches have passed almost into the sphere of expert study, so much time and research have been expended on them. On the other hand, the really valuable history of parish life in the reign—the ordinary every-day existence — has been too largely neglected. Revolts, agricultural and economic questions, and the controversies of rival religious bodies, occupy such a large place in the history that we are liable to forget the storm and stress of actual life during the reign, the varieties of religious experience, the ceaseless eddies of change in which the nation moved.

No body of documents can afford us a better insight into this actual life than the Visitation Articles and Injunctions which were issued from time to time during the period to the parishes of England. They sum up, as it were, the current policy, and help us to obtain a wider and more consistent view of the country, or at least of entire dioceses, than documents dealing with the *minutiæ* of ceremonial or local parochial history. They record the ebb and flow of the great religious fluctuations of the reign, and provide us with a view—kaleidoscopic in its changes—of men and women tossed about from one religious position to another. We see life in all the process of disorganization and disintegration. We see strong revolutionary passions and strong loyalty to the past. The pageant of change passes before our eyes in chronological order; we can almost see the daily, monthly, or yearly vicissitudes through which the people of England passed during the reign.

Before entering on the study of these documents it is well to gaze back in order to obtain a general idea of conditions at the death of Henry VIII. After the break with the Pope Henry assumed ecclesiastical jurisdiction, and twice—in 1536 and 1538—Thomas Cromwell, acting for the King, issued Royal Injunctions to all the parishes of England. The former set were administered by royal visitors, while the ordinary ecclesiastical machinery was suspended, and they reflected the changes brought about by the Henrician policy. Several of the new orders must be recorded. Henry's new style as Supreme Head of the Church is laid down as a theme for parochial sermons. English Bibles become a feature of church furniture. Several holy days are abrogated, including the patronal festivals of the parishes, which had been hallowed for generations and surrounded with much joviality. The latter set appear to have been administered by the diocesan Bishops acting under royal command. For the first time we find among its orders a violent attack on images and pilgrimages, which led to much licence in later years. Not much of value can be gained from these documents. Henry died with the Act of the Six Articles in force, and thus civil law lent its support to Catholic dogmas and practices which earlier had been called in question. Indeed, the fluctuations of Henry's policy left very little impression on the lives of the people. In the lone parishes of England, apart from the great highways of national life, men and women — spite of a well-controlled pulpit—still lived unconcerned in the King's affairs, and believed the religion of their fore-fathers.

On the accession of Edward VI. it was at once apparent that parish life would have little chance to move along the old lines. The power passed into the hands of a body of men bent on reform. We must at once exonerate the influence of the boy King. He was neither the fierce anti-Papist nor the reforming saint of party historians. His public actions were, with some few exceptions, those of his Council. It soon became clear that there would be high handed dealings in ecclesiastical affairs, which are admirably illus-

trated by the documents referred to. My object
is to interpret these documents, illustrated by
letters and reports, in their relationship to
certain phases of Edwardine life. The dealings
gathering round the Prayer Books and the Great
Pillage need not delay the history, except by
way of reference. The parish churches, certain
aspects of old devotional practices, education,
and morals are far more valuable than ceremonial
research, and it is to these points of view, to a
large extent, that this study of Edwardine life
is confined.

At the beginning of the reign the parish
churches remained almost intact, and the
services and practices of the Catholic Church
continued to be observed. The old parochial life
preserved its traditional lines, all unconscious
of its dissolution. But wavering policy of
Henry VIII., if anything Tudor can be so
described, gave way to a set purpose; and before
the reign closed a revolution had taken place in
parish life perhaps unparalleled in such a short
period in the history of the Christian Church.
We are hurled along at an appalling speed
amid divergencies in every sphere, and the
grimness of parochial factions, where legality
and illegality seem to be matters of little import.
In this connection it is well to point out that
the term " legality " is used almost uniformly
in this study in reference to civil law. Thus,
when such and such a Bishop is said to have acted
illegally with regard to certain things at a

certain moment in his administration, the meaning applied to the term is that Parliament had made no regulations at the moment of application. The First Edwardine Act of Uniformity was not passed until January, 1549, and *The First Prayer Book* had no statutory force until Whitsuntide of that year. In the months previous to that date ecclesiastical matters were largely governed by Orders in Council. There is much in these months which has been largely obscured.

Edward's councillors at once began preparations for a Royal Visitation of all the dioceses of England, following the Henrician precedents. The country was divided into sections among lay and clerical visitors, and the visitorial powers of the Ordinaries were suspended. The Visitors carried with them a set of seventy-two enquiries and enforced a set of thirty-six Injunctions. This was a convenient method for changing the face of parochial life. Before long a complete break was made with all previous traditions in preaching and teaching. The pulpit became carefully tuned—a characteristic of the period. When the reign began the parish clergy were allowed to preach in their own parishes without a licence, but they could admit no substitute unless he possessed written permission from the Bishop. This state of affairs appears to have continued, with certain fluctuations, to February, 1548, when all clergy were confined to their own cures, as far as preaching was concerned, and

they were required to possess a licence not only
from the Archbishop or Bishop of the diocese,
but also from the King or the Royal Visitors.
In the following April the parish clergy were
silenced, and preaching was confined to the
Bishops and certain licensed preachers, who were
not to be denied a hearing when they arrived in
a parish.   This policy was outlined in a letter
from the Council dated two months later, and
the clergy were ordered to follow diligently the
orders given and not to think themselves wiser
than the King and Council.   If no licensed
preacher appeared, the people were provided for
by the reading of a printed discourse of unimpeachable orthodoxy.   The Council, however,
could not even trust the licensed preachers, and
in September of the same year the King was
pleased " to inhibit all preachers generally until
further pleasure."   This regulation appears to
have lasted until removed by *The First Prayer
Book,* and with it came back the earlier system.
Royal licences for preaching were required, and
the power lay in the hands of the King, Archbishop, or a few laymen.   Of course, the
Henrician model of a sermon against the Pope
was continued in all the churches four times a
year.   But highly controversial matter comes
into prominence.   The clergy were forced to
emphasize the new place of Holy Scripture as
the sole standard of faith and practice.   The
Bible, however, was guarded.   If anyone wished
to read the Bible provided in his parish church,

or to read it aloud to others, he could not do so without a licence. This, however, was an advance from the *status quo* at Henry's death, as he had prohibited by Act of Parliament all Bible reading, both in public and private, as there were too many " meddlers with the Bible," according to a contemporary document. In addition to violent controversial sermons, the people were compelled to listen every Sunday, if there was no other discourse, to an extract from the *Book of Homilies,* which appeared in July, 1547. With regard to actual teaching, the clergy still examined their penitents in Lent on the Creed, Our Father, and Ten Commandments, as they had done for centuries before. It is noticeable, however, that knowledge of the *Ave Maria* was no longer required. It is true that it was not mentioned in the Henrician Injunctions of 1538, but it was referred to in the subsequent Henrician documents. There appears to have been no condemnation of invocation until invocations were removed from the *Primer* by Act of Parliament in 1549. It is interesting, however, to note that this Act was anticipated in 1547, when the invocations disappeared from Grafton's *Primer* of that year. There was evidently some debate over the question in official circles, but for the present, as far as the people were concerned, the matter was left in an ambiguous position.

Before turning to some consideration of worship and customs it is well to note certain

changes in the fabrics and ornaments of the
Edwardine churches.   Under Henry images had,
as we have seen, suffered.   Henry, however,
made an effort to discriminate between them by
ordering only " abused images " to be taken
down.   This differentiation was, at least in
theory, continued by the Edwardine Visitors,
with this important difference : under Henry it
would appear that the final decision lay with the
diocesan authorities, while under Edward this
decision passed into local hands.   As a result,
a spirit of iconoclasm was let loose, much wider
in its reach than the mere letter of the Visitors'
injunction demanded.   A single complaint in
a parish was sufficient to convince the visitors
that an image was abused.   Protest was useless,
and an era of destruction began far in advance
of anything Henrician in this connection.
Indeed, the discretionary powers left by the
Council to the Royal Visitors soon disappeared,
as the French Ambassador in England had
anticipated.   Writing on September 27, 1547,
that while the image-war had somewhat subsided
owing to the general offence which it caused, yet
he concluded that the excesses had the approval
of the Government and that all images would be
included in one class.   On February 11, 1548,
an Order in Council abolished the distinction
between abused and non-abused images, and
ordered that all images should be destroyed.
From that point onward the work of destruction
went on throughout the country.   Cranmer

cleared the Diocese of Canterbury of them in 1548. The Oxford Colleges witnessed a like outbreak of zeal in the spring of 1549, when even the niches of the statues were destroyed. Bishop Ridley swept the Diocese of London in 1550, and in the following year Bishop Bulkeley followed suit in Northern Wales. In the same year Bishop Hooper's zeal outran the law, as he ordered all the effigies on tombs to be destroyed in the Dioceses of Gloucester and Worcester, though " images upon tombs " were specially exempted from destruction by Act of Parliament. In dealing with pictures, mural paintings, and stained windows, no quarter was allowed from the beginning of the reign. From the year of the Royal Visitation a wholesale destruction in connection with these pious gifts was carried on. Nor was the destruction confined to the churches alone. The Royal Visitors invaded the privacy of the people's homes, and the clergy were commanded to see that their parishioners destroyed all symbols and pictures in their houses. Indeed, Ridley went so far as to demand for punishment the names of those who " kept in their houses undefaced any monuments of superstition." Economic reasons alone saved many windows from destruction ; but when repair was necessary, through ordinary wear and tear, the repair was to be in glass of " posies taken out of Holy Scripture." This use of Scripture for church decoration was one of the features of the reign. The Royal Visitors in

1547 had ordered the setting up of the Ten Commandments. Daniele Barbaro, however, who was Venetian Ambassador from 1548 to 1550, noticed that it was quite common to ornament the walls of the churches with texts of Scripture. Indeed, it would seem that even before the images were destroyed a custom had grown up of painting near them texts of Scripture condemning idolatry. Archbishop Holgate of York found texts from the Bible useful for ornamenting the bricked-up niches, while the rood-lofts in London were found useful for a similar purpose. In concluding this short review of the fabrics of the churches, it is well to mention the fate of the organs and altars. The Royal Visitors made no general order in connection with them, and it seems clear that the destruction of them during the years 1549 and 1550 was carried out either by private instructions from the Government, on the diocesan Bishop's authority, or on purely local opinion. Evidence, however, is not wanting that organ music was a " monument of superstition," and that for this reason organs were destroyed by Royal Visitors for special places. Thus at All Souls' College, Oxford, in the early summer of 1549, organs were removed, and it seems likely that the order applied to the entire University. Ridley, in May, 1550, glanced askance at them in the London churches. The Royal Visitors removed them from St. George's Chapel, Windsor, in the same year. Holgate silenced all music at York Minster in 1552.

Many of the Reformers had strong objections to organs, and this may help to account for their destruction. Opinion, however, seems to have fluctuated, as it did later in Elizabeth's reign. Barbaro certainly mentions their use in the churches in the years of his residence in England, and evidence is also forthcoming that in certain places they were repaired, and also restored after being removed. With regard to the altars, the history up to November, 1550, is somewhat confusing. *The First Prayer Book* provided *nominater* for an altar in each parish church. Shortly before it came into use a special commission had ordered the altars to be pulled down in Jesus College, Cambridge. In December, 1549—that is, six months after the introduction of this Prayer Book—altars were changed in many places into tables. The first dealings with them on any large scale took place in London in 1550, when Ridley exhorted—and that is commanded—his churchwardens to erect " honest tables " in the churches. He at once set an example of zeal by removing the high altar of St. Paul's in June, 1550. Ridley had no respect for law. In Essex in the previous May the work of destruction went on apace, under the supervision of the Sheriff, who carried out what the young King called " the Bishop of London's orders." In a few weeks there was not an altar left in the Diocese of London, and the news was joyfully conveyed to the Continental Reformers. Indeed, whatever the law, there can be no doubt

with regard to the policy, as the Court preachers
in Lent, 1550, denounced altars and went unre-
proved. Finally, on November 24 an order was
issued ordering their general removal, to which
Ridley appended " reasons," and in future a
religious ceremony seems to have accompanied
the illegality. In connection with altars, the
thorny questions of lights and of Reservation
naturally arise—to the latter I have devoted a
separate study. Henry had allowed " the light
that commonly goeth across the church by the
rood-loft, the light before the Sacrament of the
Altar, and the light about the Easter Sepulchre."
The Edwardine Visitors removed all except " two
lights upon the high altar before the Sacrament,"
which Cranmer interpreted as ceremonial lights
during Mass. The question of the Reserved
Sacrament before the issue of *The First Prayer
Book* (which made the novel provision of carrying the Sacrament direct from a celebration to
the sick) is rather complicated and difficult.
First, with regard to the Easter Sepulchre, the
Royal Visitors did not condemn it, and it appears
to have been used at Easter, 1547. Bishop
Gardiner, however, got into trouble for using it
at Winchester in the following year. There
seems, indeed, to have been an early desire to
get rid of the old custom of Reservation, and in
1547 the Reserved Sacrament was removed from
the altars in many churches. In October, 1548,
it was removed from Worcester Cathedral, and
in the following Lent from St. Paul's. Even

when *The First Prayer Book* appeared there was a distinct tendency to do away with any kind of reservation, and Ridley disapproved of it under any form. Indeed, before long, reverence for the Sacrament sank so low that proclamations and Acts of Parliament were called in against blasphemy and abuse, but in vain. Communion by proxy became common, as Barbaro noticed. Ridley and Hooper soon had their hands full in dealing with people who hired others to receive for them, and Latimer, most zealous of Reformers, lived to see the day when Communion was utterly neglected and to bewail of the English people " we care not for it."

The history of the destruction of the details of English piety during this reign is almost too complicated for a study such as this. However, certain broad lines of action can be traced, and these are of great importance in any survey of the life of the period, as the abolition of the old customs in the daily lives of the people did more than anything else to make the break with the past more pathetic and more drastic. They were part and parcel of the very religious bone and sinew of the nation. They were the daily evidence of the older religion. Judged in them-selves, they may not seem any more valuable than a policeman compared with a complete system of government. The disappearance, however, of an entire police force will discredit authority, and in like manner the withdrawal of these pious customs did a great deal to discredit

the Catholic religion among the mass of the
people. From this point of view, then, their
history under Edward VI. deserves notice. In
1538 Henry VIII. silenced the Angelus Bell,
which had been rung in England, in some form
at any rate, from the fourteenth century. " It
had been brought in and begun by the pretence
of the Bishop of Rome's pardon," and as such
must go. The Edwardine Visitors enforced this
order and extended it to all bells " except one
bell in convenient time to be rung or knolled
before the sermon." This order silenced the
Sacring Bell, which, with the Angelus, kept constantly before the people the mysteries of their
worship and redemption. The custom of saying
the Angelus in the fields or lanes was as common
in Catholic England as in Ireland or Brittany
to-day. Indeed, Archbishop Peckham had
specially ordered the ringing of the Sacring Bell,
" that the people who have not leisure daily to
be present at Mass may, wherever they be, in
houses or fields, bow their knees." The new
Edwardine orders were rigidly enforced. It is
true that in 1548 Cranmer appears to have
allowed a " non-abused " ringing of " holy
bells," but he definitely forbade the Sacring Bell.
The whole question, however, becomes so confusing that it is wellnigh impossible to trace the
fluctuations of its history. It is clear, however,
that the two already mentioned were effectually
silenced; and before long " knells and forth-
fares " became mere memories of bygone days.

" Hallowing of bells " disappeared along with other abuses and superstitions.

The history of various other customs is very voluminous, but it will be necessary to treat it in some detail, not only for the reasons mentioned, but because it figures so prominently in the Visitation records of the period, and because the customs died more slowly than anything else connected with the old religion. On the other hand, this survey of them must not be taken as in any way complete, as it would be impossible within the space of a short study even to deal adequately with the evidence provided by the documents to which I have largely confined myself. In addition, the history could be elaborated from the Edwardine Inventories and Churchwardens' Accounts, and evidence drawn from them would be required to fill in the details of the picture, which we are only drawing in broad outline. But the outline will be sufficiently clear to enable us to see how far-reaching were the effects of the Edwardine Reformation in relation to the lives and devotions of the people. It will make the history clearer to study several customs in some sort of chronological order, and to lead up from point to point until the custom was definitely abrogated by the Council. Of course, it would be impossible to decide how far this abrogation affected individuals. That is to say, we cannot arrive at any estimate of the number of people who obeyed the orders issued by the Government or Bishops,

but at the same time the history of these orders
will illustrate serious fluctuations in parish life,
and will help us to understand some of the
difficult conditions of parochial existence during
the period.

The use of holy water dated back to time
immemorial, and it was solemnly blessed before
the parochial High Mass every Sunday.   It stood
in every parish church in the land, and saint
and sinner shared in its provision.   In addition,
the parish clerk—called from this office the
aquæbajulus—carried it round weekly to the
homes of the people.   The Edwardine Government found these customs in full use.   The Ten
Articles of 1536 permitted the use of holy water
as one of the " good and laudable things to put
us in memory of what they signify."   When
there was further reform in the air in 1539, a
Royal Proclamation ordered the clergy to preach
against any superstitious use of it, and to
declare from the pulpit every Sunday " that it
was sprinkled of remembrance of Baptism and
of the sprinkling of the Blood of Christ."   The
Edwardine Visitors cautiously glanced at the
custom, and ordered that no one should condemn
it, as it was a " laudable custom of the Church,
by the King commanded to be observed, and not
as yet abrogated."   No other reference was made
to it in the Royal Injunctions of 1547, but the
Homilies, which they enforced, condemned it
without comment.   However, this condemnation
does not seem for the moment to have had much

weight, as there is extant an order in connection
with it, made by the Edwardine Visitors for the
Deanery of Doncaster and probably for the
province of York : " You shall every Sunday at
the time of your going about the church with
holy water, into three or four places where most
audience and assembly of people is . . . say
distinctly and plainly, that your parishioners
may well hear and perceive the same, these
words : *Remember Christ's blood shedding, by
the which most holy sprinkling of all your sins
you have free pardon.*" The same Visitors,
however, abrogated the custom of holy water
being carried by the parish clerk to the houses
of the people, and his visits to them were now
confined to collecting a new parochial poor-rate.
But reform soon advanced. An Order in
Council of February, 1548, abolished the use of
holy water, and henceforth it was generally
condemned. Holy water stocks, and vessels for
carrying it, were widely destroyed. Thus, for
example, the parishes of Middlesex and Essex
were brought into line in this connection in 1550.
In the following year the counties of North Wales
followed suit, and in 1552 Bishop Hooper forbade
the use of holy water in the parishes of Worcester
and Gloucester. To this evidence for its suppression may be added the fact that a Royal
Proclamation was necessary for its general
restoration in December, 1553.

Another practice must be noted in some detail,
as during the Henrician Reformation it came in

for not a few veiled attacks.   This is the use
of rosaries, which existed among all classes of the
English people, and was the most universal form
of private devotion.   The Edwardine Visitors
did not forbid rosaries, but attacked them as
among superstitious practices " which have not
only no promise of reward in Scripture . . .
but contrariwise great threats and maledictions
of God, for that they be things tending to
idolatry and superstition, which of all other
offences God Almighty doth most detest and
abhor, for that the same diminish most His
honour and glory."   They were condemned in
general terms by the *Homilies,* but so far I
have been unable to discover any condemnation
of them during the reign by the Government,
unless it was implied by the prohibition of invocation already referred to.   On the other hand,
it became quite common to forbid their use in
diocesan administration.   Thus those who used
them were ejected from church in 1549, and in
1550 a diocesan order for London forbade all
praying upon beads.   Hooper provided for a
general search for them in the homes of the
people in 1552.   He ordered all that were found
to be destroyed by the churchwardens.   The
history of Holy Bread, Palms, Ashes, Creeping to
the Cross, all the Easter ceremonies, and Kissing
the Pax, could be traced in like detail.   It is
not too much to say that before *The First Prayer
Book* appeared almost every old religious custom
had received diligent attention on the part of

the Government, and that no small array of
authority was brought to bear against them in
every parish in the land.   The churchwardens
became in this connection Government officials,
and it was a dangerous experiment to attempt
any adherence to the past where either the
Council or diocesan Bishop had spoken.   The
opinions of the people were in no way consulted.
Their private devotions were at the mercy of a
religious oligarchy in London, and it soon became
evident that Government meant during the reign
tyranny in a very real sense.   One other subject
deserves attention here before we turn to the
consideration of education and morals.

With the general loosing of restraint produced
by the ever-recurring changes, there soon arose
the question of fasting.   It would seem that in
some places the people, already growing lax
under a new and disorganized system, had begun
to play fast and loose with the fasting days.
The Royal Injunctions forbade any private action
until such time as changes were made by the
King's authority.   The opening of the reign
inherited some confusion from Henry VIII., and
in April, 1547, " Dr. Glasier preached at Paul's
Cross and affirmed that Lent was not ordained
by God to be fasted, neither the eating of flesh
to be forborne, but that the same was a politic
ordinance of men, and might therefore be broken
by men at their pleasure."   The French
Ambassador informs us that in the same month
a preacher who had previously spoken against

those who did not observe Lent was compelled
to retract publicly and to declare at St. Paul's
that the observance of Lent was a matter for
each individual conscience, adding that he made
this declaration by the command of the King
and Council. The whole movement against Lent
was characterized by profane and gross discussions and preachings. The preachers gave way
to the most wilful praise of " belly cheer " as
they called it, and said that fasting interfered
with nature. It would be possible to cull
passage after passage from contemporary literature to show how depraved were the discourses
of the preachers with respect to fasting, and how
the whole subject was dragged through the mire
of abuse, while the Council and Bishops even
turned Good Friday into a day " for jolly belly
cheer." On the other hand, a reaction set in
for economic reasons, and a Royal Proclamation
ordered the keeping of Lent in order to save
flesh and to benefit the fishermen. *The First
Prayer Book* made no provision for vigils and
fasting days, and the same Parliament which
gave it statutory force also made void " all
manner of statutes, laws, constitutions, and
usages concerning any manner of fasting and
abstinence from any kinds of meat heretofore in
this realm made or used." This statute made
no provision from fasting as distinct from
abstinence; but with regard to the latter it
enacted that in Lent, on Ember days, on Fridays
and Saturdays, and on any other day that should

be declared a fish day, no one should eat flesh. On this authority abstinence seems to have rested until the abstinence days were regulated *nominater* by a later Act of Parliament.

We have now surveyed in some detail certain aspects of Edwardine life, and this survey helps us to see how precarious and fluctuating were its conditions. The instability in religious affairs bore abundant fruit in the low state of education and morals. Edward VI. has received much credit for the work which he did in connection with education, and the Reformation in his reign has been claimed not infrequently as beneficial to morality and discipline. It is only within recent years that these two claims have begun to lose their hold. The former, if of wider import, can be dealt with in a narrower and more compact manner. The latter brings up a problem which, had it to be solved from diocesan documents alone, would not be satisfactorily answered.

Before the suppression of the Chantries the Church, through the Chantry priests, provided elementary education in most of the parishes in England. The Edwardine Visitors for the moment continued this state of affairs, and ordered them " to exercise themselves in teaching youth to read and write, and bring them up in good manners and other virtuous exercises." With the destruction of the Chantries many changes took place, and while some Chantry schools were for a time continued, the school-

masters were paid at a rate nominally fixed,
but gradually becoming less and less as the value
of the currency depreciated.   This in itself
spelled failure, and the Church could only stand
idly by and see her rich Chantry lands—destined
to become more and more valuable—pass into
royal or private hands.   Generally, however,
Edwardine parochial education was a ghastly
fiasco, while the Edwardine Grammar Schools
were merely the continuation of older foundations which it pleased the Government to spare.
Professor Pollard writes : " The greatest educa-
tional opportunity in English history was lost,
and the interests of the nation were sacrificed to
those of its aristocracy : between the endowment
of Seymours and ' superstition ' there was not
very much to choose."   In connection with the
cathedrals and collegiate churches certain provisions were made for education, but any
advances that were made were maintained by
money primarily intended for other objects, and
diverted summarily from other endowments.   A
few new schools were founded throughout the
country, chiefly, however, through money
obtained from the sale of Chantry property.
Edward VI.'s Government was in far too difficult
a financial predicament during the entire reign
to spend money, however obtained, on educa-
tional foundations.   An authoritative attempt
to educate the people was characterized by a
parsimonious expression of the Council's goodwill, and while the Government pursued its

policy of plunder it threw the burden of carrying out its orders on other shoulders. In a
typically Tudor manner they appropriated and
enforced an Henrician injunction, by which
clergy with a certain income were ordered to
maintain students at Oxford, Cambridge, or
some grammar school. This eminently burden-
some policy did not seem in the least incongruous
to the Government. To add additional expenses
to the clergy while the Church was being robbed
was something grimly Tudor. Nor was the order
a dead letter. Ridley and Cranmer saw that
there was no loophole for escape in their
dioceses. Elsewhere other efforts were made to
furnish the Universities with students. Thus,
at St. George's, Windsor, fines for omission of
clerical duty were partly applied for this object,
while all moneys of the foundation not otherwise
assigned helped the fund. Spite of all, the decay
of schools and Universities became a byword.
At Oxford priceless manuscripts and books were
burned at the instigation of the Earl of Warwick.
At Cambridge, Somerset himself superintended
the unparalleled vandalism. Ascham and
Latimer both bewailed the state of the Universities, which may be judged from the fact that
no one took a degree at Oxford in 1547 and 1548,
and Gardiner feared the closing of Cambridge
University. On the other hand, the previous
study has shown us that the Government were
not slow to encourage reading among the people,
provided they read books in keeping with the

religious policy. Bibles flowed from the press, emphasizing the wickedness of the Pope, the futility of Sacramental life, and the abolition of the old faith. In addition to this flood, countless streams of pamphlet literature reached the public, blessed by the authorities, in which all that was sacred in the religious part of the nation was held up to the most scurrilous ridicule. It is only necessary to glance down the list of printed books of the period in order to see the type of reading fostered by the Government, and abuse of the Mass has rarely reached a higher pitch of profanity.

When we turn to clerical education we find much enthusiasm on the part of the officials— civil and ecclesiastical—and apparently small practical results. The early dealings with the subject did not aim very high. The clergy were ordered in 1547 to study the New Testament in Latin and English with *The Paraphrase* of Erasmus, and examinations on these subjects were provided at the various future Visitations. This order seems to have been applied to the dioceses very widely and in various forms. For example, it was enforced in Kent and Middlesex in almost identical terms in 1548. At Winchester College the New Testament became the scholar's *vade mecum,* at the expense of all " profane authors." In York in 1552 memory lessons in the Pauline epistles were varied with studies every fortnight in the Gospels and Acts. At Lincoln the cathedral body were compelled to study a chapter of the Bible every day, while in the Deanery of Doncaster the standard rose to two chapters. How far these orders were carried out cannot now be estimated, but it is clear that examinations of all the clergy at regular intervals were aimed at. I have made close search for the records of such examinations, but all that seems to be extant is a long account of an examination of the clergy of Gloucester and Worcester held in May, 1551. The return, in addition to its splendid isolation for the reign, is a painful illustration of the depths to which clerical learning had sunk, and it is not unfair to make it a criterion for the rest of the country. Hooper asked nine questions : What are the Ten Commandments? Where are they written? Can you recite them? What are the Articles of the Christian Faith? Can you recite them? Can you prove them from Scripture? Can you recite the petitions of the Lord's Prayer? How do you know that it is the Lord's Prayer? Where is it written? For this not very formidable examination three hundred and eleven clergy presented themselves. Sixty-two incumbents were absent—mostly pluralists—who had been examined elsewhere. Of those present, one hundred and seventy-one were unable to repeat the Commandments, though all except thirty-three could tell the chapter in which they were found. Ten were unable to repeat the Lord's Prayer. Twenty-seven could not tell who wrote it. Thirty could not tell where it could be found. In some cases an incumbent could repeat the

Lord's Prayer, though he could not tell who wrote it or where it was written. Some further painful light is thrown on the state of clerical learning when we examine some of the remarks made by the clergy during the examination. The parson of Haresfield : " Repeated and knows it to be the Lord's Prayer because Christ at His Passion delivered it to His disciples, saying, ' Watch and pray.' " The parson of Harscom " repeated it, but knows not whether it be the Lord's Prayer or not." The minister of Staverton "knows it to be the Lord's Prayer· because written in Matthew vi. ; but by whom written *penitus ignorat.*" The minister of Buckland " repeated *sed a quo tradita aut ubi scripta nescit.*" The parson of Bladington " can repeat and knows it as the Lord's Prayer, *propterea quod a Christo (ut credit) tradita sit, sed ubi scripta penitus ignorat.*" The parson of Northcerney " can repeat Articles of Faith, but not prove from Scripture, *quia satis erit sibi credere propterea traditus* (sic) *authoritate regia.*" The parson of Southcerney " can repeat and knows it as the Lord's Prayer, *propterea quod tradita sit a Domino Rege, ac scripta in libro regio de communi oracione.*" The parson of Farmcote is thus summed up : " *Invenitur vir præ cœteris ignorans.*" It can hardly be wondered at if England became a byword for ignorance ; and the matter becomes all the more deplorable when we remember that Hooper imposed on the same clergy at the same time a series of dogmatic articles full of the most intricate theological problems and of highly controversial terms which they must have been utterly incapable of understanding. A strange contrast is presented between the state of learning in England at the beginning of the sixteenth century and fifty years later. When Henry VIII. ascended the throne the revival of learning had already made itself felt in England, and before long it had extended its influence outside a narrow group of scholars to both Universities. At Oxford the Benedictine Order supplied a considerable number of graduates for more than a third of the century, while at Cambridge priests and monks furnished not a few colleges with students. Monastery and monastery vied with one another in scholastic enthusiasm. Under Edward VI. all the old conditions — even immediate — changed. The revival of learning and its early gifts soon became memories, and England lost touch with the intellectual enthusiasms of the Continent as the old faith died. The Elizabethan age in literature owed its greatness to other sources.

In turning to consider moral conditions under Edward VI., we enter on an aspect of Edwardine life which is full of difficulties, not only owing to the forces of instability which had been let loose at the time, but because of the fact that the evidences have never been completely worked. However, it is possible to form a comparatively accurate idea of the condition of morals—and by that we mean general public order and decency—by considering the statements of contemporary writers and by studying the efforts, such as they were, to bring about improvement. Before entering this division of our study it is well to point out that no effort will be made to make this a comparative study. We shall deal with the broad facts of the history, and leave other ages to bear their own burden. Firstly, the religious changes, spite of Bucer's warnings, had been brought about at such an appalling and illogical pace that the whole balance of self-control among the people was upset, and unseemly riots characterized the entire reign. Towns and villages and rural parishes were split into rival factions, which watched the fluctuation of events, and scanned eagerly the religious horizon for any sign of triumph for their religious party. The pulpits rang with fierce denunciations, and the people naturally enough reflected in their actions and talk the spirit of the preachers. From the very beginning of the reign efforts were made to prevent the preachers getting beyond control; but there can be little doubt that, with the whole religious system of the country in the melting-pot, restraint in controversy was wellnigh impossible. The reign began with warnings against unneighbourly feuds, and the people were also warned not to pour uncharitable scorn on the clergy, even though " they favoured fantasies rather than God's truth." Nor were the services of the Church free from disturbances. At Canterbury " talking and jangling and lewd demeanour in choir " were common, and deprivation was hung over the heads of the clerical

delinquents as a warning.   In addition, the
ordinary amenities of life disappeared among the
personnel of the same Church, to make way for
" contention, brawling, chiding, and blows."
Indeed, Canterbury seems to have sunk to pretty
low depths at this time, and the porters' lodges
were notorious centres of card-playing and
gambling.   Throughout the Province the conduct
during the public services was deplorable, while
brawling and discord between neighbour and
neighbour characterized the daily life of the
parish.   Cranmer did his best to improve
matters, but in vain.   In London disputes
reached a climax, as was to be expected with the
presence of the foreign Ambassadors and of such
a miscellaneous class of people as crowded to
the Metropolis.   In 1550 Ridley found his clergy
" common brawlers " and stirrers up of discord
and strife.   Many defended private insurrections
and seditions, and there seems to have existed
among them an element of communism which
favoured anarchy.   Among the people there were
disturbers of worship by noises, talking,
quarrelling, or by departing out of church in a
manner sufficiently emphatic to betoken disapproval.   Indeed, it became necessary to stir
up the churchwardens to enforce order, not only
in the churches, but in the churchyards and
porches.   In the West, Hooper did his utmost.
Noises and fighting were common in the churches
of his vast diocese, and on Sundays many people
got no farther than the churchyards, where they
spent the service time in unedifying disputes.

Examples could be multiplied, but would only overburden the picture. On all sides there was abroad a spirit of revolt, irreverence, and personal bitterness, which extended from the parochial life outside the churches to the parochial worship within them.

Nor is the picture anything better when we come to deal with morals in the more technical sense of the word. It would almost seem as though the nation gave itself over to unbridled licence. Latimer, in his last sermon before the King, spoke in no unmeasured terms of the moral condition of the country : " Never was so much adultery, so much divorcing; lechery is now a trifle." The dioceses were notorious for " unparalleled immorality." He suggested excommunication from the congregation as a remedy, but, as Elizabeth found, the strength of excommunication proved ineffective in new hands, and it could have had little weight when wielded by Bishops who held their office "*durante bene placito*" and "*quamdiu se bene gesserint.*" Indeed, among them there was scandal enough. Ponet, Bishop of Winchester, was divorced after his elevation to the bench, and Archbishop Holgate of York was compelled to defend a suit of a similar nature. When we turn to details in the dioceses we are confronted with a black picture. Every conceivable breach of the moral law seems to have been common. In the first year of the reign the clergy were notorious for drinking, rioting, resorting to ale-houses, and gambling at cards and dice.   In the cathedrals there was, in addition to similar laxity, widespread hunting among the dignitaries, while suspected women visited them in their rooms or houses, or were resorted to in different places outside.   Compared with this, the bad language complained of was of small importance. Adultery, fornication, and even incest seemed to have been common among the cathedral clergy, while at Winchester College the general demeanour was so filthy and uncomely that the Royal Visitors were compelled to interfere in the interests of the students.   In the Diocese of Canterbury the state of morality among the laity was deplorable, and every document in this connection confirms Latimer's estimate.   Indeed, matters reached such a crisis that an effort was made to stir up the Church to more diligence against bigamists and fornicators, while the Lord Chancellor was compelled to deliver a speech urging the judges to deal more severely with similar offences.   The whole country was in a pitiable moral condition.

In conclusion, in no respect did the example of the Government exercise a more evil influence than in presentations to benefices.   Gain directed the policy among the Council and its officials, and those below them bartered any ecclesiastical appointments in their gift.   It may safely be said that from this point down to the death of Elizabeth the Established Church was a byword for corruption, and this not among enemies alone, but among her own best children, such as

Parker, who strove in vain to stem the tide of corruption in such relationships. From the parishes of London and Kent, from the Western Counties, from the Welsh Borders, from every cathedral, evidence is forthcoming that simony was one of the plague-spots of the reign. We cannot be surprised, then, that an Act of Parliament was required to compel the people to pay their tithes. The stream of corruption trickled down from the Government through the Bishops and clergy to the people. Among every class there was widespread greed and dishonesty. Bucer looked aghast and saw that moral reform was more necessary " than snatching the instruments of impiety " from the people " by proclamations " and imposing " the true religion by royal command." He pleaded for moderation in zeal when there was neither teaching nor example. " It is greatly to be feared that the enemy actuates men of this mind, who strive to hand the government of the religion of Christ to men who are both unfit for it, and who do not suffer themselves to be advised, and who thus make way for the greed of men to seize the wealth of the Church, and little by little to do away altogether with Christ's religion." The " greed of men " is one of the most consistent features of the life of the period, and it never stayed its hand while there remained any ecclesiastical property. Bucer might appeal, Latimer might denounce, Bullinger might tremble, but the moral law must always give way " to the King's godly proceedings." Debauchery, immorality, and dishonesty were widespread. The inns were crowded on Sundays and festivals because, as the Second Act of Uniformity said, the people " wilfully and damnably refused to come to their parish churches." Not a few of the Reformers considered that England under Edward VI. was worse than ever it had been under the Pope, and that the immorality of the age cast into the shade anything previously known in the country. Camden spoke of the " downright frenzy " of the nation. Ridley has left us a picture which is not likely to be overdrawn of the monsters of vice and lust which stalked the country. Cox declared that there would have been no Reformation had there been no property. Everything —crosses, chalices, candlesticks, all the pious offerings of generations, with the few exceptions of those hidden " against a day "—passed into the gulf of Tudor avarice, to which everything was welcome and from which nothing returned. Even the plate from the petit-canons' table at St. George's, Windsor, was inventoried as " fit for His Majesty's service, and tending to superstitious uses." And behind all stands the grim figure of Calvin urging Cranmer on against all moderation, which " is the bane of genuine improvement." Bankrupt in faith, in morals, in finance, and in the politics of Europe, England presented at Edward VI.'s death a picture perhaps unparalleled in her history, while it became a capricious and scornful jest to cry " Where is now her God?"

V

THE DIFFICULTIES OF QUEEN MARY

THE problems which lay before Mary Tudor were far more complicated than those with which her grandfather had to deal. To a large extent Henry VII.'s difficulties were clear-cut, and his energies were directed not so much in examining and balancing them as in developing a strong statesmanship in dealing with them. His very successes, however, became sources of weakness and strength to his granddaughter. He had strengthened loyalty to the throne and had carefully nurtured the new nationalism, thus helping in no small degree to render possible the rule and policy of his son. Loyalty to the throne became undoubtedly a source of strength to Mary in her early difficulties, but the new nationalism was full of intricate problems for her, as it had in it all those elements of sturdy independence, which would challenge some of her dearest aims. In addition, Henry VII. had to deal with the people inexperienced in religious upheavals and questionings; his difficulties were confined to home and foreign politics. Mary was called on to govern a people who had gone through a religious experience unparalleled in history for its compressed and swift variations. To civil and political issues had been added the far more dangerous complications of national religious differences. Henry VII. brought to his work experience of life and men and a determination to accept his limitations and to carry out his duties within them. Mary was perhaps the least suited English Sovereign who ever attempted to deal with the task of government. Her failure as a Queen was almost assured from the beginning, however heroically she might have tried to develop tact and statecraft. We shall consider, then, her personal difficulties, which severely handicapped her in dealing with the political and religious problems which lay before her—and these we shall survey in detail.

Before entering on the subject, however, it will be well to point out that Mary has been hardly dealt with by both friends and foes. On the one hand she has been almost canonized, on the other she has been remembered by comprehensive epithets of infamy. The air will be somewhat cleared if we try to grasp some of the contemporary ideas and principles. In the sixteenth century nothing could be reformed or retained without persecution. Once the student of history realizes that he will have acquired one of the essential elements in forming a judgment of Mary. In addition, if we take the old comparison between Mary and Elizabeth, we must concede at once that Mary was by far the more conscientious. The question then is, What is the value of conscience in a ruler? The lessons of history—if there are such—clearly prove that incompetence causes more suffering than unscrupulousness in statesmen, that efficiency in a ruler is more essential than conscience, partly because efficiency—if complete—will make him outwardly conscientious in his dealings with others, while no amount of conscience will make him efficient. Mary was the very refinement of conscience, but she was an infinitely worse Queen than Elizabeth, and a sincere and conscientious bigot will inflict more suffering than an unscrupulous politician like Elizabeth. Mary would have been an excellent nun ; she was one of the worst possible rulers. Of course, I would exact as high a standard of private morality in rulers as possible, but in the final analysis it is all a question of expediency in politics. Absolute principles cannot be afforded, they can only be enforced to the extent that circumstances will permit, and the most successful ruler—and the best friend of morality—is he who can discern how far he can apply moral principles without ruining the experiment by pressing it too far. On the other hand, Mary cannot, I feel, be dismissed merely by a recognition of current theories or of the defects of her virtues. It seems clear that a survey of her difficulties is emphatically necessary if an adequate estimate of her character and reign can be formed. These difficulties will not excuse her failures as a

Queen, but they deserve a greater consideration than they have received when judgment has to be pronounced on those failures. She faced them heroically, and she failed because she was not born to be a ruler or a *politique* like her father or her sister.

From her earliest years Mary was a strange figure in Tudor projects. When she was a mere child various marriage proposals gathered round her, all part of the fluctuating foreign policy of Henry VIII. and Wolsey. The tragic history of the royal divorce entered bitterly into her life, ending not merely in separation from her mother, but in public disgrace. She was robbed of her title of Princess and of intercourse with her friends. Acts of Parliament discussed her birth at intervals. Her execution was regularly pressed on her father. Her mother's death was celebrated at Court with wanton rejoicings. Humiliating proposals were submitted to her, in which she was asked to acknowledge her own illegitimacy. She sacrificed her loyalty to Rome, her mother's honour, and her own conscience by yielding to the specious arguments of the Emperor, to whom she adhered, all unconscious of his political duplicity. When her brother succeeded to the throne her religion was proscribed, and she saw England decay in influence and morals, owing to private ambitions and religious bitterness. Finally the King of France prepared to help Northumberland's project for bringing the Crown into his own

family, and Mary stood once more in the thick
perils of intrigue. It is little wonder, then, that
there must be a bitter tenacity of purpose in her
character. But there were other defects. Mary
looked towards the past, England towards the
future. She had grasped none of the new spirit
or the new tendencies, and her conception of
sovereignty was entirely mediæval. She was
called to direct a people full of the new, and she
could only offer them the wisdom of the old. In
addition, the tragedy of her early life had made
her suspicious of the national changes, every one
of which seemed to have brought her its own
peculiar burden of sorrow. Her own misfortunes
appeared to be bound up with the death of the
past and the birth and development of the new.
There can be little doubt that she loved her
country and her people, and that her whole-
hearted aim was to benefit them, but her benefits
were not such as were advantageous to a transformed nation. Child of the old, she had seen
little in the new progress which was not full of
personal tragedy, and she was so blinded by it
that she could not distinguish its principles from
its excesses. She was completely—in everything
—behind her age, and her failure is all the more
pathetic because she failed through the use of
means which half a century before would have
been successful. Such were her limitations, and
to them was added the severest of all limitations
—she did not know them. She took up the reins
of government as though the Renaissance, the

breach with Rome, and the religious anarchy had never happened. England to her was England before 1536, and the national spirit was that of an age before Luther had rebelled, before the New Learning and the New World had been heard of. In addition, she had no valuable experience of the new life or of the new politics, and what she had had confirmed her in her mistrust of the new and in her adherence to the old. Worst of all, she considered the Emperor her only friend, and the new England had little use for anything foreign. Perhaps no English Sovereign ever ascended the throne more severely handicapped by personal limitations for the difficulties which presented themselves for solution. Mary's aspirations for good government might have carried her through had she not had a conscience. To bring back her people to the bosom of the Church was to her more than all else in home or foreign politics. She regarded unity with the Church as absolutely essential to national welfare, and she attempted to bring about that unity by an appeal to the methods which were undoubtedly justified when the world was Catholic. She had learned nothing of the changes in England, or even of her brother's failure to make England Protestant by Act of Parliament. She failed to appreciate the changes in the aristocratic and landed classes, who had grown up out of the banishment of the Pope. Conscientious, sincere, and devout, she could not believe that most men at the time were not primarily Catholics or even Protestants, but simply nationalists or *politiques*. Her faith was so foolishly splendid that she thought that England could not but welcome back the Pope and the Catholic Faith, and that the restoration of them would more than satisfy the national needs. It is possible to understand Mary when we remember her limitations, and possible to appreciate her difficulties when we recall the solution which she offered to them.

Northumberland's conspiracy to put Lady Jane Grey on the throne was surrounded by many favourable circumstances. Signatures of importance were obtained to the Instrument which lent it value. Charles V. was hardly in a position to interfere actively, as his hands were full. It seemed advantageous to France not to prevent a plan which would disgrace the Emperor's cousin, and Northumberland might even hope for Henry II.'s military support. The French King knew that it would be easier to depose Lady Jane than Mary, and thus to carry out his project of uniting England to France through Mary Queen of Scots. Before Mary Tudor, then, lay an ambiguous outlook. Her best friend, the Emperor, advised a compromise, while his Ambassadors told her that anything like resistance would be hopeless. But Mary was made of sterner stuff, and the people were not likely to accept a ruler of Northumberland's choice. When Edward VI. died, Mary anticipated a summons from the Council, and fled to

Framlingham, while the people waited in gloom for the disclosure of Northumberland's hand. The proclamation against her, though couched in the arrogant language of assurance and misguided patriotism, did not move the nation to favour the project, and Ridley's sermon proclaiming her and Elizabeth bastards produced open resentment. Mary's summons to the Council demanding her rights showed, however, that there were strong forces against her, but the counties were rallying in her cause. Before long Northumberland's tools in London saw that the game was up, and Suffolk actually proclaimed Mary in London ; while Northumberland, making a virtue of necessity, did the same at Cambridge. The revolution was at an end. With it, however, began Mary's first difficulties. Undoubtedly the people welcomed her, but those who had experience in government, and who were necessary for the administration, had almost to a man been guilty of treason. She was thus compelled to begin her reign with an unwieldy body of advisers, composed of her personal friends and of the treasonable Council. The Council was a compromise. Of the restored councillors were Tunstall, Gardiner, Thirlby, Norfolk, Southwell, Rich, and Paget. Several of Northumberland's faction managed to retain their places—Winchester, Arundel, Bedford, Pembroke, Shrewsbury, Westmoreland, Baker, Cheyne, Gage, Mason, and Petre. In the national joy, however, the past was forgotten, and Mary dealt out merciful measures which were the beginning of that defect which could pardon treason, but not heresy. Northumberland, of course, suffered with a doubtful confession of conversion to Catholicism on his lips. Two of his supporters met the same fate, but the remainder of the chief conspirators were merely convicted and imprisoned. Mary's success, however, was no guarantee for the future. The Emperor and the foreign Ambassadors did not see in it any promise that she would be able to abandon the Royal Supremacy, which she specially desired to do. The national joy was purely an expression of nationalism, and Pole was retained on the Continent by various means for fear he should precipitate affairs by strengthening the Queen's intentions. Quiet changes took place at once. The Mass was gradually restored, extreme Reformers were sent to prison, and Cranmer was confined to the Tower, ostensibly for his treason, but in reality for defending the Edwardine reforms. The Edwardine Bishops who remained firm were deprived, and the Catholic Bishops were restored. Up to this point Mary acted as Supreme Head of the Church—the Act was as yet unrepealed. Two important problems faced her before she met her first Parliament—would she marry, and what would she do with regard to the Catholic Faith? With regard to the former, she considered it her duty to the nation, but she appealed to the Emperor. It was clearly advantageous to Charles that Mary should marry his son, as it would counteract the influence of Henry II. Before long it was well known that Philip's chances were good, and Gardiner felt bound to show the Queen that if she chose him she would alienate her people, who hated foreigners, and Spaniards above all. Other members of the Council supported the Chancellor, but Norfolk, Arundel, and Paget were in favour of the Spanish match. Thus almost at the beginning of her reign a serious difficulty arose. Out of it came a further complication. The French Ambassador Noailles began his career of treasonable duplicity. He encouraged young Courtenay to hope for his aid, and he threw out suggestions in favour of Mary Queen of Scots. With regard to religion, Charles, in reply to Mary's declaration that she would restore the old Faith, advised caution, and told her to wait for the deliberation of Parliament. On the other hand, Julius III. had welcomed her determination, and immediately appointed Cardinal Pole Legate, as a preliminary to the restoration of the Papal jurisdiction. The first Parliament did not advance Mary's supreme object, and it served to disclose the growing difficulties. Her mother's divorce was annulled and her own legitimacy established, but no relief was given with regard to the Royal Supremacy. In addition, it was made clear that any proposal for restoring Church lands would not be accepted. The marriage problem accentuated the dangers. Mary curtly told Parliament to mind its own business when it asked her to marry an Englishman, and abruptly broke off its address. This independent note disclosed the gravity of the position. Up to this time it may be said that religion had not entered largely into the difficulties. Here and there there were undoubtedly Protestants, but like the miscellaneous tracts and the violent preachers they were not of sufficient importance to disturb the situation. The proposed Spanish match, however, was a serious matter — the nation was against it. It strengthened Protestants, and then the religious difficulty came in, and it split Catholics into opposing camps, thus emphasizing the difficulties of government. When the marriage arrangements were completed in October, 1553, it was clear that Mary had entered on a dangerous course. Noailles was furious, for it represented the complete failure of his diplomacy. Intrigue followed intrigue until it culminated in Wyatt's Rebellion. This revolt can hardly be called religious. It might almost be called the popular réply to the high-sounding marriage treaty in which Gardiner had done his best to safeguard English interests. But Englishmen had no reason to believe in Spanish promises, and the very possibility of the most serious attack ever made on a Tudor throne showed that the nation was against the alliance. Wyatt, it is true, gathered to his forces Protestants who were displeased at the restoration of Catholic worship, and who had originally supported the Queen; but he relied on the political issue as his principal battle-call, clearly showing that the religious problem had not yet reached such complications as to make it an effective recruiting incentive for revolt. In addition to armed revolt dangerous undercurrents of discontent were abroad. Philip and the Queen were mercilessly slandered. Courtenay and Elizabeth figured in treasonable negotiations. The revolt and the obscure dealings of Noailles and Soranzo, the Venetian Ambassador, might have taught Mary a lesson in more ways than one. Lady Jane Grey was offered up an innocent victim to new treasons with which she had no connection. Her father and husband suffered with greater justice, but to the rank and file Mary extended her usual impolitic clemency. Charles V. and Renard urged severity. The Council was more hopelessly divided than ever, and Pole was waiting to take his departure for England full of scorn for the religious compromise with which Mary had begun, and prepared to do his utmost to second the Queen's resolve to restore the Pope, and at the same time to join with Gardiner against the Spanish match. Pole knew as little of the new England as Mary did. Had she at once restored the Pope Wyatt's revolt might have been more formidable. If the Emperor were alienated, the Papal cause would lose an almost essential support in England. Pole, however, believed that Spain was more hated than Catholicism, and in the result Catholicism came back with Spain, and hatred of the Spaniard emphasized hatred of the Pope.

The new Parliament only served to emphasize the difficulties. It is absurd to accept the sweeping statement that it was entirely packed. Soranzo undoubtedly said so, but his estimate is based on no evidence. Its deliberations were marked by ugly discussions. It was ready to confirm the right of a woman to rule. Wyatt's failure silenced opposition to the marriage treaty. Proposals, however, to allow the Queen to pass over Elizabeth and to bequeath the Crown were only suggested to be abandoned. The plan to revive the heresy laws, which evidently was a private venture on the part of Gardiner, and to discontinue the pensions to the religious who had married, was equally futile. Even the extension of the treason laws to protect Philip was refused. Gardiner and Paget were at loggerheads. The real issue was passing to questions of religion, and Renard informed the Emperor that religion was the cause of all the troubles. On all sides fear was growing up among Catholics, and Protestants were gaining courage. Essex and Suffolk almost broke into revolt. Paget was supposed to be arranging a secret conspiracy to arrest Gardiner and the Papal party in the Council. He represented to a large extent the new mind of England. Mary wanted to restore the Church lands—that was the great difficulty. Paget and his party cannot be called Protestants, and nothing was to be feared by the Queen from conscientious Protestants. But Paget saw that if Mary interfered with the new strength in the nation which had arisen from the destruction of the Church it would join hands with conscientious Protestantism and destroy her influence, if not her throne. In addition, Paget saw that if Mary refounded Monasticism in England along the old lines, the nationalism of the country would be outraged by a clerical majority in the House of Lords, and the day for such a position had, for good or evil, passed. When Paget appealed to the Emperor he hoped that Charles V. would support him with his son against an extreme reaction such as Mary and Gardiner contemplated. The secular side of Henry VIII.'s changes must not be destroyed. Indeed, Mary could not hope to restore the Pope until it was confirmed. The Queen, however, was clearly under clerical control, and Paget's party—the supporters of the Spanish match—hoped from their knowledge of Charles V. and his policy that his son would use his influence on the side of the Henrician settlement with regard to Church lands. If that were done, none of them cared very much whether the Pope or the Sultan became head of the Church. Charles used his influence. Efforts were made to smooth matters over before the session ended, but ugly difficulties had showed themselves. One aim alone predominated in Mary's mind, and it blinded her to the obvious fact that no Government could expect to hold together when she remained unamenable to reason. However, the comparative calm of the closing days of Parliament acted on her as the victory over Wyatt had done. She was content with the apparent success, and the fact that she was not defeated strengthened her determination to carry out her policy, when it ought to have taught her to reconsider it. The marriage took place with Mary still blind to the disruption in her Government and to the discontent among her people.

Charles V. had now no object in preventing Pole from coming to England. No more suitable Legate could have been provided from the Papal point of view. Pole had clean hands and a clear conscience. He had never deviated from allegiance to the Pope nor gone through any variety of religious experience. He looked on England as a land almost miraculously given an opportunity, by Mary's accession, of returning to the ancient Faith, and he understood nothing of the new England or of the public hatred of the Pope which had been fostered for almost a generation. He was an Englishman in his objections to the Spanish match, but when it came to a question of restoring the Papal jurisdiction he was heart and soul on the side of Mary, even to the extent of wishing to restore Church lands. The position, then, when his arrival was determined on was this : He was a traitor already attainted, and there was no possibility of his being received in England and of having this difficulty removed by Parliament unless some concession was made. Gardiner now saw that it meant that past alienations must be confirmed by Rome. The new Parliament, chosen by Mary's advice on letters sent round to the Sheriffs and county officials, would do nothing for the Pope or Pole until the secular question of property was settled to their advantage. It is not necessary to discuss the composition of this Parliament—forty per cent. of the old members were returned—but Mary found it quite tractable as soon as it became known that the wealth diverted from the Church would not be restored and that its holders would be confirmed in their possession of it. All this was arranged by Renard before Pole left Brussels for England. His attainder was hurriedly repealed, and he was received by Parliament with such an expression of joy as relief from the fear of personal loss can produce. The Bills for reunion with Rome passed unanimously, and Lords and Commons, on behalf of themselves and the nation, on St. Andrew's Day, 1554, were absolved from schism. To the simple-minded Catholic the reunion with the Church must have been a source of real joy. To the Queen it must have meant the crown of all her hopes—but the whole thing was unreal. Many of the people were devout Catholics, and many of the northern gentry were prepared then, as in the future, to fight on behalf of the Catholic Faith; but the vast majority of the country gentry were ready to become Jews or Mohammedans if it suited them to do so. The religious changes had made them indifferent. In addition, there was scarcely a wealthy or moderately wealthy family in England that had not benefited materially by the Acts of Henry VIII., and these were only ready to become " good " Catholics on condition that they retained the worldly benefits of their sin. Now Mary was quite blind to the true state of affairs. There was not a sufficient leaven of Catholicism left in the country to bind England to the Church. Most of the people were ready to accept outwardly the religion of their Sovereign. Renard and Suriano saw this, while Mary did not. Lords and Commons were quite ready to accept an absolution which did not hurt their pockets in this world, whatever effect it may have had on the next. Mary saw in the pitiful hypocrisy of St. Andrew's Day a nation conscientiously returning to its ancient Faith. Hundreds of people attended Church, like Cecil and Elizabeth, because the State had made it the legal thing to do. They deceived no one. The foreign correspondence now opens to us the real state of many conformists. They obeyed the law, but they did not believe. Parliament revived the heresy statutes, abolished the Henrician Acts against the Pope, and left the Faith and Church government to ecclesiastics. There lies the real solution to the persecutions. Parliament revived the heresy laws, but the Church must convict, and Mary and her Council must issue a writ for burning a heretic thus convicted. We are not called on to excuse Gardiner or Bonner or any of the Bishops. They have suffered all the penalties which prejudice can produce, and they were not as bad as they have been painted. It seems to me that the issue lies plainer than almost anything in Tudor history. The heresy laws were permissive, not coercive, and Parliament cannot be entirely saddled with an odium which belongs to the ecclesiastical courts and to the Queen and Council. Burnings were permitted by law, but no law compelled their being carried out. To the Queen and Council history must lay the greatest blame. The latter could undoubtedly have held the Queen's hand had it been able; but Mary had tuned it to her likings, and she conscientiously liked to persecute. Of course, every schoolboy knows that in this she stood on the same platform as the Reformers, as Cranmer himself. That, however, is not in question. When this argument is produced, why not make it clear in whose hands lay the decision as to whether persecution should take place or not? Persecution in the sixteenth century is nothing to be ashamed of. When we blame, as we shall do later, Elizabeth and her Council and Parliament, it is foolhardy and fatuous to excuse Mary and her Council and to throw all the burden on Parliament. Elizabeth shrewdly placed treason in the forefront, and invented new treasons to cover religion. Mary at least held by the old laws of England and burned for heresy, although she might in many cases have included treason ; but the blame is almost entirely hers. It is in this connection that her greatest failure lay. The most elementary form of political foresight might have taught her that it would be fatal to put in motion the new machinery which Parliament had given her when its own material interests were saved. Once more the inherent weakness of being satisfied with apparent success blinded her, and the dealings with heretics began which, on the top of the Spanish match, lost her the love and devotion of her people.. Gardiner's death, after opening the new Parliament in October, 1555, deprived her of one of the stanchest Englishmen in her Council. She leaned more than ever on Pole, who had no political interests apart from the Church. In addition, Philip, who had left England in the previous September, began to urge her to obtain Parliamentary sanction for his coronation, and failing that to have it carried out on her own authority. Mary could no more oblige him in that than give him an heir to the throne, but everyone knew that she would have done so had she not feared a national revolt. The closing difficulties of the reign gather round Spanish policy, and may well be considered in connection with it. Before doing this, however, it may be well to refer to a difficulty of a somewhat serious nature which faced Mary and her Government. The Press got out of hand, and the authorities completely failed to control it, although there was no small display of attempts to do so. The national dislike for the Spanish marriage was emphasized by the reports which Noailles circulated. There were few possibilities of misfortune which he did not make use of as certain to happen. He played on every note— national suffering, personal suffering, religious and political chaos. There was hardly a dis- contented party in England—or one liable to discontent—which in some way or other did not come in contact with his methods. The way was thus prepared for the most scurrilous literature which ever attacked an English Sovereign. Care must be taken that the influence of this literature is not overestimated. Not a few writers, in their desire to provide excuses for Mary, have laid more weight on the effects which it produced than can be justified. All that can be said is that it accentuated discontent, decreased loyalty to the throne, and lowered the royal ideal. To claim for it more than this is to lose historical propor- tion. The most influential productions came from abroad. Goodman and Ponet encouraged rebel- lion against the throne. Knox attacked the Queen as a woman, and therefore under the curse of God and incapable of ruling. These three combined with Bradford and Bale to make the Spanish match odious. Seldom has language been used with more vitriolic force, or calumny and scurrility been more harmoniously blended. The very fact that such a literature was possible shows the failure of Mary's rule. Doubtless it accentuated that failure and made government all the more difficult. Its circulation could not but do Mary and her rule harm, as she was already discredited, and her advisers had proved inadequate; but it would be a mistake to assign the discredit and hatred of the Government to the literature. It complicated the situation, it did not create it. Seditious literature only flourishes where sedition already exists.

The final scenes of the reign gather round a national awakening against Spain. This unity— for such it may be called—was not against Spain *per se;* it would have been as strong against any other nation under similar circumstances. On every side men saw favour meted out to Spanish interests. Mary was ready to strengthen Philip's position in England. Her ships became in reality Spanish ships. Her subjects, inspired by the call of new worlds, were uniformly sacrificed to Spanish interests. Rumours came of Spanish forces ready to compel the English nation to agree to Philip's coronation. Contemporary observers noted the nation's mind and foretold disaster. Discontent soon made itself felt. Although there was a public peace between France and Spain, yet Henry II. welcomed refugees from England. A formidable plot was formed to set Elizabeth on the throne and to marry her to Courtenay. Treason gathered forces not merely among the gentlemen of the West but among Members of Parliament. Noailles knew everything, though it is difficult to find out how far he was impli-cated. It was small consolation for Mary to have

built up the outward fabric of the Church when
her partiality for her husband was not only a
fruitful source of active treason but was driving
her into more difficult relations than ever with
France, where Englishmen fled to plot against
her throne. The position was rendered all the
more tragic by Philip's continued absence at
Brussels, where his life was one of gross immorality. He was preparing for another war with
France, and Mary knew that this would bring
her husband into difficulties with the Pope, for
whom she had laboured regardless of cost.
Before long Paul IV. excommunicated Philip,
and stood with France against Spain, Tuscany,
and Savoy. This war was the crowning difficulty
of Mary's life. Would she stand with her
husband against the Papacy? Spiritual reasons
called on her to remain at least neutral, and
Pole advocated peace. On the other hand, if she
decided to support her husband she knew that
the vast majority of her people and all her
Council—Paget excepted—would be against a
French war. Paget was at least consistent in
his support of Spain, but his private influence
failed to overcome national feelings, and Philip
at last came to England, drawn by a desire to
implicate the country in the most unpopular of
wars. Mary felt that she had failed to bring him
back, that only his own ambitions caused his
return ; but once more she hoped to present him
with an heir and thus to bind him to herself.
Pole failed hopelessly to move either the French
King or the Pope in the direction of peace. The

Council remained obdurate, but Henry II. and Paul IV. judged England from the point of view of Philip's presence there. The former encouraged more than ever the plots of English refugees, and Paul IV. denounced Spain in no very delicate terms, and invited the French to try conclusions once more with the Spaniards in Italy. Stafford's attack on the coast of Yorkshire was Henry's answer to Philip's visit to England. It proved a failure, but not, as has been claimed, because loyalty was widespread, but because the attempt was ill-managed and Stafford was not in touch with English discontent, which, in addition, could hardly be called organized. It succeeded, however, in making a French war possible, and in June, 1557, the English Government publicly declared it, and the English Ambassador left Paris. The military details need not delay us. As a matter of course, Pole, who was the living representative of Mary's fondest aims, lost his authority as Legate, and an old and insignificant friar, William Peto, was given his authority. It was a cruel return for all that had been done, and the Pope filled the bitter cup when he connected Pole's name with a charge of heresy and summoned him to Rome. Nor was there any consolation among the people. The naval and military forces were ready to rebel. Martial law enforced by German mercenaries was necessary. Money had to be raised by forced loans, which were stoutly resisted. A momentary peace prepared the way for the loss of Calais. For that loss there can be little excuse. Crudely stated, the reason that Calais fell was because the English Government had failed to prepare it for defence, and on sea there was no English fleet ready. There may have been treachery, but if there was it only served to emphasize military and naval incompetence, against which the Government had received adequate warnings. Nor was its loss the only source of disgrace. The nation saw itself sacrificed to Spanish ends. Philip told his wife not to trouble herself with attempting to recover Calais. He erected other fortresses. He seized English arms. He did his best to ruin English trade. He filled to the brim the cup of Mary's misfortunes. When the dull November day brought the news of her death, church bells rang; bonfires and merry-making greeted the new Queen, and Feria, the new Spanish Ambassador, welcomed Elizabeth on the footsteps of the throne.

We have now surveyed the problems which lay before the Queen, the difficulties which she created, and her methods in dealing with them. Her reign can only be called a conscientious failure. In every case Mary followed what her conscience dictated. Her very virtues, leniency to traitors, and compassion, became serious defects. That she could pardon treason and could not condone heresy shows how far she was distant from the England of her day. She was not the person to handle the difficult problem of the English Reformation, and her sincere piety was wasted, for we look in vain for any evidence of widespread piety during the reign. Catholic zeal did not exist apart from the Queen and Cardinal Pole. The vast majority of the clergy and people accepted Protestantism under Elizabeth, just as they had accepted a Catholicism under Mary, which knew nothing of the enthusiasm of the counter-Reformation or of the whole-hearted zeal of the new Catholic piety. There was no national spirit of fervour under either Sovereign. Mary did not understand her people. Her one aim was to make them Catholics, and they were much more anxious to become Englishmen in the new sense of the word. Her only consistency of action was with regard to religion, and the energies of her rule were spent on persecution alone. Her Government was inefficient and her nation decayed through lack of proper handling. She could have succeeded, perhaps, had she allowed the reaction against Northumberland and the Edwardine religious excesses to grow strong within an atmosphere of national development, and had she been content to let her country wait for such aid from outside as would have encouraged the growth of Catholic piety. Her enthusiasm served to make a pitiful future for those who were Catholics in more than a Parliamentary sense, while it made possible a settlement of religion based on neither piety nor fervour, but on a general reaction against the sacrifice of good government to conscientious zeal. It is the vocation of a ruler to be able and efficient, to understand the mind of his people, and to train himself in the art of government,

and especially to attempt to remedy personal
defects which would be detrimental to the forma-
tion of an adequate estimate of the immediate
problems which lay before him. No amount of
piety or goodness can take the place of lack of
ability, and no amount of conscientious energies
expended in the direction of religion can make
up for the want of some effort to produce an
administrative ability suited to the national
needs. A pious and good ruler who has ability
and who is efficient is the ideal, but when a
choice has to be made in government between a
pious incapacity and a capable religious indifference there can be little doubt as to which is the
better. All Mary's religious fervour cannot
make up for her incapacity; indeed, it accentuated it under the circumstances. All her
charity, all her purity, all the cleanness of her
Court, all the lack of corruption in her Government, which stand out in brilliant contrast to
Elizabethan days, cannot blind the student of
history to the fact that she was a failure as a
Sovereign. Her failure is made all the more
pathetic because she failed as a woman conscientiously convinced that she acted honestly.
Her ambitions for England were sincere. Her
love for her people was sincere. The tragedy lies
in the fact that her aspirations were out of tune
with the age, and that her love was not tempered
with a patience emphatically necessary amid the
changes and movements of new worlds, new
tendencies, and new reconstructions.

VI

THE EARLY HISTORY OF
THE ELIZABETHAN COMPROMISE
IN CEREMONIAL

WHEN Queen Elizabeth came to the throne it was at once clear that there would be some religious change. The only serious question was how far the change would go. Would it be along the conservative lines as represented at the death of Henry VIII., or would it advance along the lines of the Edwardine Reformation? At first the Government proceeded with caution. The new Queen and Cecil made a powerful combination of tactful statecraft. Nothing was done in a hurry. The writs summoning the first Parliament of the reign included a non-committal " Etc." instead of the title " Supreme Head of the Church." Although Cox preached a violent sermon at the opening, yet Bacon, the Lord Keeper, advised moderation in speech. It is true that certain Acts showed the direction in which the Government was preparing to move, and that Convocation immediately passed a series of strong resolutions in favour of the old religion. In due course the Act of Supremacy was passed. With regard to public worship, a penal Act—the Elizabethan Act of Uniformity—brought back

The Second Prayer Book of Edward VI., with certain modifications and changes. It is with a section of this Act that we have to deal in discussing the question of Elizabethan ceremonial. We shall see in another chapter what parochial problems centred round the whole matter; here we are only concerned to trace, as carefully as possible, the history of the policy during the first few years of the reign. The troubles connected with it will be considered later.

It will be remembered that in *The Second Prayer Book* of 1552 the Mass vestments, which had been retained by *The First Prayer Book,* were discontinued, and the celebrating minister was ordered to "wear a surplice only." A special section of the Elizabethan Act of Uniformity overrode this rubric—" Provided always, and be it enacted that such ornaments of the Church and of the ministers thereof shall be retained and be in use as was in this Church of England by authority of Parliament in the second year of the reign of King Edward VI. until other order shall be therein taken by the authority of the Queen's Majesty with the advice of the Commissioners appointed and authorized under the great seal of England for causes ecclesiastical or of the metropolitan of this realm." In the printed Prayer Books of 1559 this section was turned into the following rubric : " And here it shall be noted that the minister, at the time of the Communion and at other times in his ministration, shall use such ornaments in the Church as were in use by authority of Parliament in the second year of the reign of King Edward VI., according to the Act of Parliament set in the beginning of this book." Before continuing the history an awkward question has to be faced. Was this rubric legal? The Act of Uniformity had clearly stated the only changes made in the final book of Edward VI., and no reference was made to the introduction of this new rubric restoring the Mass vestments. Thus it is argued that the rubric was inserted without Parliamentary authority as a concession to the Queen, and the section of the Act just quoted is explained as meaning that the churchwardens were to act as trustees of the ornaments of the Church and ministers which had been confiscated to the Crown, until such times as the Crown was prepared to dispose of them or to destroy them. It must be conceded at once that much can be said in favour of this contention. On the other hand, there are grave considerations which the evidence in its favour cannot overcome. For example, when the Elizabethan ceremonial controversy was at its height, would it not have been tactful to omit the rubric, had it no Parliamentary authority? It is well known that this was not done, and no Elizabethan Prayer Book has been found in which the Ornaments Rubric was expunged. All along the extreme Reformers argued that it was illogical for the Bishops to try and make them wear the surplice when they themselves did not obey the rubric by wearing the Mass vestments. In addition, it is almost impossible to conceive that a Prayer Book was issued restoring these vestments in an illegal manner, and that all record of contemporary protests should have been lost. We possess such a voluminous history of the ceremonial controversy that, had this rubric been illegal, there could hardly have been wanting some reference to it. No such reference has been discovered. Besides, vestments survived in use which the Ornaments Rubric alone could cover. The weighty arguments in favour of illegality do not answer these objections. Evidence justifies us in accepting the section of the Act of Uniformity and the rubric as one and the same thing, and that the Elizabethan law provided for the use of vestments during the actual celebration of the Eucharist. Into the vexed question of the exact standard ordered it would be rash to venture. Indeed, I have merely included the subject of ceremonial in this volume in order to illustrate Elizabethan policy, to throw some light on the actual workings out of the Reformation in her reign, and to establish the value of some little known and disparaged documents.

The next point in the history is connected with the Royal Injunctions which were administered throughout the country in 1559 by the Royal Visitors. Two of these Injunctions obviously bear on the question of ornaments of the Church and minister; a third is in dispute, and will receive separate treatment. The two obvious items are—" That they shall take away utterly extinct and destroy all shrines, coverings of shrines, all tables, candlesticks, trindals, and rolls of wax, pictures, paintings, and all other monuments of feigned miracles, pilgrimages, idolatry, and superstition, so that there remain no memory of the same in walls, glasses, windows, or elsewhere within their churches and houses . . . ," and " that the churchwardens of every parish shall deliver unto our Visitors the inventories of vestments, copes, and other ornaments, plate, books, and specially of grails, couchers, legends, processionals, manuals, portuesses, and such-like appertaining to their church." These two Injunctions, considered together, help to explain the fate of vestments and ornaments during the Royal Visitation. There was a general destruction of vestments and church goods. These could easily be classed as " monuments of idolatry and superstition." This is exactly what happened, and they were destroyed under the first Injunction just referred to. Their destruction was notorious. In August, 1559, the Spanish Ambassador noticed that altars, crosses, and images had disappeared from the London churches. At the same time Machyn, the contemporary diarist, records that a huge bonfire had been made of church furnishings. Tunstall deplored that his vast Diocese of Durham was denuded of church ornaments. The Churchwardens' Accounts of 1559 provide us with details of the wholesale

destruction of " Papistical books, idols and
pictures, banners, chrismatories, paxes, bells
pyxes, vestments, roods, and all other idols."
These could not have been destroyed as illegal,
for at this point in the history their preservation
at least was covered by the Act of Uniformity.
In the violence of the reaction from the failure
of Mary's reign they were included by the churchwardens as coming under the Injunction ordering
the destruction of anything connected with
"idolatry." In the final issues of the Elizabethan
Reformation this destruction was encouraged,
and we shall refer to this at the conclusion of
this study; for the present it is only necessary
to notice that in some places certain portions of
church furnishings were retained, and this could
only be done on the grounds of their legality.
For example, we find that in Canterbury
Cathedral copes, chasubles, etc., survived in
1563, but Cardinal Pole's gifts and vestments
were " defaced." The churchwardens or local
authorities decided what should be destroyed, not
on the basis of law, but on their own decision as
to what was a monument of superstition and
what was not. I have endeavoured in vain to
find any other reasonable explanation of the
history. What I have suggested seems to be as
reasonable a view of the question as the history
will warrant, and the subsequent history of the
reign seems to confirm it. Of course, I do not
set it down as final, and I am conscious of
Stubbs' " ever open court of appeal," but at

least it serves as the most workable hypothesis at which I have been able to arrive.

Before leaving the Royal Injunctions we must refer to one round which much controversy has arisen, commonly known as " the Thirtieth Injunction." It ran as follows : " Her Majesty being desirous to have the prelacy and clergy of this realm to be had as well in outward reverence as otherwise regarded for the worthiness of their ministries, and thinking it necessary to have them known to the people in all places and assemblies, both in the Church and without, and thereby to receive the honour and estimation due to the special messengers and ministers of Almighty God, willeth and commandeth that all Archbishops and Bishops, and all other that be called or admitted to preaching or ministry of the Sacraments, or that be admitted into any vocation ecclesiastical, or into any society of learning in either of the Universities, or elsewhere, shall use and wear such seemly habits, garments and such square caps as were most commonly and orderly received in the latter year of the reign of King Edward VI.; not thereby meaning to attribute any holiness or special worthiness to the said garments, but as St. Paul writeth, *Omnia decenter et secundum ordinem fiant* (1 Cor. xiv. cap.)." There are several interpretations of this Injunction. Those who hold that the Ornaments Rubric was illegal explain the Injunction as merely administrative. We need not deal with this explanation, as we have already decided in favour of the rubric. Once more, it has been argued that it is a taking of " other order " under the section of the Act of Uniformity which we have already quoted. This view will not fit into the history, for on the permanence of the Ornaments Rubric depended the use of the cope and almuce which survived, and also the dilemma in which the Puritans placed the Bishops later in the reign—to which we have referred—a dilemma which would have been meaningless and easily answered had this Injunction been either administrative or a taking of " other order " under the Act of Uniformity. Other objections, less strong but worthy of consideration, may be urged. It is by no means clear that the Royal Injunctions were drawn up by the advice of the Ecclesiastical Commission or Metropolitan, and this was necessary under the proviso of the Act. At the moment there was no Metropolitan, and it cannot be proved that the Ecclesiastical Commission was in existence when these orders were drawn up. Then we might reasonably suppose that " other order " would have been taken in a clearer form—that is to say, not mixed up with a body of miscellaneous Injunctions without any reference to the regulations done away with or to the Act of Parliament under which action was taken. Of course, this objection has obvious weaknesses. The Crown could issue " other order " in any form and include it in any document that it liked. But no contemporary evidence refers to this Injunction as "other order." The Puritan dilemma is against it, and the two instances of which we know when other order was taken—with regard to wafer bread and altars—differ the one in fòrm and the other in place from this Thirtieth Injunction. A third view—that the Injunction refers only to outdoor dress, has much to say for itself; but the use made of the Injunction seems to show that this was not held by contemporaries to be the exclusive meaning. As we proceed this will become clear.

At this point we must go aside from the general history to consider the services in the Royal Chapel. Catholics and Protestants alike had carefully watched the ceremonial there in the hopes of drawing some consoling hopes for their future. To the former there was much to encourage, to the latter much to dread. The altar still remained with cross and lights. The ministers wore chasuble and copes. The Catholic champions hailed such news with joy, and could not believe that their cause was hopeless. On the other hand, the Reformers were dismayed by the retention of Papistical vestments, altar with cross and lights, and the Lord's Supper without a sermon. Attempts were made to persuade the Queen to moderate the ceremonial until a synod had been held. The position was a difficult one. The Queen had the Act of Uniformity behind her. The Reformers could appeal to the dealings with church furnishings during the Royal Visitation.

It is not clear what the real issue was. The Queen forced a disputation on the Bishops on the advisability of restoring in all the churches the Rood and Holy Family, and opposition to her ceremonial seems to have died out before such a sweeping and reactionary step. Indeed, when the new Bishops began to deal with the parishes they found that they had more than enough to do, and were content to leave the Royal Chapel alone.

The task before the new episcopate was one of almost inconceivable difficulty. The Queen could not be relied on, and it was not clear if she would support the letter of the law for the parishes, no matter how well she obeyed it in private. However that may be, the Ornaments Rubric and the Act of Uniformity presented to the Bishops and ordinaries the requirements of the law in connection with church ornaments. Obvious reasons prevented these requirements from being put into force. The Bishops themselves presented no united front in either doctrine or the standard of ceremonies desirable for public worship. It is not too much to say that not one of them would have been prepared to enforce the Ornaments Rubric in detail, though Parker and Jewel might have done so had the Queen insisted. The vast majority of them had returned from exile on the Continent, and they had fallen in with foreign conceptions of ceremonial. Indeed, shortly after the passing of the Act of Uniformity Bishop Sandys had reported to the

Primate that he and his friends interpreted the law in the widest sense, and that authority would not compel them to wear vestments and to use the old ornaments, which were merely retained as the Queen's property. Nor was there any demand among the people for them. On all sides the forces of Protestantism were growing, accentuated by the presence of those who had learned Continental ways during their enforced exile under Mary, and encouraged by an ever increasing literature. Almost immediately a compromise was evident. Surplices and copes were in use, of course covered by the Ornaments Rubric, but Parker and his assistants performed the memorial service for Henry II. in square cap, hood and gown, while during Lent, 1560, many of the Bishops preached in rochet and chimere, which had been their original outdoor dress. Considering the episcopal opinions and the state of public opinion, it is clear that the Ornaments Rubric could not be fulfilled. The whole religious life of the country was in a turmoil, and however desirous the Bishops might have been to enforce the law, it was evident to the Government that it would be tactless to do so. The Elizabethan aim was to hold the nation together in a National Church, and a hard and fast line in ornaments and ceremonial would have defeated that aim from the beginning. In addition, the restoration or retention of vestments, as soon as the new episcopate began their way, was a practical impossibility, for the wholesale destruction of them during the Royal Visitation simply ruled the Ornaments Rubric out of practical politics. Even in those places where the old furnishings survived they were little in use, for the approved dealings during the Visitation were too recent object-lessons to be lightly disregarded. On the other hand, it was clear that the Queen and Government would never be satisfied with the dull bareness of Continental ideals in worship. The Bishops therefore decided on a compromise, such as would carry with it not only the royal support, but the goodwill of as many of the clergy and people as possible. Their decision appears to have been something like this : to base their demands as little as possible on the strict letter of the law as laid down in the Act of Uniformity and the Ornaments Rubric, and to fall back on such items in it as might be considered as reinforced by the Thirtieth Injunction, if interpreted to refer to church dress. This contention must now be considered in some detail.

Two documents survive—two copies among the Petyt MSS. in the Inner Temple and one among the Parker MSS. in Corpus Christi College, Cambridge—which illustrate this division of the subject. The first Petyt manuscript is a draft copy with corrections in Parker's hand. It consists of some notes on the Royal Injunctions of 1559, on the Prayer Book, on burial, on matrimony, on collation of benefices; a set of Latin Articles of Religion, and certain injunc-

tions for deacons and readers. It has a general
title — " Resolutions concerning the Injunctions." The second Petyt manuscript is similar,
but there are important differences. Its general
title is a better description of the contents—
" Declarations of Injunctions and Articles for
Ministers and Readers." It is a fair copy and
not a draft. It is endorsed in different writing
(which, while it resembles Cecil's, appears to be
later than the document itself)—" A declaration
to have been made of the Injunctions by Dr.
Cox." This endorsement presents difficulties.
Probably Cox drew up the document and sent it
to Parker for correction. The first Petyt manuscript would represent these corrections, and the
second a copy passed by the Primate and written
out again by Cox. This copy will serve to answer
any objections that have been made against these
documents on the grounds that they are purely
tentative drafts. It is as finished and perfect
as hundreds of Elizabethan MSS. which are
relied on, without controversy, as authoritative. The Parker manuscript is not so wide
and is not subdivided. The Articles of Religion
have been deleted as well as the directions for
deacons and readers. All the manuscripts belong
to the early months after the Royal Visitation,
and we shall refer to them as ." The Episcopal
Regulations." Two items deal with clerical
dress, and are found in all the manuscripts.
" Item : That all ministers and others having
any living ecclesiastical shall go in apparel

agreeable, or else, within two monitions given by
the ordinary, to be deposed or sequestered from
his fruits according to the discretion of the said
ordinary or his lawful deputy," and, " First,
that there be used but only one apparel, as the
cope in the ministration of the Lord's Supper
and the surplice at all other ministrations."
When these two items are read together it is
perfectly clear that the first refers to outdoor
clerical dress, and that the second refers to dress
during clerical ministrations in the churches.
The Petyt MSS. make this perfectly clear, as the
first item quoted is found in the section headed
" Resolutions concerning the Injunctions," while
the second is found in the section headed " Concerning the Service Book." A further examination of the manuscripts brings to light an
important fact. The items in the fair Petyt
manuscript are numbered consecutively throughout. The first thirteen of them—that is, the
section entitled " Resolutions concerning the
Injunctions "—deal with various items in the
Royal Injunctions of 1559, and the number of
the item in these Royal Injunctions which is
dealt with is placed to the left of the number of
the episcopal " Resolution " on it. Now, in
this fair Petyt manuscript the first item which
we have quoted is numbered " 8," and to the
left of this " 8 " is placed the number " 30."
This latter number refers to the famous Thirtieth
Royal Injunction, which has been quoted earlier
in full. It is obvious, therefore, that the Bishops

explained this Thirtieth Injunction as referring only to outdoor clerical dress. When this is taken into consideration it helps to prove that this Thirtieth Injunction was not administrative on the theory that the Ornaments Rubric was illegal, and that it was not a taking of " other order " under the section of the Act of Uniformity. It is a difficult problem, and its difficulty must be recognized. I believe that the Bishops fell back on the words " in the Church " in this Thirtieth Injunction in order to make them an excuse for enforcing the minimum of the surplice, while at the same time they wished to preserve the use of the cope, if only to please Elizabeth. The cope could not be included in a " resolution " covering the Thirtieth Injunction, and so an item was introduced in The Episcopal Regulations providing for the use of cope and surplice, and included in the section entitled " Concerning the Service Book." When the struggle came over the surplice the Bishops could and did say that they were enforcing the Royal Injunction. As for the cope, they never appear to have carried out their regulation. What is of importance, however, is the fact that they clearly laid it down at this point in their administration as the dress required for the minister celebrating the Eucharist; and they could not have done so had they not realized that, if their regulation was disputed by zealots, they had the full legality of the Act of Uniformity and the Ornaments Rubric to fall back on.

The question now arises, granted that The Episcopal Resolutions are of sufficient value as manuscripts to be used by the historian, is there sufficient evidence to prove that they were authoritative? This question is forced on the student of Elizabethan history from the fact that there is no official evidence extant—either printed or manuscript—in which the documents are mentioned by any of their titles or subdivisions. It is possible, however, to establish a strong argument in favour of them, and to show that they represented a system of episcopal policy. The evidence in favour of this position may be classified under three heads. Firstly, that the Bishops did draw up some articles for their common guidance. Secondly, the ceremonial compromise suggested by The Episcopal Regulations was in certain places carried out. Thirdly, extracts from the Episcopal Regulations were used in diocesan administration. We shall deal with the documents from these three points of view.

The Parker manuscript has a general heading covering the whole document : " Resolutions and orders taken by common consent of the Bishops, for the present time until a synod may be had, for observation and maintenance of uniformity in matters ecclesiastical throughout all dioceses in both provinces." Now, the Bishops were in session at Lambeth on April 12, 1561, and passed a series of Articles, entitled " Articles agreed upon . . . by the most reverend fathers

in God, Matthew, Lord Archbishop of Canterbury, Thomas, Lord Archbishop of York,
with the assent of their brethren the Bishops
to the same." It would seem from these
Articles that The Episcopal Regulations were
finally passed then : " First, the Articles
agreed on at the first session be ratified,
confirmed, and put in execution accordingly." Of course, this is merely a suggestion ;
but, comparing the general title of the Parker
manuscript with this first Lambeth Article, it
seems a reasonable conjecture. Indeed, I believe
that the conjecture can be supported from
Parker's *Correspondence,* in a letter evidently
written after February, 1561. Writing to the
Queen, he says : " We have of late in our consul-
tations devised certain orders for uniform and
quiet ministration in religion. We trust your
gracious zeal towards Christ's religion will not
improve our doings, though such opportunity of
time hath not offered itself as yet to be suitors
to your princely authority to have a public set
synod to the full determination of such cases."
The reference to the synod not yet held in
Parker's letter and in the Parker manuscript
leads me to believe that the " certain orders "
to which he refers were The Episcopal Regulations. There is no evidence to prove that the
Queen ratified them ; indeed, all that Parker
asked was that she would not disapprove of them.
Secondly, evidence is forthcoming to prove that
the ceremonial standard set up by The Episcopal

Regulations was accepted. Copes were purchased by some churches in 1560. When Convocation met in 1563 a resolution was suggested dealing with vestments : " That the use of copes and surplices may be taken away." Such a resolution would never have been suggested if some churches at least were not falling into line with The Episcopal Regulations. On the failure of this resolution to reach a vote, another was brought forward. Convocation divided on it and defeated it by one vote. It was proposed " that it be sufficient for the minister in time of saying Divine Service and ministering the Sacraments to use a surplice only." Once more, this motion, which actually divided Convocation, would have been absurd had some clergy not been using at least a cope. Further, in January, 1565, when the Queen asked Archbishop Parker to provide her with a return of the varieties in ceremonial, etc., which then existed in the dioceses, we find that in one of these returns, commonly believed to belong to the London Diocese, and dated February 14, 1565, it is recorded that some ministers celebrated the Eucharist " with surplice and cope, some with surplice alone." In addition, a similar but undated return is extant referring to Canterbury Cathedral. It appears to belong to the same year as the return already referred to, and it discloses the fact that copes were in use there. Further evidence in this connection could be drawn from entries among parochial manuscripts belonging to the same months in which it is noted that copes are retained. Thirdly, the most convincing evidence in favour of The Episcopal Regulations is derived from the use of large extracts from them in diocesan administration. Bishop Scambler in 1561, during his first visitation of Peterborough Diocese, required his cathedral clergy to subscribe to the Latin Articles of Religion which are found in the Petyt MSS. It seems reasonable to suppose that these had at least full episcopal approval behind them, otherwise it would have been a bold thing for Scambler to enforce a series of dogmatic Articles entirely on his own authority. But the strongest evidence in favour of The Episcopal Regulations is to be found among the manuscripts of Bishop Guest at Rochester. During his visitation of that diocese in 1565 Guest deliberately follows, in five of the Injunctions which he gave to his clergy, the wording of The Episcopal Regulations. It is just a conjecture that he had a copy of them lying beside him when he drew up his Injunctions —otherwise it is impossible to account for the use of the same words after the lapse of four years— and that he incorporated these five items not only as suitable for his peculiar needs at the moment, but because they had behind them the opinions of the episcopal body on matters of importance applicable to the Church at large. Another point of interest can be found among the Cecil MSS. at Hatfield. Bishop Cox, writing to the Council in November, 1564, and making suggestions to them for dealing with certain classes who disturbed the religious settlement, asks their approval to put in force an item from The Episcopal Regulations, which he quotes exactly from the Petyt manuscript with which the endorsement already noted connects his name. Finally, in this connection, the Latin Articles of Religion in the Petyt MSS. disappear in the Parker manuscript. The reason for this is that the Bishops had drawn up a new series of dogmatic Articles between the months of February and April, 1561, known as the Eleven Articles, or the Declaration of Certain Principal Articles of Religion. This new formulary is referred to in the Parker manuscript—" That the Declaration devised for unity of doctrine be enjoined to be used throughout the realm uniformly "—and it was confirmed by the assembled episcopate at their Lambeth meeting, to which reference has already been made. This regulation of the Parker manuscript was carried out. For example, the Bishops of Lichfield and of Ely enforced it during their diocesan visitations. These considerations will, I think, establish a reasonable case in favour of The Episcopal Regulations, and will lift the documents out of obscurity and doubt into their just place in the history of Elizabethan ceremonial. The Queen from the very beginning was prepared to make the Bishops do the dirty work of getting the parishes into line, and the Bishops began their task in connection with ceremonial by a compromise. They were prepared to be satisfied with the use of a cope for the Eucharist in parish churches in place of the

full and legal Mass vestments, and when this
failed they tried to enforce the cope in cathedrals
only. Personally, I believe that most of them
would have preferred to see it disappear entirely,
and, as later history shows, some of them did not
approve even of the surplice. But the Queen was
a doubtful quantity, and it was well to have something in hand. Finally, when the Puritan controversy broke in 1566, it had become a question
of getting the surplice worn; copes and such-
like had long since passed out of the
sphere of practical policies. One point must
be noticed in conclusion. It soon became
customary for the Bishops to issue orders
that a surplice should be worn "according
to the Queen's Majesty's Injunctions." This is a
difficult phrase to explain taken by itself and
isolated from all the history. I am inclined to
believe that The Episcopal Regulations, dealing
as they did largely with the Royal Injunctions of
1559, became mixed up with the Queen's name.
It would seem clear, at any rate, after the evidence which we have been considering, that the
Royal Injunctions were not a taking of " other
order " under the Act of Uniformity, for the
episcopate attempted to retain the cope in parish
churches a few months after the Royal Visitation,
a thing which they could not have done had the
Ornaments Rubric been abrogated. On the other
hand, the surplice became connected with " the
Queen's Majesty's Injunctions " in diocesan visitation Articles and Injunctions. The two things
appear, on the surface, contradictory, and on the

surface it appears hard to reconcile them. I believe that the episcopate were tolerated in using the phrase at a time when the question of vestments had disappeared, and when there was grave danger that the bare minimum of a surplice could not be enforced. It was a difficult position when, as early as 1563, almost half the members of Convocation were ready to abandon its use. The surplice soon became as much a badge of Popery as the vestments themselves.

It may be asked, considering the circumstances, why was the Ornaments Rubric not legally abandoned ? To that question I have found no adequate answer. Ecclesiastical government was finally carried out as though it had been. The final demand made by authority was a surplice only, and the parishes of England were regularly searched for the old vestments and ornaments. On the other hand, I believe that these facts do not prove that " other order " was taken ; the evidence on the other side is too strong for such a conclusion. The whole history fits into the tactful policy of the Crown. The law was left clear at the beginning, and could be used if the overwhelming majority of the nation demanded it. Later, when a bare minimum was all that was in dispute, it did not suit the Queen, for some reason which I have never discovered, to have the law changed. That this was never done seems clear from the Puritan taunt to the Bishops : " Why make us wear the surplice when you yourselves do not obey the rubric ?"

VII

THE ELIZABETHAN REFORMATION AND PAROCHIAL LIFE

ALTHOUGH much has been written about Elizabethan ecclesiastical history and the drastic changes which took place in England during the closing half of the sixteenth century, yet few students know how these changes affected the actual lives of the people during those years, and how parish life was transformed from Catholic into something quite different than what we know as Anglicanism, which is, in its present form, largely a product of the Oxford Movement. My object in this study is to present a picture of Elizabethan parish life based on a study of manuscripts, which are preserved in the Record Office, the British Museum, London, and in the diocesan libraries up and down England.

Before entering on the subject it is necessary to recall the outstanding changes made by the Queen and Parliament at the beginning of the reign. The Protestant Prayer Book of 1552 was restored, as we have seen, and its use made compulsory in every parish in England on and after Midsummer Day, 1559. Any breach of this law was severely punishable—for the first offence by a heavy fine, for the second offence by six months' imprisonment, and for the third offence by deprivation and lifelong imprisonment. Thus, Catholic worship on the part of both priests and people became a severe offence under the statute law. In addition, the jurisdiction of the Pope was abolished by Act of Parliament, and all Bishops and clergy, as well as judges, mayors, magistrates, etc., were required to take an oath that they acknowledged the Queen as Supreme Governor of the Church. The history of this oath-taking is well known, and the devotion of a loyal episcopate witnessed to the solidarity of the English Catholic Hierarchy.

As soon as the sees were filled with reforming Prelates it was incumbent on the Government to apply the new machinery to diocesan life. All episcopal jurisdiction was suspended, and a body of Royal Visitors went through the country administering the oath and enforcing a body of regulations on the parishes up and down England. From these regulations of 1559 we get a general idea of how the parochial life was changed. Thus, with regard to preaching, the clergy were ordered to praise and uphold the Queen's supremacy and to preach against "Papal usurpation." The English Bible must be open in every parish church, so that anyone could read it unhindered and undirected, while side by side with it must lie some of the Reformers' works. Strict orders were given that anyone who

favoured the old religion was to be reported to
the magistrates, and everyone absent from the
Protestant service on Sundays was compelled to
pay a fine of 12d. for each offence. Almost immediately a spirit of iconoclasm was let loose, as
the Royal Visitors ordered the churchwardens in
every parish to destroy all shrines, images, and
stained glass windows as monuments of the gross
superstition abolished by Act of Parliament.
Nor was the sacredness of the homes of the
people respected. Search was made in them for
any images of the saints, and for holy pictures,
and these were ruthlessly offered up to the new
religion, any attempt to retain or conceal them
being severely punished. In addition, the Royal
Visitors demanded from each parish a list of
everything connected with Catholic worship—an
eloquent commentary on their fate which I shall
consider later. Nor are we surprised to learn
that the old altars were destroyed and tables set
up in their place. The only touch of humour in
the entire dealings of the Royal Visitors is one
characteristically Tudor. Any clergyman who
wished to marry was ordered to bring the lady of
his choice to the diocesan Bishop and two magistrates for inspection, and only with their sanction
could the marriage take place. Licences for
clerical marriage, after such an examination, are
extant among the Loseley and Parker MSS., and
the custom seems to have continued to the middle
of Elizabeth's reign.

We can well imagine how these royal orders

turned the entire country into not only a camp of
religious warfare, but also into a vast field of
wanton destruction. Every shrine and picture,
every tabernacle and altar, every image and relic
of the saints was handed over to brutal sacrilege;
while above all sounded the voice of the new
State Minister denouncing the ancient Faith of
England and encouraging the work of demolition.
Indeed, things reached such a pass that the
Government was compelled to step in a few years
later and attempt to save the chancels from
complete destruction. Even the new holy table
called for little respect. It was moved in and
out of the choir at will : hats and dust lay on it
more frequently than the Sacrament, and when
the Holy Communion was administered some
stood, some sat, some knelt. Records remain
among the parochial manuscripts of the purchase
of rude forms for the communicants to sit on
during reception, or of rude planks to kneel on.
The expulsion of Catholic worship soon brought
with it that spirit of irreverence and familiarity
which even partizan writers have noted as one of
the products of the reign.

What happened to the vestments? I want here
for a moment to go back and to point out that
under Mary the church vestments were rigidly
restored. It is unnecessary to emphasize this
point except by saying that Cardinal Pole ordered
the churchwardens to restore everything connected with Catholic worship, and evidence is
extant to prove that this was done. The state-

ment that many parishes at the beginning of Elizabeth's reign were unprovided with the necessaries of worship is either a gratuitous falsification of history or inexcusable ignorance. We have seen that the Royal Visitors of 1559 ordered lists of vestments to be drawn up; but among their orders was also one ordering the destruction of " monuments of superstition." In many cases the vestments provided by the self-denial of Catholics during the poverty of Mary's reign were at once destroyed as superstitious. On the other hand, some were sold to provide funds for the promoters of the new régime; some were made into garments for the poor ; some were cut up to provide coverings for the pulpits. Cushions in pews often reflected some beautiful piece of work once dedicated to the service of the altar, while in not a few cases we find that the chasubles were made into players' coats or rustic doublets. The records of sales and destructions from 1559 onwards are pretty full. It makes little matter to history if it pleased the Queen to play for a time with Catholic ceremonial in the Royal Chapel. From the very first a blow was struck at the great mystery of Catholic worship, and in the large majority of parishes the people were forced to stand by and see the hallowed objects of their charity and self-denial destroyed or outraged by the commands of Queen and Parliament In dealing with the vestments it will be more convenient to sum up the history of the chalices and patens. Here again we touch a sacred place in the hearts of the people. Not a few of the sacred vessels were their own gifts after the pillage under Edward VI., and many of them were memorials of friends. In the early years of the reign I have not succeeded in discovering much evidence in this connection. The paten is rarely mentioned; but it seems clear that there was some general order given forbidding the use of the old chalices, which is not now forthcoming. In some places they escaped, but as early as 1559 we find that they were sold, and from 1565 on we find that the record of sales becomes more detailed. However, I am inclined to think that the Government meant these beautiful works of the goldsmiths' art to be destroyed from the very first, as there is a record among the *Canterbury MSS.* for 1560, when a clergyman was reported for using " a Popish chalice." In 1565 the *Rochester MSS.* record that the Bishop ordered his cathedral clergy to use, " instead of their chalice, a decent cup of silver." In 1567 there is a record that the clergy of all the parishes in the Diocese of Norwich were ordered to abandon the use of " the superstitious chalices," and to provide " decent Communion cups." In 1571 a similar order was made in every parish in the Province of York. On the other hand, there are two noteworthy records with regard to the chalices. First, Bishop Guest of Rochester has left among his MSS. an order for his churchwardens, in which he enjoins them to transform " the chalice into a decent cup "; and secondly, there is preserved among the State Papers a document dated 1569, in which it is reported that in many parishes in the Diocese of Chichester the people have hidden their chalices, " hoping for the Mass again," and that they were wilfully disobeying the order to turn them into Communion cups. I have failed to discover the order; but there was a motion passed in Convocation in 1563 that " chalices be altered to decent cups."

Leaving, as it were, the altar, we pass to the rood screen and loft which guarded the " holy of holies," with beautiful figures of the Crucified Redeemer and of Our Lady and St. John. The destruction of these works of art and piety began early in the reign. It must be remembered that the vast majority of them were erected by people then alive, as the " reforming zeal " under Edward VI. had dealt with them in the severest possible manner, and few, if any, had been allowed to remain. There was no definite order made for their destruction in 1559, but the Royal Visitors encouraged the work, and, in many cases, figures and lofts shared the fate of other " monuments of superstition." There is quite a strong catena of evidence which goes to show that the Elizabethan Visitors were not behind their Edwardine predecessors. Roods and lofts were destroyed and sold in London, in Bedfordshire, in Exeter, for example, in 1559, and in not a few cases where sales took place there is a record that the wood of the roods and lofts was used for making bridges, for testers for beds, for ceilings, and for the Communion table. It was one of the most usual sights in an Elizabethan parish from 1559 to 1563 to find the beautiful carvings at the entrance to the chancel being carted off to repair some waterway or the floor or roof of some secular building. On the other hand, it must be recorded that an effort was made in 1563 by the Government to preserve the chancel-screen, and in some cases this was successful. In connection with the roods, it may be well to consider the fonts, as the documents almost always mention them together. There is not much evidence to go on, but such as it is shows that there had been a good deal of wanton destruction, and the Government order of 1563, above referred to, forbade the removal of the fonts from " the accustomed place."

The crosses and the crucifixes (and these names were almost always used as convertible terms) seem early to have suffered the fate of images. They were destroyed in St. Paul's Cathedral in 1559, and this noteworthy example in London seems to have inspired destructive zeal throughout the provinces. We have valuable manuscript returns for Lincolnshire, extending over the years 1559-1566, and only nine crosses stood in the latter year, and this in one of the largest counties and in one thickly studded with churches. The general evidence is not very full as to the fate of these " superstitious relics of Popery." In a few cases we have a record of sale in the Churchwardens' MSS.; but as a general rule I think we must conclude that they were demolished, as there is little reliable evidence to show that they were converted into money for parish purposes. On the other hand there is much manuscript evidence which goes to show the hatred which the Elizabethan Reformers bore to the Sign of our Redemption. For example, we find from the *Lansdowne MSS.* in the British Museum that every parish in the Diocese of Worcester was ordered in 1569 to destroy all crosses as " monuments of idolatry and superstition." In 1571 a searching enquiry was made in the Province of York, and " every cross " was singled out to be " utterly defaced, broken, and destroyed." Those retaining them were to be reported and dealt with by law. In 1565 an interesting document among the State Papers records that the people in every parish of the Diocese of Lichfield and Coventry were ordered not to " set down the corpse of any dead body where a cross had stood by the wayside, nor to say *De Profundis* there for the dead." As a concluding example, we may note that the *Winchester MSS.* tell us that the stone crosses in graveyards were destroyed in 1571 by episcopal commands. It would be possible to multiply examples, but I think sufficient evidence has been given from original sources to show not only how late in the reign the devotion to the cross survived, but also how energetically the Government pursued its destruction. Once again, it must be recalled that all the crosses and crucifixes in the church, on the waysides, and in the graveyards, were the pious gifts of men and

women still alive or but lately dead; and once
again the Queen and Parliament invaded the
people's personal works of devotion.

I now turn to consider the service books. The
most unrestrained destruction under Edward VI.
has practically denuded England of them. Under
Mary parochial piety carried out Pole's order for
their reprovision, and almost without exception
we find every church in possession of an adequate
set of service books, many of them of great beauty
and value. When Elizabeth restored the Protestant service book her Visitors, as we have seen,
ordered each parish to make a list of books in its
possession, but as a general rule they shared the
fate of " monuments of superstition," and were
destroyed in the Parochial Visitations of 1559
and 1560. Few have found a place among the
treasures of the nation or of private individuals.
But the work was not confined to these earlier
years, as the Government were determined, as
far as possible, to destroy every trace of " superstitious Popish books of worship." Records
extend over many years, and show that the
Queen's searchers did not confine themselves to
the old service books, but invaded private houses
in order to destroy every possible copy of " Latin
books of private superstition." To follow the
details would be impossible, as my notebooks
show extracts form diocesan documents extending over many pages. A few examples, however, will be sufficient to prove the zeal of the
Queen's inquisitorial methods. In 1561 we learn
from a record in the British Museum that the

parishes of Norwich Diocese were searched for "books of devotion and service forbidden by law," and the names of those who possessed them were demanded for "further dealings." In the same year there is a record among the *Corpus Christi MSS.* at Cambridge to the effect that the Protestant Prelates met at Lambeth Palace, and made an order that "all old service books, grails, antiphonars, and other be defaced and abolished by order in Visitations." This order was strictly enforced. In 1565 the State Papers record that the people in the parishes of Worcestershire, Warwickshire, Staffordshire, and Derbyshire were commanded by their parsons and church-wardens to "cast away your Mass books, your portesses, and all other books of the Latin service." In 1569 the churchwardens of Norfolk and Suffolk were asked to search private houses and to return names, and in the same year this order was extended to the counties of Worcester and Stafford. As late as 1571 many old service books survived, especially in the north, and in that year a close search was made by the church-wardens through the private houses of the northern parishes, drawing a line across the map from Chester to Hull. Even London and the neighbourhood of the Government's central activity were not free from them. In 1571 a British Museum record informs us that the churchwardens of the London parishes were diligently inquisitioned about "books of the Latin Popish service" and "in whose custody the same is, and what be the parcels thereof."

The county of Kent was searched in the autumn of the same year. The churchwardens of the counties bordering on Wales (*Cecil MSS.,* British Museum) were diligently enjoined to destroy books of " private superstitious devotions " in the year 1569; and the *Rochester MSS.* contain a record that a similar search in private houses was again necessary in Kent in the year 1572. There is no necessity to elaborate the history. It is quite clear that there was no intention on the part of the Government to tolerate, even in private, Catholic piety. Few historians have hinted at this wholesale invasion of the privacy of home life on the part of the Queen's servants. The evidence is overwhelming, and it goes to prove that the aim of Elizabeth's rule was not a mere outward conformity on the part of the nation, but a wholesale extirpation of every relic of Catholic times in the homes of the people. In my opinion, Tudor despotism reached its highest point when the family devotions in private were brought within the spying sphere of parochial supervision.

I now turn from these broader elements of the religious policy to other details of parochial life, which possess a history none the less valuable, and certainly much less widely known, if known at all. Once again, I can only hint at the overwhelming changes which were carried out in every parish; but I have examined practically all the documents of the reign, and I shall not state any position which is not supported by ample documentary evidence, and this of an indisputable kind. At the beginning I am confronted with the serious difficulty of selecting from a mass of material, all of which is of fascinating interest to students. Thus, for example, there exist sufficient manuscripts to make a volume of history dealing with parochial life in its relation to the old holy days, the deckings of the altars, marriages, the reading of the Bible, the burial of the dead, the enforcing of attendance at church, the parish clerk, the stamping out of confession, fasting, holy water, church music, the poor, education, and many like details. In fact, it may be said that the life of every parish in the country was watched with scrupulous diligence from week to week, and that even such a detail as the saying of grace in English in private did not escape the careful supervision of churchwardens and questmen, who became, in a very real sense, spies of the Government. It would be quite possible from the existing evidence to form such a conception of parish life under Queen Elizabeth as could scarcely be paralleled in the whole range of modern history. The infinite variety of the enquiries, the ceaseless vigilance of the spy system, the long record of orders and injunctions —in a word, the elaborate organization of a well-considered policy on the part of the Queen and Government has left us, in manuscript evidence, an almost inconceivable insight into the parish life of the period. In addition, the history of almost every cathedral and of Oxford and Cambridge could be traced practically from year to year. These, however, lie outside the scope of this article. I wish, however, to draw attention to certain subjects which are of wider interest than those to which I have just referred.

Firstly, mention has already been made of the " extirpation of the Pope's usurped power," and. of the regulations enforced regarding the Royal Supremacy and the new preachers. We have also seen how attendance at the Protestant services was enforced, and I may add that the most diligent enquiries after absentees was carried out to the very end of the reign. When the Government, by means of an elaborate system of fining and spying, had filled the churches, the greatest care was taken to see that the pulpit in every parish church in the country was carefully tuned to the new system, and that the position of the Pope was diligently denounced by the licensed preachers, who were men carefully tried by Government officials. It is a mistake to think that all the new clergy preached. Licences were confined to those on whose Protestantism the Government could rely, especially with regard to the " Pope and all his superstitious usurpations." For the rest, they confined themselves to reading printed homilies on the dullest points of theological controversy. This denunciation of the Pope became part and parcel of the parochial system, evidently on the principle that some part at least of regular denunciation would find its way to the hearts of the people, carefully guarded from the priests—a matter to which I shall refer later. Thus, for example, in 1565 every parish in Kent was provided with special preachers " to speak against the supremacy of the Pope, and to maintain the Queen's Majesty to be Supreme Governor of this Church " (*Rochester MSS.*). Throughout the parishes of Norwich the " just taking away of the Pope's usurped power " was prescribed in 1561 as the sole subject for a quarterly discourse. In 1569 the Channel Islands (belonging to Winchester Diocese) were brought into line, when six annual sermons were ordered in all the parishes on the theme " to confirm the Queen's Majesty's royal authority in all causes ecclesiastical against the late usurped power of the Bishop of Rome " (*Winchester MSS.*). These examples might be multiplied from every diocese in England. Nor were the Government satisfied merely with preaching against the Pope's power; they extended their diligence to those who maintained it in conversation. The neighbourhood of Eastern London was searched by the church-wardens in 1566 for " favourers of the Romish power." In 1569 the counties of Worcester and Warwick and the borders of Gloucester and Oxford were searched for any " in the parish who, either by word or writing, maintain the usurped authority of the Bishop of Rome " (*Lansdowne MSS.*). In 1571 an order was issued to the churchwardens in every parish north of Chester and Hull to the effect that " the church-wardens of every parish church shall present half-yearly the names of all persons that be

favourers of the Romish power " (*York MSS.*).
In the same year the churchwardens of the city
of London instituted, by order, similar enquiries,
and in the following year it became necessary to
extend the enquiry once more to Kent, and even
" the suspicion of favouring the Pope " became
a presentable offence. Thus it is clear the
Government was determined to see that the
pulpits and the private conversations should
reflect the "abjuration of the Pope's blasphemous
jurisdiction." But a further trouble was in
store, and this forms the second part of my
review in this division of the subject.

We have seen that Elizabeth's first Parliament
provided for the use of the Protestant service
book under severe penalties. A biassed statement still survives that the Queen was prepared
to a large extent to wink at the Mass in secret,
and that there was no serious effort to suppress the secret work of priests until after the
Bull of Excommunication in 1570. *A priori,* we
should at once say, considering the treatment
meted out to the objects of Catholic piety, and
considering how the Pope was denounced, that
such a position could not be maintained. When
we come to examine the documents we find that
almost from the beginning it is clear that no
quarter was to be given to priest or Mass either
in public or in private. The system which followed service books, crosses, images, and pictures
into the houses of the people was not likely to
connive at the secret practice of Catholic
worship. The documents speak for themselves.

In 1560 enquiries were made over the entire
South of England (*i.e.*, south of Chester and
Hull) for priests who did not exclusively use the
Protestant service book and conform to the
established religion (*Lambeth MSS.*). In 1565
this enquiry was specially repeated in the north-
western parishes of Kent, with the additional
enquiry " if any in your parish openly or
privately say or hear Mass " (*Rochester MSS.*).
In 1560 the Eastern Counties underwent a severe
inquisition from the parochial churchwardens in
order to find out if " any man is known to have
said or heard Mass since it was abrogated by
law." This enquiry was again gone through in
the same counties in the following year. In 1563
search was made in the parishes of Eastern Kent
for hearers of Mass in private. In 1569 the
churchwardens carried out enquiries in several
Western Counties for any who " had forsaken
the ministry . . . and in corners say Mass "
(*Lansdowne MSS.*). Much additional evidence
could be produced to show that there never was
the smallest intention on the part of the Government to suffer even secret deviation from the law
during the first ten years of the reign. After
1570 the enquiries became fuller, and the parishes
were regularly invaded by enquiries for priests
and secret Masses. I do not intend to pursue the
question further. The policy of Elizabeth's
Government was consistent from the beginning.
It is well summed up in an extant sermon by one
of her Bishops : " [The Queen] hath caused the
vessels that were made for Baal and for the host

of heaven to be defaced ; she has broken down the lofts that were builded for idolatry; she hath turned out the priests that burned incense unto false gods; she hath overthrown all polluted and defiled altars; she hath abolished darkness and caused the eternal truth gloriously to shine, as we see it doth in England at this day." And here it is well once and finally to contradict the statement that Catholics were permitted by the Pope to attend Protestant services, and that the Pope was prepared to acknowledge the Protestant Prayer Book if the Queen acknowledged his supremacy—statements found in many histories. It is true that a memorial was sent to Rome on behalf of the English Catholics showing that church attendance was compulsory under penalty, and asking if presence at " mere prayers and psalms," under any circumstances, were to be permitted. In October, 1562, an answer came from Pius IV. returning a decided " No " to the question, and this in spite of the fact that the Spanish Ambassador, who presented the question, had said that the punishment was hanging, not fining.

Finally, I want to refer to the moral condition of the parochial life. An article such as this does not admit of detail, and even a close study of this division of parochial life in the reign would necessarily be short, owing to the impossibility of giving a minute account of the deplorable depths to which morality sank. Document after document goes to prove that not merely did real **religion decay, but vice of the grossest kind** sprang up on every side. Mr. Hubert Hall, who has been a careful student of the Elizabethan State Papers for many years, has summed up the parochial life in this connection in his *Society in the Elizabethan Age* : " The state of society was the worst that had ever before been in the land. And where all this time was the influence of the Church at work ? There was no pretence even at such an influence." All research confirms this conclusion ; and if Mr. Hall could write so strongly after a close study of the Elizabethan State Papers, language would have failed him had he gone into the ecclesiastical documents.

Parochial life was thus given over to a complete imposition of a new system. No sphere of parochial life escaped, and from the very beginning care was taken to subject Catholic authority to regular abuse, and to leave no room for argument in public or private. Destruction carried off the materials of Catholic worship and the memorials of Catholic piety. Preaching poisoned the sources of parochial opinion, and priest-hunting deprived the people of their natural defenders and teachers. It is a pitiable picture, which no one has yet painted in detail, though the colours stand ready mixed in countless documents. There is not a ray of light in the proceedings of the Government, and it is one of the glories of the old Religion that so many men and women were found who stood true amid parochial desolation, and were made worthy to become confessors and martyrs of the Church.

VIII

TWO ELIZABETHAN CHAMPIONS
OF CATHOLICISM : BLESSED EDMUND
CAMPION AND CARDINAL ALLEN

OUT of the dust of religious controversy during the reign of Queen Elizabeth the names of two Catholics emerge which are worthy of a permanent place in history—Edmund Campion and Cardinal William Allen. Most, if not all, of their contemporaries in the deplorable religious struggle of the times were men of strong tempers and illogical minds, and incapable of presenting their case with anything like equanimity and moderation. These two, however, were men of disciplined lives, high motives, and conscientious zeal, and they stand out as by far the most noteworthy Catholic champions of the age, while their writings are not unworthy of consideration in the history of prose literature. In order to understand them the modern student must be prepared to throw himself back into Elizabethan England, and to try as far as possible to look out on their aims and fears and struggles and convictions with contemporary eyes. He may not be prejudiced in their favour—and all the better if he is not. He may not be convinced

after his study of their wisdom, of the cause
which they conceived just and right, of the
validity of their arguments. That makes little
matter. At any rate, if he approaches their
history in a detached frame of mind, he cannot
complete it without knowing a great deal of
Elizabethan life and methods, and without seeing
that something at least may be said on behalf of
Elizabethan Catholics. Above all, he must try
to keep in his mind that he is dealing with men
who lived in the sixteenth century, when the
Papacy had not abandoned any of its political
claims, when, though weakened by the Reformation and not renewed in full by the Counter-
Reformation, men still feared its power in the
councils of nations—a century in England when
the throne was everything and the individual
apart from the throne less than nothing. He
must remember in dealing with the history of
Elizabethan Catholicism, as in dealing with that
of Elizabethan Puritanism, that both were contrary to the national ideal in religion—one State
with one Church. In addition, it is necessary to
remember that the former appeared far the more
dangerous to the Government, as it might become
allied with its co-religionists abroad, especially
with the strength of Spain, and might overturn
the State in England, while the latter never had
the appearance of a national force likely to
receive foreign aid of any value. Indeed, even
after the defeat of the Spanish Armada, in which
English Catholics took their full share, there still

remained the fear in the mind of the Government
that political Catholic aid from abroad might be
forthcoming. It must be conceded once for all
that they had good reasons for their fear; but
when this concession is made, it must not be
forgotten that the history does not lie in the
twentieth century, and that many men then felt
deeply about religious questions, especially when
these questions had been astutely mixed up by the
Government with those of loyalty or disloyalty to
the throne.

In order to place Allen and Campion in their
historical setting it is necessary to review the
religious policy and legislation of the reign.
Firstly, the Queen had been declared Supreme
Governor of the Church under a severe penal
statute, which made it, for the third offence, high
treason to maintain the Pope's spiritual jurisdiction in England. Catholic worship had been
banished by the Act of Uniformity. Priests
using the Catholic forms of worship were liable
to six months' imprisonment for the first offence,
twelve months for the second, and for the third
imprisonment for life, in addition to being
deprived of all their spiritual promotions. If
they did not possess any, the six months became
a year, and the year imprisonment for life. In
addition, Catholics were compelled to be present
at Common Prayer on Sundays and holy days,
upon pain of paying for each offence the sum of
twelve pence; and they had seen, as we have

pointed out, the destruction of all the pious furniture connected with their worship, which their ancestors had preserved with many risks during the reign of Edward VI., or which had. been reprovided by their fathers or themselves during Mary's reign. It was not long before their Bishops were deprived, with many of their clergy, for refusing the Oath of Supremacy. In 1563 further penal measures were dealt out to them. An Act was passed entitled *An Act for the Assurance of the Queen's Majesty's Royal Power over all Estates and Subjects within Her Highness' Dominions,* which made it *præmunire* to maintain the jurisdiction of the Bishop of Rome for the first offence, and high treason for the second. Similar penalties were enacted for those who refused to take the Oath of Supremacy as defined in the Royal Injunctions of 1559.

During the years 1559 to 1570 Catholics were harried all over the country, and were driven into secret worship, carried out by those Marian priests who remained faithful. The evidence for the severity of the Government's persecution, which only stopped short of taking life during these years, is overwhelming. Document after document of unimpeachable authority goes to prove that the parishes of England were searched regularly by the parochial officials for the smallest relic of Catholic piety. The homes of the people were at the mercy of the churchwardens, and Catholicism at home was as severely enquired into as absence from church. In addition, it has been too frequently stated that fines for non-attendance at the new worship were not actively enforced. Such a position is unhistorical. Evidence exists from 1561 to 1570 (and, indeed, we may say to the end of the reign) of a character which cannot be disputed, proving that fines for non-conformity were levied with unfailing consistency, and that the churchwardens were compelled, without any possibility of escape, to carry out their duties in this respect. Nor are lists of Catholic prisoners wanting for the period. The next phase of anti-Catholic legislation is in connection with the Northern Rebellion of 1570. It is hardly possible to consider this revolt apart from religion, and the rebels themselves claimed that it was a religious crusade. The whole problem is full of difficulties, and the best defence can be read in Knox's *Record of the English Catholics*. Personally, from a modern point of view, I cannot defend it, and even from a sixteenth-century point of view I consider it one of the most foolhardy undertakings ever attempted. It never had any hope of success, and it did not even carry with it the goodwill of the majority of English Catholics at home. It was forced on the Northern Catholics by their friends abroad, who did not in the least understand English conditions, and forced on people, too, who, proscribed and outlawed for their religion, did not themselves understand them. On February 25, 1570, Pius V.

excommunicated Queen Elizabeth, and the Star
Chamber made an effort, in an official declaration, to disentangle politics and religion; but
when Parliament assembled in the following
April it was at once clear that they were insepar-
ably connected. Severe penal legislation marked
the session. It was made treason to dispute the
Queen's claim to the throne, or to call her heretic
or schismatic. It was made treason to bring into
the realm any Bull, absolution, or reconciliation;
to absolve or to receive absolution; to obtain any
new Bulls or instruments from Rome. Aiders
and abettors were made liable to *præmunire,* as
well as those who brought into England any
Agnus Dei; crosses, pictures, beads, and such-
like, or gave them to others to be worn. The
persecution became active. The prisons were
soon full of Catholics, many of whom could have
had no connection with the treasonable plots of
Norfolk and the Spanish Ambassador. But the
organization of Catholicism was passing into
other hands. When Archbishop Parker died in
1575, of those Marian priests who survived none
were under forty, and their ranks were rapidly
thinning. To keep the Faith alive it became
necessary to train men abroad, and when these
missionaries came to England they understood
little or nothing of English life, and their worldly
wisdom was in an inverse ratio to their zeal.
Foreign literature, characterized by neither tact
nor exact knowledge of facts, flooded the country.
The Government were affected by the national

panic, and Cuthbert Mayne was condemned
under the Act of 1571 as a missionary from Rome.
It must be conceded by the honest historian that
he stated at his trial that he was free to serve
the Crown and to aid his country against foreign
invaders. He was guilty of legal treason—he
carried a Bull of Jubilee and an *Agnus Dei*. He
persisted against the law in saying Mass. It
would be hard to find the evidence of political
treason in his life or work. In the spring of
1580 the first Jesuit missionaries arrived in
England, in the persons of Robert Parsons and
Edmund Campion. The first soldiers of the
Church's new army did not pass unnoticed among
the Government's spies, and Parliament, already
in a state of nerves over plots and invasions and
rumours of plots and invasions, passed a further
penal Act, entitled *An Act to retain the Queen's
Majesty's Subjects in their due Obedience*. Any
efforts made to procure converts to Catholicism,
to withdraw people from the established worship,
to move them to obey the Pope's authority, were
declared equal to attempts to withdraw the
Queen's subjects from allegiance to the throne,
and therefore treasonable. Aiders and abettors
in these offences were declared guilty of mis-
prision of treason. The penalty for saying Mass
was laid at a fine of two hundred marks and a
year's imprisonment, and after that indefinitely
until the fine was paid. Every person hearing
Mass was punishable with a fine of one hundred
marks and a year's imprisonment. Every person

over the age of sixteen absent from church was punishable with a fine of £20 per month during absence. Absence for a whole year necessitated two securities of £200 each. Any person keeping a schoolmaster who did not conform was punishable with a fine of £10 for every month that he had remained in the family, and every unconforming schoolmaster was liable to imprisonment for one year. In 1585 the activity of the missionary priests had become so great that *An Act Against Jesuits, Seminary Priests, and such other like Disobedient Persons* was passed. It ordered that all priests ordained since the Feast of St. John the Baptist, 1559, should depart from the realm within forty days after the session of Parliament had concluded. Any such remaining after this time were held to be guilty of high treason, those who kept or supported them being pronounced felons and condemned to a felon's death. Those English subjects in the foreign seminaries who were not yet ordained were ordered to return and submit to the Acts of Supremacy and Uniformity. If they returned and did not do so they were guilty of high treason. Those who subscribed to the support of such seminaries were guilty of *præmunire*. Those who sent their children abroad to be educated without special licence were fined £100 for every offence. Legislation followed legislation. In 1587 another Act was passed reinforcing the fines for non-conformity of the previous years. Nor did the defeat of the Armada, bringing with it as it did relief from fear of Spain, lessen the persecution. In 1593 the most severe of all the Acts against non-conformity was passed. Absence from the Protestant services and refusal to attend them was, in future, punishable by imprisonment until conformity and a public declaration of submission were forthcoming. Harbouring non-conformists was punishable by a fine of £10 for every month during which they were sheltered and entertained. It is true that this Act aimed at the Puritans, but its terms were applicable equally to Catholics. However, in order that there might be no loophole, the same Parliament passed an Act against them, in which loyal and disloyal Catholics were treated as one. They were not to travel farther than five miles from their dwellings. Breach of this law rendered them liable to banishment. Any priest refusing to declare directly that he was a priest was imprisoned. These Acts, with many proclamations, fill up the story of repression. Before the reign closed 124 priests and 63 men and women of the laity were executed in the most revolting manner. On the other hand, it has too often been overlooked that, when the fears died down somewhat after the Armada, the Government, whatever the strict law may have been, endeavoured in actual practice to distinguish between loyal and disloyal Catholics, and the executions lessened accordingly. The fines, however, were enforced in increasing oppression, and many families were

completely ruined by their efforts to compound
or to pay, and the prisons were filled with
Catholics of all sorts. Indeed, the fining and
imprisonments became so heavy that the old
question of outward conformity, which the Pope
had forbidden early in the reign, was reopened,
only once more to be pronounced against. After
1591 executions almost disappeared, but death
would have been better than life in the average
recusant's prison, with torture in the Tower ever
at hand. Even at the close of the reign, when
Catholics were disgraced by the most unedifying
disputes among themselves, and even when the
majority of them had completely abandoned the
foreign advice which had cost them, by its ignorance, rash advice, and political folly, so dear,
the Government made it clear that persecution
and repression would not cease, however self-
evident the loyalty of Catholics might be. There
could be " no toleration of two religions within
the realm." Banishment was held out over the
loyal Catholic's head if he did not conform. This
closing scene of the reign has been obscured. It
must be granted, and fully granted, that the Bull
of Pius V. was a fatal blunder, that it placed
English Catholics—no matter what reservations
were issued in connection with it—in a tragic
position. It must be granted, and fully granted,
that zealots who had fled from England, and who
enjoyed security on the Continent, were the worst
possible advisers whom the Pope could have had,
as they simply saw life in England from the

vantage-ground of their own safety, through the eyes of enthusiasm, and knew nothing of that new national *nescio quid* which had grown up in the country. It must be granted, and fully granted, that they were full of political plans which only unpractical enthusiasts could have formed, which, unfortunately, however, raised storms of persecution round their countrymen at home, and made the names Catholic and traitor synonymous in the ears of the nation. On the other hand, the final dealings to which reference has just been made make it clear that, in the final analysis, the profession of the Catholic religion was sufficient to bring banishment, if not death. Here Catholicism and Puritanism join hands.

Into such a world of religious warfare Cardinal Allen and Edmund Campion were born. I have selected them for the reason that they represent two special phases of Catholic life during the period, and each is the best in his class. Allen was a political-religious champion, and Campion was purely a missionary fired with religious zeal on behalf of his fellow-Catholics in suffering. The general survey of the history which we have just made has been necessary if we are to understand, even in a small degree, the lives and aims of both men. For the moment, details of that history have to be omitted, but as their personal history is considered many of them will appear and take their place in the history of the reign. We have already seen something of the Elizabethan ideal and its workings in the daily lives of the people. This ideal, and the survey made at the beginning of this chapter, must be kept carefully in mind if real justice is to be done to Allen and Campion. Every part of that ideal, and every Act and proclamation on the part of the Government, influenced them, while the active repression of Catholicism, whether by fines, imprisonments, or executions, was the reason which made each of them in his own sphere an active champion of his Faith. Nor is it possible to doubt their sincerity, while we may dispute their wisdom. It may be said of them in a lesser degree, as we said of Queen Mary, that their very conscientiousness rendered them inefficient in public affairs. We must judge them, however, just as they were, and in severe connection with the history which lay round them in such tragic forms. Out of their history will, I think, emerge something of value for the student, and something of help to the general reader in forming or reforming his opinions of Elizabethan Catholicism.

Cardinal William Allen is least known of all the English Cardinals of the sixteenth century. Wolsey has lived in the unenviable fame surrounding the Royal Divorce which we have considered. Reginald Pole is part and parcel of the history of Mary's reign; but Allen is only a name to the majority of his countrymen. Even his latest biography leaves much to be desired in clearness, historical details, and an adequate understanding of sixteenth-century life. Yet

Allen has many claims on the student of Elizabethan history. He excelled his predecessors in
many respects. He was a finer scholar than
Wolsey, and he was by nature utterly incapable
of Wolsey's duplicity and dishonesty. He was a
man of stronger character and intellect than
Cardinal Pole, and he was far above both in his
powers as a writer. In addition, he shares with
them something which has always aroused the
interest of men, however they may differ. He is
one of that band of men who gave themselves
whole-heartedly to a cause and lived to see it
ruined. Wolsey's diplomacy broke round him in
angry fragments before he died. Pope followed
his Queen with the heart-rending cries of a lost
cause in his ears. Allen lived to see his methods
recoil on those for whom he had lived and worked
whole-heartedly during his entire life. He was
born in December, 1532, at Rossall Grange, in
Lancashire, of an old and sturdy race. His early
education was carried out at home, under
parental supervision, during those pregnant
years when Henry VIII. was breaking the ties
which in later life Allen was to attempt to
reknot. When he was a lad of fifteen years he
entered Oriel College, Oxford, from which he
graduated in 1550 with a reputation for learning,
industry, seriousness of purpose, and humility
of bearing. He was at once elected to a Fellowship of his College. Allen's history during the
reign of Edward VI. is obscure, and I cannot
pronounce on his state of mind then; but he

proceeded M.A. in 1554, and was promoted as Principal and Proctor of St. Mary's Hall in 1556. His active connection with religion during Mary's reign cannot be proved. With the accession of Elizabeth, life at the Universities became impossible for a Catholic who refused to take the Oath of Supremacy. Accordingly, he resigned his appointments in 1560, and his successor, John Raw, was appointed in the same year. He continued at Oxford till 1561, encouraging his colleagues and students to remain steadfast in the Faith. His zeal, however, became too pronounced, and in the same year he crossed to Flanders and settled at the University of Louvain. Failing health brought him back in the following year to England, where he found that many Catholics were conforming outwardly to the Protestant worship. In the early winter of the same year Pius IV. had pronounced against such conformity, and Allen—still a layman—went about the country bringing to the attention of Catholics the Papal decision. He supported his mission by circulating in manuscript a work entitled *Certain Brief Reasons concerning the Catholic Faith.* His activities and success, especially in Lancashire, forced him to fly from England in 1565. He retired to Malines, where he was ordained priest, and published his work on *Purgatory,* which he had written during his first exile. At Malines he lectured for two years, while his writings were causing trouble to the Government at home, who issued an order for his arrest in February, 1568. His reply was a further set of writings, which showed that he was now capable of the best form of controversial literature. In 1567 he went to Rome with his old Oxford tutor, Morgan Philips, and Vendeville, Professor of Canon Law at Douay, and afterwards Bishop of Tournay. Vendeville failed to see Pius V. in connection with a missionary project which is not clear. His failure, however, led Allen to lay before him the state of Catholics in England, and out of the conversations on the subject came the founding of the seminary college at Douay, which was opened on St. Michael's Day, 1568, for the special purpose of supporting and spreading the Catholic Faith in England. Allen was made President, and among the later students was Edmund Campion. Seventy-four priests left the new college during the first ten years of its existence, and of these, fifteen, including Cuthbert Mayne, were put to death. Allen's work, *A Brief History of the Glorious Martyrdom of Twelve Reverend Priests,* was published in 1582, and supplies us with much of the earlier history. In 1578 the college, after a precarious financial struggle—owing to the fact that it was impossible to get money from England—and the success of revolutionary forces in Douay, removed to Rheims. Before this removal, however, Allen had begun those political activities on behalf of English Catholicism which were fraught with such tragic results. The purpose of the seminary—aid by spiritual means,

and the purpose of Allen's political propaganda
—aid by force, lie in modern eyes far apart.
To-day we can appreciate and see the justice of
the one, while we condemn the other. In the
sixteenth century both were agreeable to current
principles. It is well, however, to point out that
in Allen's college the discussion of all political
questions was absolutely forbidden, and in
college debates and arguments the question of
the deposition of rulers was emphatically ruled
out of discussion. It is not often in history that
a man has succeeded, even as far as Allen did, in
keeping apart two methods so dear to his heart in
which his conscience and the theories of his age
allowed him to believe.

It will be well to state clearly Allen's connection with treasonable schemes, and to leave the
student to form his own opinions on them. From
the year 1577 at least he was active against
Elizabeth, and mixed up later in all the plans
for her deposition and for helping Mary Queen
of Scots. Allen was consulted by Gregory XIII.
when there was some idea of sending an expedition to England. The whole thing, including
Stukeley's attempt on Ireland, was foolhardy in
the extreme, especially as Philip II. had no
active hand in it. It seems impossible, however,
to disconnect Allen's influence from the affair,
although it proves him to be severely lacking in
political foresight and wisdom. Later on Allen
went to Paris. Certainly by April, 1582, he was
actively connected with the plots of Esmé Stuart,

Seigneur d'Aubigny. For two years various negotiations were carried on with Philip and the Duke of Guise to further Aubigny's plan for the destruction of Elizabeth's rule in England. The whole thing was equally futile, but Allen was now under the influence of such a zealot as Father Parsons, and this fact, coupled with his long absence from England, made it impossible for him to temper his zeal with an accurate estimate of the real state of affairs. If any further proof of this were needed, it can be found in the praise which Allen bestowed on Sir W. Stanley for the surrender of Deventer, in the Low Countries, to the Spanish forces. This work so outraged the patriotism of the majority of English Catholics, who were ready to fight the Spaniard, no matter how strengthened with Papal sanctions, that they believed that it was a forgery to injure their religion in the name of its most prominent champion. Indeed, Allen's political activities largely accounted for his elevation to the purple. Document after document goes to prove that his support of Philip II. in his claims to the English Crown was brought forward to further his elevation. It was commonly stated that, if Allen were made a Cardinal, Philip would hurry on his attack. Accordingly, he was created Cardinal Priest of the Church by Sixtus V. on August 7, 1587, with the title St. Martinus in Montibus. The Pope stated that his object was to console English Catholics for the death of Mary Queen of Scots, heir-presumptive

to the throne of England, in whom their hopes
had been placed, and to prevent them despairing
while Elizabeth, " that impious Jezebel," lived.
The years were big with purpose. Allen outlined a plan for restoring and administering the
Church in England when Philip gained the
Crown. Plan and hope went to the winds a year
later with the destruction of the Armada. To the
end of his life Allen remained hopeful of Spanish
success, and defeat did not dim the vision of his
political schemes. It must be one of the most
pitiable regrets in Catholic history that a man
of such sincere religion should have marred the
splendid work which he did for the Catholic
Faith, and for the persecuted Catholics in
England, by becoming an alien to the new spirit
among Englishmen. The most callous student
of history cannot but acknowledge the heroic
self-sacrifice of the seminary priests who came
from Allen's college to minister to the broken
members of the Church, nor can he deny, no
matter how hard it may be for him to be unpreju-
diced, that intense piety and simple loyalty to
the Faith characterized the vast majority of
Allen's students, helped them in the perils of the
duty, and supported them in misery and in
death, which in no small degree Allen's political
activities forced on them. This is, I think, a
just estimate of the case.

It is now necessary to turn to Allen's literary
work. In addition to that already referred to
he wrote a *Life of Edmund Campion, An Apology*

for the English colleges at Douay and Rome, *Instructions concerning the Government of Seminaries,* and a *Defence of English Catholics,* to which I shall return. That his controversial writings were of more than average importance and more skilled than those of his fellows was recognized at the time. Walsingham, with a zeal characteristic of the age, plotted his assassination through the hands of the infamous Egremont Radcliffe. One of the most interesting events, however, in Allen's life is his connection with the official versions of the Scriptures. One of the greatest aims of the Popes after the Council of Trent was to bring out a carefully corrected edition of the Latin Vulgate. In 1579 Cardinal Caraffa, under the direction of Gregory XIII., got together a band of scholars to prepare an accurate edition of the Septuagint as a preparation for the work. Among these was Cardinal Allen. We have no accurate information as to what part he took in this edition, which appeared in 1587, but it is reasonable to suppose that during his various visits to Rome he assisted his colleagues. A new Commission was appointed in 1591 to carry out the plan of Gregory XIII., and Allen's first biographer, fourteen years after his death, speaks of his work in connection with this Commission. More interesting still was his work in connection with the Catholic Version of the Bible in English. When the Douay college was transferred to Rheims, Allen ordered Gregory Martin, an

English student from the Diocese of Chichester, to begin a translation. Martin's work began in October, 1578, and each page was carefully revised by Cardinal Allen and Richard Bristow, one of the original exiles at the college, and a Fellow of Exeter College, Oxford. The New Testament was completed in 1582, and the Old in 1611, all the money necessary for the undertaking having been collected by Allen before his death. It is hardly necessary to recall its connection with the Authorized Version of King James and its influence on it.

Before concluding this study of Allen it will be well to refer to his *Defence of English Catholics,* which appeared in 1584. As it is intimately connected with the spiritual side of Allen's work, and as it deserves no small place in the history of English prose literature, it calls for consideration, as well as for the fact that it throws some considerable light on the inner history of the reign. In addition, it is a work largely unknown, and the use made of it by Elizabethan historians is out of all proportion to its value. The full title is, *A true, sincere, and modest Defence of English Catholics, that suffer for their Faith both at home and abroad, against a false, seditious, and slanderous libel, entitled: " The Execution of Justice in England."* The tract to which it was an answer is commonly ascribed to Lord Burghley, and was apparently issued as the official apologia for Elizabeth's dealings with Catholics, and as an

explanation of the severe Penal Act of 1581. Its
full title is, *The Execution of Justice in England,
for Maintenance of Public and Christian Peace,
against certain stirrers of sedition and adherents
to the Traitors and Enemies of The Realm, without any persecution of them for questions of
Religion, as is falsely reported and published by
the fautors and fosterers of their Treasons.* In
the eyes of the Government there were grave
reasons that their actions should be defended.
Their religious policy had failed. They had not
reckoned on the devotion of the old Marian
priests and their ability to keep the Catholic
Church alive in England, nor were they prepared
for the new missionaries, trained in modern controversy and fired with the greatest enthusiasm
and devotion, who began to invade the country
and to stir up the weak faith of their brethren.
Severer measures were necessary, and the
authorities appear, towards the close of 1575, to
have begun by dealings with the gentlemen of
Staffordshire, which soon extended through all
the Southern Counties. In addition, efforts of a
determined character were made to prevent
the circulation of the controversial literature from the Continent. Not only were the
Channel ports carefully watched, but the Bishops
carried out strict inquisitions for such books in
the parishes, even invading the homes of the
people, so great was the Government's anxiety.
Among the earliest missionaries was Cuthbert
Mayne, who returned to England in April, 1576,

in company with John Paine. They were soon followed by others. The Government grew alarmed, and Mayne, with his host Tregian and others, was arrested in June, 1577. Mayne was tried in September, and the official charges laid against him were that he had brought a Bull into England, carried an *Agnus Dei,* said Mass, and administered the Lord's Supper in a " Papistical manner." The Bull was only an expired Bull of Jubilee, and there was no positive evidence forthcoming of saying Mass or of distributing " Papal trinkets." Contemporary reports tell of dissension among the judges and of pressure on them from above. Mayne was sentenced to death for treason under the Act of 1571. The charges against him are of the utmost importance in view of Burghley's tract and Allen's reply. There was no evidence brought forward at the trial that he was mixed up in political affairs. The method of his execution need not surprise us or call for any comment. Hagiologists have not been wanting in their duty in this connection. Mayne was followed within a year by John Nelson and William Sherwood. These severe dealings did not produce the desired effect. Before long the Bishops found that Catholicism was increasing on all sides, and enquiries and repression once more began in a more diligent manner. Two replies were forthcoming : a foolish invasion of Ireland, suported by neither common sense nor men, and the coming of the Jesuits. Parsons and Campion arrived in England in the summer of 1580. Within a short time they left London and went on tour through the country, while the Government issued a proclamation against the harbouring of Jesuits, and the available prisons were filled up and others provided. The paper war began over a tractate written by Campion, which we shall consider later. The final reply was the Act of 1581. Lesser men were captured and tortured—Ralph Sherwin, Hart, Bosgrave, Briant—until in July Campion himself was taken. The trial leads us up to the publication of *The Execution of Justice,* and must be examined and recalled in connection with that of Mayne. The preliminaries were rackings and disputations. These proved of no material value, and the scene was shifted to the law court. Even here the triumph would be difficult. Campion had, by written and spoken word, acknowledged Elizabeth as his Sovereign. This may have been discounted by the fact that the official gloss on the Bull *Regnas in Excelsis* only allowed such acknowledgment for the present. However, it could be answered that no one could be condemned for treason on account of his future conduct. No aggressive acts of treason were proved against Campion and his companions. Of legal treason under Elizabethan Acts they certainly were guilty, and against such Acts defence was hopeless. Conviction was certain before the verdict was returned. Campion, Briant, and Sherwin were executed on

December 1, 1581. In the following May seven more followed. Within a short time the number of priests executed since Mayne's death reached eighteen. The execution of Campion and his companions raised an angry storm, not merely in England, but in Europe. On all sides discussions, bitter as the age, went on. An official defence was necessary, and Burghley came forward as the champion with *The Execution of Justice,* which must be analyzed in detail. As Allen's *Defence* is the best that can be said for the Catholic side, so this tract is the best that can be said for the Protestant. The names Catholic and Protestant are used without apology, as they are the only two which appear in the discussion.

Burghley begins by a general statement that rebels always advance excuses for their rebellion. He evidently refers to the Northern Rebellion of 1570 and the attempt in Ireland in 1579, pointing out that their suppression was necessary as treasonable acts to dethrone the Queen, and because they would have promoted general civil war. He denies that the revolts were religious— this excuse was merely a cloak for rebellion, and he brings to the front the merciful measures dealt out to the rebels—" Some few of them suffered." The fact that Sussex condemned almost twenty per cent. of the Northern rebels to death was omitted for obvious reasons. Charles Neville, Earl of Westmorland, and Thomas Stukeley come in for some severe personal abuse, which is char-

acteristic of the age, and does not affect the history. The Bull of Deposition is next considered,
together with its effects. Among the different
classes of exiles were those who could not live at
home " but in beggary, some discontented for
lack of preferments, which they gaped for un-
worthily in Universities and other places." The
new seminaries are then referred to. They are
uniformly classed as nurseries of treason, and
their spiritual aims are mentioned only as
" Romish trash." It is accepted as true that
those who should be reconciled to the old religion
would be *ipso facto* traitors, " in their hearts
and consciences secret traitors." For these
reasons some of the obvious stirrers of rebellion
had been openly condemned for treasons, but
only after " all manner of gentle ways of persuasion used." Then comes the important statement : " These, I say, have justly suffered death,
not by force, or form of any new law established
either for religion or against the Pope's
Supremacy, as the slanderous libellers would
have it seem to be, but by the ancient temporal
laws of the realm, and, namely, by the laws of
Parliament made in King Edward the Third's
time, about the year of our Lord 1330, which is
about 200 years and more past, when the Bishops
of Rome and Popes were suffered to have their
authority ecclesiastical in this realm, as they had
in many other countries." The Queen's clemency
is dealt with and her desire not " to have any
blood spilt " pointed out, in spite of which the

seminarists come in secretly. Their open avowal of a spiritual mission is categorically denied, and they are one and all classed as those ready to take up arms against the Queen, to assist a foreign invasion, and to break the peace with foreign countries which had lasted since the reign began. The duty of the Government is outlined, and its methods laid down in one particular in an important sentence : " And though there are many subjects known in this realm that differ in some opinions of religion from the Church of England, and that do also not forbear to profess the same, yet in that they do also profess loyalty and obedience to Her Majesty, and offer readily in Her Majesty's defence to impugn and resist any foreign force, though it should come or be procured from the Pope himself, none of these sort are for their contrary opinions in religion prosecuted or charged with any crimes or pains of treason, nor yet willingly searched in their consciences for their contrary opinions that savour not of treason." The dealings with the Catholic Bishops and clergy who would not accept the new religion are referred to at length, and the fact that none of them had been " burdened with capital pains " pointed out. Their fluctuations during the various changes in religion are also referred to. The treatment of lay people who held to the Catholic Faith is then pointed out. There had been no executions, " no loss of life, member, or inheritance " for the profession of religion, even though the Government knew that many believed in the Pope's Supremacy and denied the Supreme Governorship of the Queen in ecclesiastical matters. The executions after 1570 are defended as solely due to maintaining the Bull of Deposition, and as being carried out under "the ancient laws temporal of the realm." Sanders and Morton and their plans and plots receive, in turn, consideration, and Parsons and Campion are dealt with in the same connection. No distinction can exist between treason and the religion of the Pope. The outcry against the executions is answered by an appeal to the small number executed during many years compared with the great number executed in a few years under Queen Mary, and by the statement that the Marian martyrs never knew any other religion than that for which they suffered, while the Elizabethan traitors over thirty years of age impugned a religion which they had learned in their youth. Burghley then advances into wider questions. The Papal claims to depose Kings and Princes are dangerous to all rulers, but the Popes had behaved themselves in this respect until the time of Hildebrand. Historical examples of those who resisted the Popes in the past are called in to support Elizabeth. The sack of Rome, the siege by the Duke of Alva, Mary and Pole's resistance of Pope Paul IV., are in turn pressed into the argument. Suggestions are made for the canonization of other rebels and traitors. England's prosperity and " generally

all kinds of worldly felicity " under his curses
sufficiently discount his methods to make them
like the maledictions of Balaam. Four reasons
are given to persuade readers that no one was
executed for religion, but only for treason : the
Queen suffered Bulls and excommunications to
come in, and took no notice of them until,
secondly, Pius V. sent his Bull, and Felton
suffered for nailing it up in London ; thirdly, the
Northern Rebellion changed her attitude—the
Pope's treason in connection with it was
manifest; fourthly, the invasion of Ireland confirmed Her Majesty in her actions. To the objection that those executed are but scholars, priests,
Jesuits, and unarmed, Burghley replies that
arms are not necessary to traitors, and that the
secret teachings of these men had stirred treason
to open acts. The execution of the seminarists
is justified for six reasons along similar lines.
The tract concludes : " If these seminarists,
secret wanderers, and explorers in the dark
would employ their travels in the works of light
and doctrine, according to the usage of their
schools, and content themselves with their profession and devotion, and that the remnant of
the wicked flock of the seedmen of sedition would
cease from their rebellious, false, and infamous
railings and libellings altogether contrary to
Christian charity, there is no doubt, by God's
grace (Her Majesty being so much given to mercy
and devoted to peace), but all colour and occasion
of shedding of blood of any more of her natural

subjects of this land, yea all further bodily
punishments should utterly cease . . . *Magna
est veritas et prœvalet.*" The tract is remarkable for its mildness of tone compared with the
controversial literature of the reign. This was
doubtless due to the fact that it was intended for
circulation not only in England, but abroad.

In considering Allen's reply, it must be remembered that we are not concerned either with a
discussion in Church history or theology—
Catholic or Protestant. We merely take
Burghley's tract and Allen's tract as they are.
The rights and wrongs of their statements do not
concern us, and we have still less to do with how
they might have strengthened their respective
cases, or how they may have weakened them by
what they actually said. Allen's work, however,
may be mentioned in its relation to English
prose. It is remarkable that it has escaped all
mention in this connection. At a time when
English prose was largely unformed, and when
it was most successful only in controversy,
Allen's style has a note of practicability about it
which reaches its hand out to Dryden. It is not
so discursive and elusive as Sidney's, nor so
ponderous and complicated as Hooker's. It has,
considering the period in which it was written,
no small amount of dignity and ease, and it
comes nearer the conversation of an educated
man than any other book of the day.

Allen begins by pointing out that the
charge of treason in matters of religion

had been made in the history of the early
Christians, though they, as the Elizabethan
sufferers, had claimed that their religion
alone was the cause of their persecution.
He also points out that his charge of covering
their real causes by pretences applies equally to
Kings and Princes and rebels, and he brings
forward the names of Richard III., the promoters
of Lady Jane Grey's rebellion, and of the Scotch
against their lawful Sovereign. He then proceeds to deal with one of the most important of
Burghley's statements, and to prove that none
of the martyrs were prosecuted and condemned
under the treason laws of Edward III., as
Burghley had dogmatically stated, but under the
Acts of 1571 and 1581. Mayne suffered for an old
Bull and an *Agnus Dei,* as the records of his
trial proved—things unknown to the laws of
Edward III. Sherwood suffered for denying the
Supreme Governorship; Nelson for saying that
the Queen's religion was heretical and
schismatical; Hanse for maintaining the Pope's
spiritual authority. These were obviously new
treasons, and Hanse and Nelson were severely
interrogated as to their conscientious beliefs,
contrary to Burghley's statement that none were
charged in their consciences by any inquisition
to bring them into danger of capital law. Other
martyrs are then considered, and Allen proves
that in no case were the treason laws of
Edward III. appealed to. He then discusses the
reference to the Queen's position in ecclesiastical

affairs, especially the matters of "Supreme
Head" and "Supreme Governor." Allen traces
the history of the question, and shows that the
official explanation of the Oath of Supremacy
proved that the difference was merely in words,
as Elizabeth claimed that her rule in ecclesiastical affairs corresponded to the Supreme Head-
ship of Henry VIII. and Edward VI. He next
refers to the use of the rack, which Burghley had
not spoken of in *The Execution of Justice*, but
had referred to in a pamphlet entitled *A Declaration of the Favourable Dealings of Her Majesty's
Commissioners appointed for the examination of
certain Traitors and of tortures unjustly reported
to be done upon them for matters of Religion,
1583.* Here Burghley stated that it was never
used "in any question of their supposed conscience as to what they believed in any point of
doctrine or faith" in the dealings with the
seminarists and their friends. Allen replied that
it had been used to find out where Mass was
said, where priests were harboured, where
children were sent to school, where Catholic
books were printed—things which he claimed
affected conscience and religion. Campion's
examination, among others, is brought forward
in proof. He then deals with the horrors of the
imprisonments, to which Burghley had made no
reference, and brings forward in his support the
deaths of Catholics in York through their treatment in confinement. In Chapter II. a return
is made to the treason laws of Edward III., on

which Burghley had entirely relied. He considers the arraignment of Campion and his brethren : " To conspire and compass the death of the Sovereign or to levy arms against him," under which clause a charge was laid. It was alleged that " at Rome and Rheims, the last days of March and May in the 22nd year of Her Majesty's reign, they compassed the Queen's death, the subversion of the State, and the invasion of the realm." It is easy to see that the old treason laws had no connection with the actual trial. Allen then considers the four reasons towards the close of Burghley's tract. First, no Bulls were issued or came into England before that of Pius V. Secondly, the bringing in of a Bull of Excommunication was not treason under Edward III. Thirdly, the Northern Rebellion had no connection with the seminarists. Fourthly, they had no connection with the Irish affair. Nor had it been proved that they were secret promoters of rebellion. Walsingham's disreputable spies come in for some strong remarks, and the evidence with regard to plots at Rome and Rheims is shown to prove too much, for some of those to whom it referred had never been in either place. Stress is laid on the fact that religion must have been in question, as the martyrs would not have suffered had they acknowledged the Queen as Head of the Church. The next chapter deals with the Marian persecutions from several points of view. Mary did not invent new heresies; she

only executed old laws of England and of all
Christendom against heretics. It was absurd to
say that the Marian martyrs only knew of the
religion for which they suffered. Life is not all ;
it may become to a multitude a living death, as
Elizabeth has made it by spoil of goods and
liberty, by fines of £20 per month, by taking
away children to bring them up in another faith,
by enclosing women in dishonourable prisons.
Cranmer's character is severely analyzed, and a
petty comparison is drawn between the intellectual and social state of the respective martyrs.
In answer to Burghley's assertion that the
Marian martyrs never denied at their death their
lawful Queen, nor maintained her enemies, Allen
brings forward Cranmer, condemned for high
treason ; Ridley, who preached during Lady Jane
Grey's rule that Mary and Elizabeth were both
bastards, and all of Wyatt's conspirators. He
says Burghley's " at their death " is a " deceit-
ful cobbling in of words." The answer proceeds
to deal with the questions put to prisoners on
the Bull of Pius V., " wherein, if you say
nothing, or refuse to answer something in contempt or derogation of the See Apostolic, then
you are judged no good subject, but a traitor."
The general attitude of the seminarists to
political questions is pointed out. Neither in
word or writing, nor at their executions, had
they uttered a word against the Queen, and in
their training at college they had never been
allowed to discuss deprivation or excommunica-

tion of princes, neither in general nor in particular. He contrasts their public conduct and private training with the efforts made to involve them by cross-examination in treason, and to bring their very thoughts into evidence against them. Even supposing them to hold that the Pope can depose or excommunicate a prince, yet that cannot be proved treason by the statute of Edward III., " upon which only he saith we be condemned for traitors." Even taking the new laws, no seminarist or martyrs ever called " the Queen heretic voluntarily, contemptuously, or maliciously, as your statute runneth, but when they were driven by you of set purpose to offend the law, so to have some quarrel to make them away." Allen then deals with Burghley's appeal to Kings and rulers to notice how the Pope's claim endangers their sovereignty, pointing out that Calvin, Beza, Zwingli, Knox, Luther, held that princes may be deposed by their subjects if they do not hold the Reformed Faith. Flanders and Scotland were contemporary examples. Burghley cannot have it both ways. He sums up the position thus : " Thus both schools and laws speak and resolve for the matter in hand, both Catholics and Protestants arguing that Princes may, for some causes, and especially for their defection and faith in religion, be resisted and forsaken. Though in a manner of executing the sentence and other needful circumstances Protestants follow faction and popular mutiny, we reduce all to law, order, and judgment." The

dilemma forced on Burghley is this : England
has assisted the Protestants of France and
Scotland against their rulers, supported by the
official teaching of contemporary Protestantism.
Is such mutiny right only for Protestants and
never for Catholics?   Allen then surveys Church
history in connection with this division of his
subject, coming back once more to his challenge :
In connection with any of the rebellions in
England or Ireland against the Queen, " put
down to the world (if you can) any one word,
writing, or approved witness, that any Jesuit,
priest, or seminary man of all those whom you
have executed these late years were either
authors, persuaders, or dealers therein, and then
you will have some shadow of defence for your
justice. Prove only that His Holiness ever communicated his doings or intentions (whatsoever
they were that way) to any one of them all, and
we will confess that you have reason in the rest.
If Pius V. addressed Dr. Nicholas Morton sixteen
years since about the matter of excommunication
in England, shall all priests and Jesuits be
deemed traitors therefore ?   If Dr. Saunders,
either upon his own zeal and opinion of the
justice of the quarrel, or at the Pope's appoint-
ment, were in the wars of Ireland employed for
defence of the Catholic religion against the
Protestants, may you by your laws, or any other
Divine or human ordinance, condemn therefore
to death a number that never knew either the
man or the matter? Some pretence may you

have to be offended with the Pope, and perhaps
lack no laws to punish the said two Doctors, that
never were either of the Society or seminaries;
but to make all priests and Catholics at
home or in banishment traitors thereby is
too unreasonable, and to murder so cruelly
one man for another's fault is too foul
and intolerable iniquity." Allen next considers
the cases of the Emperor, Alva, and Queen Mary,
and points out how their resistance to the Popes
was in connection with matters of temporal
policy, and not in connection with spiritual
authority. The same answer is given to the anti-
Papal statutes in England before the Reformation. In considering Burghley's argument about
the present prosperity of England without the
Pope but with his cursings, Allen sums up the
benefits derived by England in the past from the
Catholic Church; and when he comes to speak
of the reign of Elizabeth he touches a point
omitted by his opponent : " Never so much in-
justice, never so much extortion, never so much
theft, never so much pride, ebriety, glutton, riot,
and all other sin and abomination." The worldly
felicity of which Burghley alone spoke was confined to a small portion of the population. In
conclusion, Allen turns to Burghley's promise
of clemency, and points out that the past offered
little hope for the future, and that if a " few
places of the realm never so secretly " had been
allowed for Catholic worship, if " any piece of
that liberty which Catholics enjoy in . . . other

places among Protestants '' had been granted to English Catholics, he was convinced that the Elizabethan Government would never have repented their decision. He is ready to promise that, if the persecution now ceases, the seminary priests will come into the country openly and behave loyally in public as they did in secret.

Such, then, are the refinements of defence issued by Elizabeth and the Catholics in connection with the persecutions. Without trespassing the limits which we imposed on ourselves when we began this study, it must seem clear that Burghley's tract was obviously written to influence those who did not know with any accuracy English affairs. In addition, it has always been a puzzle to me to explain why he produced a defence which gave so many loopholes for attack. He could hardly have written anything to which, other things being equal, a skilled controversialist could have more easily replied. On the other hand, Allen attempts to cover the whole ground. He does not confine himself merely to a rebuttal of Burghley's main positions, but he attempts to include every point in dispute, and to give a comprehensive view of the Papal position. From this point of view his work is a failure. The tracts, however, open up aspects of Elizabethan history which, I venture to think, have been largely obscured by the too common custom of looking at them from a modern standpoint. Here we possess the best that can be said on both sides from men of the day, and beyond their defences I do not think that the modern student will make much advance. If he wants to follow the subject into endless minutiæ, he can find voluminous material in Bilson's *The True Difference between Christian Subjection and Un-Christian Rebellion,* published at Oxford in 1585. He will find there a vast array of Protestant authorities, and a detailed dissection of Allen's case, but he will not find anything which will throw light of any value on the complicated history.

It is almost a relief to turn to Blessed Edmund Campion. Acts of Parliament were not his *métier.* Political problems lay outside his life. He was consumed with a pure love of God, and his zeal was the outcome of an inner life full of singular beauty and piety. Campion was born in London on January 25, 1540, and educated at Christ's Hospital. He welcomed Queen Mary in her triumphal procession into the City, according to the customs of the day. He joined St. John's College, Oxford, on a scholarship from the Grocers' Company, and later became a Fellow of the same foundation. In 1564 he took the Oath of Supremacy. His personality and scholarship gathered round him a band of enthusiastic pupils. During his Oxford life he lived on terms of friendship with Bishop Cheney of Gloucester, by whom he was ordained a deacon in the Protestant Church. His adherence to the new principles was never sound, for immediately after his ordination the Grocers' Company suspected his opinions, and demanded a public sermon from him in London. This he refused, and finally his connection with the Grocers' Company was broken. His conscience now began to work, and his friend, Gregory Martin, to whom reference has already been made, confirmed his scruples. On August 1, 1569, Campion resigned his appointments at Oxford and retired to Ireland. His life in Ireland soon got him into trouble with the authorities. His open defence of Catholicism and his attendance at Catholic worship did not tend to quiet living at a time when the English Government was more anxious than ever over the Northern Rebellion and the Bull of Pius V. Hurrying in disguise from his exile, he returned to England, only to find the inquisitions against Catholics more severe than ever. He determined to retire to Douay, but his first attempt only ended in his arrest at sea by an English gunboat and in a compulsory return. However, his captors were not anxious to secure his person, and he finally escaped to Calais. In 1571 he joined Allen's foundation at Douay. Here he remained for a year, and in 1572 reached Rome, determined to enter the Society of Jesus. It is difficult to arrive at his reasons for leaving his fellow-countrymen at Douay. Apart from a desire to become a religious and to take part in the missionary work of the Jesuits, a case has been made out for the theory that he left Douay because his political ideas differed from those of Allen. There can be little doubt that Campion had no

interest in political questions, and that he fully
disapproved of the Bull *Regnans in Excelsis,* but
there is no conclusive evidence to prove that
his departure from Douay was due to these
opinions, or that he had heard them opposed
there in controversy. Indeed, there is positive
evidence that such discussions never took place.
In April, 1573, Campion was received as a
Jesuit novice, and in the following June began
his novitiate at Prague. In October he was
removed to Brünn, where he completed his pro-
bation. After passing through the various
spheres of work peculiar to the Society, he was
sent to Rome, where he found that Allen had
made arrangements for the Jesuits to come to
England. In due course Campion, accompanied
by Parsons, set out, and arrived there in June,
1580. It is hardly necessary to follow in detail
the story of Campion's brief mission—we have
already spoken of its end. The broader details
of his influence and of his writings will fit him
into the place chosen for him here as a champion
of Catholicism. Campion became almost at once
the most successful of missionaries. He fired
with new zeal the spirits of English Catholics,
and his writings were the clarion summons to
broken men. They kindled again the fires of
faith, which, though they smouldered for generations, survived. Apart from politics, apart from
plots, they called his countrymen to the battle
of a living religion. The gentle missionary
became the inspired apostle of his cause, and

the diligent Government found in him a greater
foe than deposing Bull or open rebel. To these
writings we turn.

At the close of June, 1580, Campion preached
at Paget House, Smithfield, to a large and
enthusiastic congregation. The event was too
public and the numbers too large to secure
secrecy, and at once Campion and Parsons were
forced to leave London owing to the diligence of
the Government. The two friends met at Hoxton
to arrange their plan of action. This had
scarcely been agreed on when a prominent
Catholic, Thomas Pounde, of Bedhampton, interviewed them. He informed them that their
dangers were many and that they would doubtless fall into the hands of the many pursuivants,
who were more active than ever. Once in prison,
they could only expect their replies and conversations to be misrepresented. Every effort would
be made to distort their answers and to implicate
them by difficult examinations. He urged each
of them to write then and there a letter which
should contain what he wished to become
public, in case he was imprisoned and unable
to answer the reports which the Government
would undoubtedly circulate as to what he
had confessed or said. After some persuasion
Campion composed, inside an hour, his letter
*To the Right Honourable the Lords of Her
Majesty's Privy Council,* commonly known in
Elizabethan history as *Campion's Brag.* The
writer kept a copy for himself, and entrusted

another, unsealed, to Thomas Pounde. Parsons
also wrote an explanation, and gave a sealed
copy to the same person, to be used in the circumstances outlined. Parsons and Campion then
separated and toured different parts of the South,
returning to London in September. Here they
found *Campion's Brag* famous. Pounde had
been prosecuted and thrown into prison at
Bishop's Stortford, but not before he had handed
round the unsealed copy of Campion's letter.
Thus fame and infamy gathered quickly round
the new missionary. The cause began to flourish
as it had never done since 1558, and the Government and their champions were placed in the
annoyingly absurd position of being invited to a
public disputation which they would not accept.
Parsons undoubtedly exaggerated the effects of
the unsought success, but the evidence is strong
that Catholicism had achieved a victory which,
small though it may have been in reality, was
sufficient to call for congratulation after more
than twenty years of public contumely. The
letter opened by a declaration that Campion had
been sent into England " for the glory of God
and the benefit of souls," and that, anticipating
capture, he had thought it wise to record at the
beginning of his mission his object and plans,
which he proceeded to explain under nine heads.
Firstly, he was a priest of the Catholic Church,
for eight years a member of the Society of Jesus,
vowed to a spiritual warfare, and dead to the
world. Secondly, acting under the orders of his

Superior, he had passed from Prague to Rome, and thence to England, as he would have done to any other part of the world had he been ordered to do so. Thirdly, his aim was " of free cost to preach the Gospel, to minister the Sacraments, to instruct the simple, to confute errors—in brief, to cry alarm spiritual against proud vice and foul ignorance, wherein many [his] dear countrymen are abused." Fourthly, he " never had mind and [was] strictly forbidden by [the] Father that sent [him] to deal in any respect with matters of State or policy of this realm, as things which appertain not to [his] vocation, and from which [he did] gladly restrain and sequester [his] thoughts." Fifthly, he asked three audiences : to discourse before the Council on religion as far as it touched them and the common weal; specially to discourse before the Doctors and Masters of both Univer-sities, and there to prove the Catholic Faith from Scripture, Councils, Fathers, history, natural and moral reasons; to discourse before the lawyers spiritual and temporal, and to justify the Catholic Faith by the common wisdom of the laws yet in force and practice. Sixthly, he was loath " to speak anything that might sound of any insolent brag or challenge," yet he was so convinced of the truth of his cause, and that no Protestant could defeat him, that he desired all the three disputations to be arranged. Seventhly, knowing the notable gifts of the Queen his Sovereign Lady, he desired her to be present at some of his suggested conferences or to listen to a few of his sermons, confident that he would move her to discontinue the hurtful proceedings against Catholics.   Eighthly, his convictions were so strong that he confidently hoped that he would convince his adversaries, and that they would hearken to those "who would spend the best blood in their bodies for your salvation." The next passage is quoted in full to illustrate Campion's zeal as well as his English style : " Many innocent hands are lifted up to heaven for you daily by those English students whose posterity shall never die, which beyond seas, gathering virtue and sufficient knowledge for the purpose, are determined never to give you over, but either to win you heaven or to die upon your pikes.   And touching our Society, be it known to you that we have made a league—all the Jesuits in the world, whose succession and multitude must overreach all the practices of England—cheerfully to carry the cross you shall lay upon us, while we have a man left to enjoy your Tyburn, or to be racked with your torments, or consumed with your prisons.   The expense is reckoned, the enterprise is begun.   It is of God, it cannot be withstood.   So the Faith was planted, so it must be restored."   Ninthly, if his offers were refused, and if he were rewarded with severities, he recommended himself and the Council to God, praying Him to set them both " at accord before the day of payment, to the end we may at last be friends in heaven, when all injuries shall be forgiven."   Such is *Campion's Brag*, which, unknown to the author, strengthened his countrymen. As a matter of policy, it was undoubtedly too confident and free-spoken in style; as a battle-call it produced unquestionably a temporary victory. The Government grew alarmed. The Bishop of Winchester was soon busy arresting those who had copies. " The protestation or challenge," he said, was " very plausible " to the people of his diocese. Before long Campion's letter was known throughout the country, and the hands of the authorities were full dealing with those who circulated it, and the lot of Catholics became worse through more severe measures. Imprisonments increased, and the confinement was made heavier by daily Common Prayer and bi-weekly sermons and conferences between each prisoner and a minister. The literary war began once more. Charke, Hanmer, Lyon, and Parsons added their books to the controversy. In the works of the first two Campion had been accused of pride and insolence in offering single-handed battle to the intellect of England. He met this charge in his next publication, which we shall shortly consider.

Parsons and Campion met after their tour at Uxbridge to discuss plans for the future, and specially to take as much advantage as possible of the commotion made by *The Brag*. The suggestion was made that the time was opportune for Campion to write a Latin address to the Universities, where his scholarship had been admired and where the memory of him still lingered. Various subjects were proposed, but finally Campion chose the paradoxical title *De hæresi desparata,* and answered objections by saying, " Even for this cause seemeth this argument most fit at this time, for that this manner of their cruel proceeding by terror is the greatest argument that may be of their destruction; for if they had any confidence at all in the truth of their cause they would never proceed in this manner." Out of this title and its explanation came, in due course, Campion's famous *Decem Rationes.* The missionaries then parted, Campion going through Yorkshire, Lancashire, and Derbyshire, while Parsons set up his press in London. In March, 1581, Parsons received Campion's manuscript : *Decem Rationes: quibus fretus Edmundus Campianus certamen adversariis obtulit in causa Fidei, Redditæ Academicis Angliæ,* etc. Parsons at once saw that the work was a valuable addition to the missionaries' resources, but he doubted the wisdom of the detailed references—had Campion the time and means to verify them? In spite of Campion's statement that they were correct, Parsons was careful to have every reference examined, and this was no easy matter under the circumstances. At length the book was ready for the press, now set up at Stonor Park, on the borders of Oxfordshire. The actual printing began about the end of April, but the book was not finished till the third week in June, owing to the necessity for secrecy, the small number of workmen, and the scarcity of type. While the book was in the press Campion carried on his missionary labours with renewed vigour. The Oxford Act took place at St. Mary's on June 27, and Hartley conveyed as many copies of Campion's book as possible to his old University. At the end of the first day he waited till everyone had gone out, and then, slipping the little books among the papers left on the seats, he quietly retired. Next day success crowned his efforts. It was soon evident that the audience were paying no attention to what was going on, but were eagerly engaged in reading the new challenge, in low conversations, which gave place to open discussion as soon as the session closed. Hartley rode off at once to convey the news to his anxious friends at Stonor. Not only at Oxford was excitement high; London was alarmed, and official replies followed, the literary controversy lasting until the succeeding reign. Outside its special interest to us, it will not seem strange that a volume written in excellent Latin, and on a religious subject, had many readers who were not even friendly to Campion, when we remember that Latin was still the language of culture, and prose writings were almost entirely confined to controversy. For us it is more important to note that Burghley urged Bishop Aylmer to prepare replies at once, and that, as a result of his anxiety, Whitaker, Professor of Divinity at Cambridge, and Humphrey, Professor of Divinity at Oxford, produced replies out of all proportion to the shortness of Campion's tract. Within a week of the publication Campion was seized, and in due course executed. The *Decem Rationes* is by no means the work of a trained theologian. It is almost too slight for controversy. It can best be considered as Campion's answer to his alleged pride —an outline of lectures which he hoped to deliver showing that he relied on the truth and justice of his cause. It is divided into ten positions, which he was prepared to defend : That Protestants have mutilated the Scriptures, and have evaded the true meaning of the parts retained ; that Catholicism shows the true nature of the Church, for an invisible Church must be inaudible and unable to testify to the truth ; that, in respect to General Councils, the acceptance by Act of Parliament of the first four imposes on the new Church many things for believing and practising which it persecuted ; that the Fathers, while read in England, rendered the Catholic controversialists superfluous, as they one and all attacked the doctrine and practices now introduced into England, and that the consent of the Fathers in their interpretation of Scripture would afford him a welcome subject for argument ; that history was a witness against Protestantism in favour of the Church ; that the writings of the Reformers are full of " paradoxes " ; that Protestants are illogical in their appeal to Scripture. Finally, the book concludes with a mixture of rhetoric and dogma—everything possible which has any connection with history is pressed into service. This note of rhetoric runs right through the little treatise ; but it served its purpose—it roused missionary zeal, and gave the missionaries their purest and most devoted martyr.

IX

ELIZABETHAN PURITANISM

WHILE the inner circles of Elizabethan diplomacy
were trying to grasp the religious situation in
the early weeks of the reign, and preparing for
the necessity of " præmunire " and " slight
prohibitions," Bishop White of Winchester
delivered a prophecy at Queen Mary's funeral
on December 14, 1558, which proved only too
true : " At this time I warn you the wolves be
coming out of Geneva and other places of
Germany, and have sent their books before, full
of pestilential doctrines, blasphemy, and heresy
to infect the people." The exiles who had left
England during Mary's reign soon began to
return from the foreign centres of reform.
Interpreting the news of Mary's death as a
favourable sign, they hastened to end their exile
—certainly a relief to their hosts as far as Frankfort was concerned—and poured back to England
in crowds. Their five years on the Continent had
changed their religious outlook, and their arrival
home brought with it all the warring elements
of Continental reform. Riots characterized the
first Christmas of the reign, " some declaring for
Geneva and some for Frankfort." Inflammatory

sermons broke up respectable congregations into factions, until the Government stepped in and silenced all preaching. Meanwhile, those whom the winter delayed abroad supplied England with literature. It was clear that there was trouble ahead. Nor did the Coronation a month later clear the air. It was a source of much heart-searching that Popish ceremonies were continued at it, and that a Catholic Bishop took part in the actual crowning of the Queen. Disputes over images followed, and dissatisfaction broadened out into a dispute over ceremonial, which finally led up to the first Puritan crisis of 1566. The " wolves " howled, but before the reign was over they had, as the Government found, learned to bite.

The Elizabethan ideal in religion was national unity. The Acts of Supremacy and Uniformity laid the foundation of that ideal. But as the exiles looked out into the new reign they had every reason to hope. They saw a bench of Protestant Bishops set up, many of whom were in close sympathy with them and had shared their exile. They saw the Pope once more banished from England, and Catholic worship placed under the ban. They held in their hands a Prayer Book which was largely the product of Edwardine extremes, and they had no reason to believe that the Elizabethan Reformation ex-cluded a better reform. As the reign advanced the high-handed dealings with the old hierarchy and clergy, the smashing of images, the overturning of altars, the abandonment of vestments, all helped to encourage their hopes that they would soon bring the Established Church into line with their own ideals. The Genevan system was held up to the highest praise in a book dedicated to Lord Robert Dudley and circulated throughout the country—a system in which " heresy and strange pestiferous doctrines were narrowly seen into," and the ecclesiastical polity " taken out of the Gospel of Jesus Christ was ordained and established with the sound of the trumpet and great bell." Indeed, they only accepted the Elizabethan Settlement in the hope that they would soon give it the impress of their foreign opinions. While they complained that much " superstition " was still retained, they painted fair pictures to their friends abroad of what they believed was their vocation, and they were confident that the day was not far distant when every trace of " Popish idolatry " would be banished from " the fair heritage where harbour is granted to the afflicted members of Christ's Body."

The Puritan has suffered much at the hands of historians. His sincerity had been called in question, his zeal sneered at, his beliefs held up to ridicule. It is true that Puritanism fell at times into the hands of unbalanced leaders, and that at times it got beyond the realms of consistency and logic ; but the fair verdict of history must place the Elizabethan Puritan, with his fellow-sufferer the Elizabethan Catholic, among

the most sincere men of his age. It was no
matter for sneering or ridicule to stand up
against the religious autocracy of Queen Elizabeth, and the questioning of her position in that
connection did more than anything else to make
the Puritan hateful to her. He had religious
convictions in an age of opinions. He believed
in a relationship between creed and character in
an age when they were never wider divorced.
From a modern point of view we may fail to
understand him, and may consider him an
illogical extremist, but we have no right to dispute his claim to appeal against the Papacy of
the Queen, which was as hard as ever the Papacy
of Rome.

The influence of Puritanism made itself felt
early in the reign, and in September, 1560, the
Government was forced to step in and attempt
to preserve the chancel screens. The Parliament
and Convocation of 1563 witnessed to its growth.
The speech of Bacon, the Lord Keeper, at the
opening made it clear that the Queen was dis-
satisfied with the manner in which the New
Religion had been received, and that there was
need of " sharp reformation." The discipline of
the Church had been neglected; ministers had
been slothful; legal ceremonies had been
neglected. The preparations for Convocation
revealed the gathering strength of the party.
Archbishop Parker had already under consideration some " general notes of matters to be moved
by the clergy," among which it was suggested

that the use of surplices should be discontinued, that the Holy Tables should stand no longer altarwise, and that organs and singing should be abandoned. During the early sessions of the Convocation he also asked some of his brethren to provide him with some notes of what they deemed necessary to be reformed. Three of these documents survive—one drawn up by Bishop Alley of Exeter and two by Bishop Sandys of Worcester—which illustrate the Puritan position. Two petitions from the Lower to the Upper House may well be considered in the same connection. The sign of the cross in Baptism was found " very superstitious." Sixty-four clergy wished an expression added to the General Confession at Holy Communion that " the communicants do detest and renounce the idolatrous Mass," and they demanded that only communicants should be present at the celebration. In addition, they demanded that all sponsors should disappear from the rite of Baptism. A further extreme petition followed : the sign of the cross, the use of surplices, kneeling at Communion, and the outdoor dress of the clergy needed reform. On February 13 it was proposed that Sundays and Feasts of our Lord should alone be kept as feast days, and that the minister should face the people in reading the prayers. Other details were added, and the motion only failed by one vote. It is not unreasonable to conclude that practically half the clergy in the Province of Canterbury were in sympathy with

Puritanism, that many of the Bishops were unreliable—" pleni rimarum, hac atque illac efflunt," as Parker described them—and that the clerical sympathies with further reform were reflected among their people. It was clear that the Queen would soon make a move to have the law respected.

The Puritan party had achieved a moral victory, and the long correspondence with the foreign Reformers opened in August, 1563, in which hopes overbalanced fears. But Elizabeth had grown impatient with the general neglect of the plainest directions of the Prayer Book. In the late summer of 1564 reports of severe legislation were in the air, and prominent sympathizers with Puritanism grew alarmed. Pilkington, the Bishop of Durham, wrote an urgent appeal to Leicester, who favoured the Puritans, asking him to use his influence with the Queen against any drastic action, and he foretold that many were prepared to abandon their livings rather than wear the dregs of superstition. Whittingham, the Dean of Durham, backed up his Bishop with a letter to the same nobleman, telling him that rumours had reached him of threatened deprivation for disobedience to the Prayer Book, and begging him to do his utmost to help " God's poor children " against " the triumphs of the Pope." Nor were the rumours altogether unjustifiable, as there was open preaching against the Established Religion in the near neighbourhood of London.

The earliest attempts to grapple with the Puritan situation took place in the early winter of 1564, when Parker made an effort to bring two Oxford champions—Humphrey, President of Magdalen College, and Sampson, Dean of Christ Church—into line. He formulated the matters in question, and they replied by objections to the surplice and cope. The correspondence widened out by the intrusion of Bishop Guest of Rochester, and attempts at conciliation by Parker, who laid down the position that distinctive dress within and without church could be worn, as there was no idea of worship of necessity. The champions accepted this position, but qualified it by saying " all things are lawful but not expedient." This early act is not of much historical importance, but it illustrates the Puritan position. To the plea that the habits were " things indifferent " they answered, " Why worry us, then, over minutiæ of dress, outside the authority of Scripture ?" To the plea that Scripture could not be considered a guide in ritual and ceremonial they replied, " The habits are not things indifferent, but relics of Papistry." It was useless to reason with men who took up such a position; but the time for reasoning soon passed. On January 25, 1565, the Queen entered the controversy with a severe letter of complaint to Parker. She pointed out that the varieties in worship which existed not only discredited the law of the land, but made for disintegration in the national ideal.

The Church alone of all the national institutions had failed to respond to the national unity. She blamed the entire bench of Bishops, to whom she had graciously entrusted her government of religion, for their moderation—if not something worse—in administration and discipline. She demanded a clear-cut account of the differences existing within the Church, and urged the Primate and his brethren to put in motion such powers as they had at their disposal. The letter took immediate effect. Parker issued it to the Southern Province with a covering letter asking for varieties of service.

One detailed return is of importance in connection with our study—that belonging apparently to the Diocese of London, and entitled " Varieties in the Service and Administration used." Before quoting this document *in extenso* as one of the most valuable evidences of the strength of Puritanism, it will be well to give a broad idea of " varieties " derived from episcopal documents. In connection with Baptism, private opinion seems to have been the rule. The fonts were removed and household basins introduced. Some of the clergy maintained that a father could christen his own child, or stand godfather; others desired seven godfathers. In places, someone not in Orders baptized. In some parishes preparation for Confirmation was carried out, in others omitted. Lay-readers at times " churched " women. In many places surplices were abandoned and the service read from the nave of the church, and at Cambridge the surplice was only worn under compulsion. The survey already referred to can, without any historical error, be applied to the whole country. " Service and Prayer : Some say the service and pray in the chancel, others in the body of the church ; some say the same in a seat made in the church ; some in the pulpit with their faces to the people ; some keep precisely the order of the book ; others intermeddle psalms in metre ; some say with a surplice, others without a surplice. Table : The Table standeth in the body of the church in some places, in others it standeth in the chancel ; in some places the Table standeth altar-like, distant from the wall a yard ; in some others in the midst of the chancel, north and south ; in some places the Table is joined, in others it standeth upon trestles ; in some the Table hath a carpet, in others it hath none. Administration of the Communion : Some with surplice and cope, some with surplice alone, others with none ; some with chalice, some with a Communion cup, others with a common cup ; some with unleavened bread, some with leavened. Receiving : Some receive kneeling, others standing, others sitting. Baptizing : Some baptize in a font, some in a basin ; some signed with the sign of the cross, others not signed ; some minister in a surplice, others without. Apparel : Some with a square cap, some with a round cap, some with a button cap, some with a hat ; some in scholar's cloak, some

in others." These varieties bear abundant
witness to the growth of Puritan opinions, and
even on the threshold of the crisis Leicester and
Cecil received letters urging the reasonableness
of the Puritan claims. Once more Parker tried
Humphrey and Sampson. The Queen urged him
on to severer measures on a wider scale. Appeals
followed appeals to the Puritan nobility. The
Bishops were divided. Grindal wavered as ever.
Pilkington threatened to resign. As the storm
gathered Puritans preached with permission
from the Government. Cathedral dignitaries
mocked at proceedings. The licensed preachers
took the side of the extreme party. The withdrawal of licences only led to secret Genevan
worship. At Cambridge violent sermons were
preached against copes and surplices, altars,
wafer bread, and kneeling. The fateful day was
only postponed, while every reforming centre in
Europe was besieged with letters. Bullinger
would not give his entire support. Grindal
for once stiffened his back. The Queen urged
Parker on, and at last, in March, 1566, *The
Advertisements,* of unhappy memory, appeared
ordering surplices and hoods in choir in parish
churches, a cope for the three ministers at a
celebration in the cathedrals, and the old outward apparel. Kneeling at Communion and the
use of the font were enforced. In addition,
future preachers must be examined as to their
conformity to the Elizabethan Settlement, and
all controversial sermons derogatory to the

Established Religion must be reported for
censure. Orders were added covering the acceptance of the Prayer Book and of the Royal
Injunctions of 1559.

At this point it is well to look back and sum
up the position. From the beginning of the reign
Puritanism had been gathering force. It is idle
to claim, quite apart from Catholics, that the
Established Church carried with it the nation.
Public opinion, as far as it existed, showed a
distinct Puritan direction, and the most influential people round the Court fostered its
development. It cannot, then, be said that
Puritanism was an insignificant force even in
1566. The question naturally arises, Why was it
attacked, and why did the Queen personally urge
the attack? It seems that there can be only
one answer. She did not really care much for
the questions at issue, but she cared greatly for
her prerogative. Individual action within her
ecclesiastical sphere was not to be tolerated. I
think this explanation has been largely overlooked. Catholics, of course, were outside the
national religious inheritance. They must conform or suffer. Others must accept the worship
and ceremonial provided; and, if they chose to
be Protestants, to be Protestants à la Elizabeth.
It was a dangerous experiment to scorn her
Governorship of the Church. She was in a very
real sense what Lord North described her, " Our
God in earth," and a Puritan appeal to Scripture was, in her eyes, political heresy, as it dis-

honoured the National Church of which she was
Supreme Governor. The insult was an insult to
the throne—and the throne was a Tudor throne.
The Puritan was a dangerous member of society,
not so much because he was a Puritan and followed his own opinion in matters of religion
and worship, but because he ventured to place
his opinion against the Queen's. All through
the Puritan history, up to the time of Bancroft,
this was the real crux. It was useless to appeal
to Scripture when the Queen was supreme in all
ecclesiastical jurisdiction. This was the weakness of the Puritan position—it failed to understand the Queen.

On March 26, 1566, the momentous meeting
between the London clergy and the authorities
took place in the Chapel of Lambeth Palace. To
make assurance doubly sure, Robert Cole was
there wearing all the hated habits. A contemporary account has come down to us from
Thomas Earl, minister of St. Mildred's, Bread
Street, who was among the clergy present. " My
masters and ministers of London, the Council's
pleasure is that strictly ye keep the unity of
apparel like to this man here—a square cap
four-cornered, a scholar's gown priestly, a
tippet, and in the church the linen surplice; and
strictly keep the rubric of the Book of our
Common Prayers, and the Queen's Majesty, her
Injunctions, and the Book of Convocation. Ye
that will presently subscribe—Volo—I will—so
write; ye that will not subscribe—Nolo, I will

not. Be brief. Make no words. So is the order : peace : peace. Apparitor, call the churches. Masters, answer presently *sub pœna contemptus* and put your names." The penalty laid down was " suspension and sequestration, with deprivation to follow in three months' time if they continued obdurate." " Subscribe," adds the diarist, " we all must to three books—the Book of Common Prayer, the Convocation Articles, the Archbishop's Book." No doubt the scene impressed Earl : " Great was the sorrow of most ministers and their mourning, saying we are killed in our soul for this pollution of yours, for that we cannot perform it in the singleness of our hearts this our ministry, so we abide in most extreme misery, our wives, and our babes : the gracious knot of Christian charity is broken." Thirty-seven refused to conform, and among these were the best of the ministers, as Parker himself declared. Subsequently some of them repented, among whom was Earl ; but the die was cast. The Puritan might expect " severe dealings " in the future. Parker followed up the Lambeth scene by sending an account of it to his brethren, and expressed hopes that equally successful results would follow elsewhere. But the success in Lambeth Chapel was only on the surface. Crowley, the minister of St. Giles, Cripplegate, took advantage of a funeral to create a riot, driving the clerks and their " porters' coats," as he described surplices, out of his church. Crowley was at once hailed before

the authorities, and in addition to being ready
" to resist the wolf if he can, being the surplice
man," he was found to hold theological opinions
contrary to the Established Religion.   Holy
Week was disfigured by disgraceful scenes.   The
substitutes for the non-conforming ministers
were ill received by the people.   In places the
doors were shut by the Puritan laity against
the assembling congregations.   In places the
wafer bread and wine were taken from the Holy
Table while the minister was reading the
Passion.   In places the church officials stubbornly
refused to provide surplices for the clergy.   The
burden of all the contumely fell on Parker.   It
is well to redeem his character from the invective
of Puritan historians.   No man could have done
more to appease the Queen, and no man could
have acted with greater kindness to the Puritan
clergy under the circumstances.   He was urged
on by Elizabeth in vindictive passion, and left
almost alone to carry out her painful commands.
His protestations had at least this effect, that
the Council at length stepped in to assist the
Ecclesiastical Commission in bearing the weight
of the new inquisition.

The letters of the Puritans to their friends
abroad now began to abandon the early note of
hope.   Several of the Bishops joined in the
voluminous correspondence, and it must have
been difficult for the Continental Reformers to
arrive at a true estimate of English affairs.   The
Puritans painted a harrowing picture of repres-

sion ; the Bishops minimized the situation. However, the sympathizers abroad were not prepared to support the extremes. Bullinger especially refused to lend aid, and with a general upward move in favour of discipline among the episcopate, the early dawn of Puritan hope faded into the grey of ominous apprehension. But the cause was not lost. Lambeth Chapel was but a skirmish—the battle of the books began, and with it a campaign which certainly lasted till the death of the Queen. This literature at every phase of the history of Elizabethan Puritanism must be carefully considered, as it is one of the most valuable sources for tracing the development of Puritan opinions. Much of it is scurrilous and violent, but this was characteristic of the age. As we clear away the scaffolding of controversy, however, we get the growing building of the Puritan position, until it emerges in complete separatism.

A few weeks after the Lambeth scene the first Puritan pamphlet appeared—*A Brief Discourse against the Outward Apparel and Ministering Garments of the Popish Church*. The title sufficiently explains the contents. The all-sufficiency of Scripture is, as of old, maintained. The " garments " offend the weak and encourage the Papist. They serve no purpose except that of Popery, and " no authority can command that which God has not commanded." Counter-attack followed. Not only did the Council prohibit and confiscate the manifesto and arrest the printers, at the instigation of the Ecclesiastical Commissioners, but Parker, encouraged by the veteran controversialist, Walter Haddon, prepared an elaborate reply, under the title, *A Brief Examination for the Time of a Certain Declaration lately put in Print in the name and defence of Certain Ministers in London refusing to wear the Apparel prescribed by the Laws and Orders of the Realm*. Haddon was delighted, and he found special cause for joy in the fact that Parker made use of the position taken up by the foreign Reformers. With surprising speed a reply was ready—*An Answer for the Time to the Examination put in Print, without the Author's name, pretending to maintain the Apparel prescribed, against the Declaration of the Ministers of London*. The method of this reply became typical. Every position was examined by being printed and answered in detail in a form of disputation between an Examiner and Answerer. We do not yet learn much from the literature. A later tract—*The Fortress of the Fathers*—however, gave a hint of the directions towards which Puritanism was tending when it declared that " neither Prince nor Prelate may, by the Word of God, make ecclesiastical laws to bind men's consciences under the pain of mortal sin to keep them." The Puritan champion of *To my Loving Brethren that are troubled about the Popish Apparel: Two short and comfortable Epistles*, with a somewhat grim humour declared that " by the use of the surplice is maintained a hypocritical opinion of holiness." Foreign correspondence for the moment created an armistice, but the battle soon continued with *A Brief and Lamentable Consideration of the Apparel now used by the Clergy of England, set out by a Faithful Servant of God for the Instruction of the Weak,* to which the Bishops replied with a skilful use of every Reformer's opinion which was on their side, under the title, *Whether it be mortal sin to transgress Civil Laws, which be the Commandments of Civil Magistrates.* It was an attempt to hoist the Puritans on their own petard.

This literature may seem to be the history of a campaign about nothing — " church-tippet, gown, or hood "—but no one can read it without seeing that Parker's fears were true that a real difference between Puritanism and the Established Church was close at hand. It was no far cry from " surplice " and " square cap " to Prayer Book, Parliamentary rites and ceremonies, and episcopacy itself. Round the last the real contest must sooner or later be waged. At the outset the Puritans do not seem to have seen in episcopacy anything more than a human arrangement for ecclesiastical affairs. But this early literature turned their minds to the question, and while as yet conditions were not ripe for separatism, there can be no doubt that before the year 1567 had closed there was abroad a new spirit in the Puritan party. As we look back it is hard for us to understand. Religious conditions under Queen Elizabeth did not favour the erection of isolated Protestant units apart from the national religion, and for the moment at any rate the controversial literature only provides us with adumbrations of secession from the National Church. Nor were these without at least one actual scene of independent worship. In June, 1567, the Government broke up a meeting in London held for worship after the model of Geneva. Puritanism now experienced its first acquaintance with an Elizabethan prison, and while Grindal's mildness mitigated the punishment, it seems clear that when he left London for York in 1570 he left behind him more types of worshipping God than those provided by the Book of Common Prayer or the Catholic Missal. On the other hand, the general adherence to the idea of remaining within the Established Church and reforming it is adequately summed up by Professor Pollard : " Episcopacy being, in the view adopted by the Puritans, no essential part of the Church, its repudiation involved in their minds no idea of separation from the Church. They considered themselves quite as much entitled to remain Churchmen in order to make the Church Presbyterian, as they were to remain Englishmen in order to make the monarchy constitutional. Their loyalty to the Church was equal to their loyalty to the State, unless episcopacy was more essential to the Church than personal monarchy to the State." In addition, there were many reasons to urge the Puritans on, quite apart from their conception of Church government or the influence of the nobility. If we eliminate the faults common to an age of religious bitterness, there can be little doubt that they were, broadly speaking, inspired by a sincere religious spirit. It may not have included toleration—we know that it did not; but toleration is a modern virtue. It certainly did include those elements of morality which have been common to Christianity from the beginning. Their very zeal was strengthened by their outlook. The Episcopate was such—Parker alone excepted—as could command no moral respect. Avarice, greed, and dishonesty were not unknown among them. The clergy of the National Church were not famed for either learning, sincerity of purpose, love for their office, morality, or righteous living. The state of society was as low as ever it had been in the history of England. If religion meant anything to the Puritan it meant life. He could not understand a creed that made no demand on men's thoughts and actions. He soon brought to his attack, as we shall see, the justifiable charge that a Church under which national morality grew worse instead of better had no moral right to bind his conscience. It is true that he, too, tried to bind men's consciences, but he would bind them at least with bonds of virtue and not of corruption. In a struggle passion and violence and bitterness are usually predominant, but there were among the Puritans many really pious men and women, whose shoe's latchet the National Church was not worthy to loose. " Nothing," writes the late Bishop of Oxford, " can have contributed so much to the opportunities, the power, the zeal, the hopes of the Puritans as did the neglect of duty in the Church. At such a time ignorance and inability among the clergy were serious enough, but avarice and plain indifference to the meaning of a spiritual change were far worse. . . . In many a parish the minister could only struggle through the service, never preached, but read, perhaps four printed sermons in the course of a year ; or, it may be, had never resided in the place at all, and had he done so, might only have made matters worse by the example of his vicious life."

Before the full force of the storm against episcopacy broke, it may be well to refer to a Puritan model of piety working within the Church and with the approval of the Bishops. *The Orders and Dealings in the Church of North- ampton* provides us with an insight into the methods and aims of Puritanism as a religious system, and shows us something of that stern search after holy living which was so emphatic- ally needed at the moment. The Prayer Book rites were employed. After Morning Prayer the people assembled at a central church for a sermon. Twice a week expositions of Scrip- ture took place. The children were examined, in Calvin's Catechism however, on Sundays and holy days. In all the churches there were quarterly Communions, prepared for by visits from the clergy and churchwardens to the homes of the people. On these Communion Sundays there were two celebrations in each parish, and three clergy ministered to the people from a Holy Table standing in the nave of the church, while Scripture was read from the pulpit. A psalm closed the service. The mayor and clergy formed a bureau of Christian discipline, and absence from Communion was enquired into on one of the week evenings assigned for Scriptural exposition. Parallel with this were meetings for the spiritual edification of the clergy. These were organized under a signed confession repudiating Papistry, rites and ceremonies not founded on the Word of God, and the necessity of an episcopate. On the other hand, the Apostles' Creed was accepted as Apostolic and Scriptural. The meetings consisted of Scriptural conferences, and may be considered as the forerunners of " prophesyings " which we shall consider later.

For some time the Government was engaged in dealing with the Catholic. opposition to the National Church, and Puritanism had to a large extent been left to itself, although there is abundant evidence to show that anything like refusal to conform to the established worship on the part of either Catholic or Puritan was diligently suppressed. The Visitation records for the years succeeding 1566 prove that there was much parochial diligence in this connection. On the other hand, Puritanism was drifting away from the definite public position taken up by its early leaders over habits, and approximating to a Presbyterian system. A new generation of Puritans was growing up to whom surplices and outdoor habits afforded no inspiration. Their challenge was to the organization of the National Church, and the gauntlet was thrown down in the summer of 1570 at Cambridge by Thomas Cartwright, the new Lady Margaret Professor of Divinity, who added to his zeal and piety sound scholarship and wide learning. From his professor's chair he boldly placed the issue in a clear light by attacking the episcopal form of Church government. The Chancellor at once grew alarmed and informed Cecil. Even Parker was moved to demand severity, and the wavering Grindal scented dissolution unless there was " some speedy course " with " the precisians." Cecil, Parker, and Grindal, however, passed into the background of the controversy as John Whitgift, Master of Trinity College, entered. Whitgift himself had not escaped suspicion in the earlier dealings with Puritanism; but now, when it became a clear-cut question between the system erected by Queen Elizabeth and a new system from abroad, he came out as the champion of the religious Settlement. He saw what was only too evident, that if Cartwright's attack against the Protestant Ordinal was not met and defeated, it would mean that at least ten years of struggle had been wasted, and that the Eliza-bethan ideal must fade into the light of Conti-

nental commonplace. In his capacity as Chancellor—which he was now appointed—he removed
Cartwright from his office and forbade him to
preach. For the moment matters rested there,
waiting with the dangerous hush of expectation
for the Parliament which was summoned to meet
on April 2, 1571.

It was quite clear that the Puritans looked
forward to the Parliamentary debates to test at
any rate their strength, if not to achieve some
success. It was also clear that the Government
was prepared for a Puritan challenge. This
Parliament illustrates not only the Puritan
history, but the tenacity of Elizabeth's purpose.
She was head of the national religion, and it is
not too much to say that she saved it by her
autocratic interpretation of her prerogative. The
House of Commons desired further reforms, and
many of them were sorely needed. Most important, however, in connection with Puritanism
was a Bill introduced by Strickland on April
14 " for the reformation of the Book of Common
Prayer." The Lord Treasurer advised discrimi-
nation, as he knew the Queen's mind, but the
debate was carried on in a clamour for immediate
reform. The House finally agreed to approach
Elizabeth and adjourned for Easter. Before it
reassembled Strickland was brought before the
Council and forbidden the House. Only astute
statecraft prevented a rupture with the Sovereign
over the liberties of the Commons. The Puritan
members, however, continued to block procedure

by various measures which proved abortive before the Queen's strong stand. At the same time, Committees of the Commons wearied Parker with interviews for further reform, and presented him with the Thirty-nine Articles, amended in such a form they were willing to accept them, notably by the omission of the Article of the Ordinal. The Primate had a severe passage-at-arms with Peter Wentworth, a Puritan member. " Surely you will refer yourselves wholly to us therein?" almost innocently asked Parker. The answer was definite and to the point : " No, by my faith I bear to God, we will pass nothing before we understand what it is, for that were but to make you Popes. Make you Popes who list, for we will make you none." The Articles, however, received Parliamentary confirmation in the form passed at the Convocation of 1563.

The Puritans were baffled, but not beaten. Exasperated with both Queen and Bishops, they prepared once more for the conflict in a new Parliament, while Sandys, the new Bishop of London, attempted to enforce conformity, and the Ecclesiastical Commissioners stirred up the churchwardens throughout the country to suppress licensed preachers and to enforce the use of the Prayer Book. Parker, with the Bishops of Ely and Winchester, took in hand the work of enforcing a new test on the Puritan ministers by demanding subscription to the apparel as defined in *The Advertisements,* to the Book of Common Prayer, and to the Thirty-nine Articles.

It becomes necessary here once again to question
the sweeping statements of the Puritan historians, who have painted overdrawn pictures of
large deprivations at this point. At the very
highest estimate a few dozen cases of even severe
dealings can be substantiated. On the other
hand, the Puritans heralded the comparative
mildness of their treatment with a new attack on
Parker, and the author—Anthony Gilby—remained unmolested. His pamphlet was entitled,
*A View of Antichrist, His Laws and Ceremonies
in our English Church unreformed: A clear glass
in which may be seen the dangers and desperate
diseases of the English Church*. Gilby made a
violent and unjustifiable attack on " the Pope
of Lambeth," which must be mentioned not only
as an example of the evil done to Puritanism at
the time by its friends, but because it represents
the stock-in-trade of those who have in later
times damaged the Puritan history by accepting
its factious controversial literature as absolute
truth. However, the quiver of Puritan literature
contained a surer and stronger and truer shaft.

When Parliament met in May, 1572, the
Puritan members, undeterred by their previous
failures, renewed the attack on the national
religion, with equally fruitless results. Their
triumph lay elsewhere. Shortly before the
adjournment of Parliament on June 30 the
famous *Admonition to Parliament* appeared.
Puritanism had at length found its voice. The
first edition sold out immediately, and three

editions followed in six weeks. Published anonymously, with no printer's name, it not only excited fear among the Bishops, but rallied the Puritan party as none of their other efforts in any direction had done. It relied on a definite statement of a certain aspect of the Puritan position; and while the second part contained much of the contemporary sneers in the contemporary style, they served to add piquancy to the solidity of the claims and arguments in the first part. A general assault was made on the Elizabethan Settlement as represented in Homilies, Articles, and Injunctions; on the luxury and idleness of the Bishops; on kneeling at Communion; on wafer bread; on the ecclesiastical courts. But this assault was insignificant compared with the attack on the established ministry. The parochial minister " should be called by the congregation, not thrust upon them by the Bishop, or ordained without a title, and should be admitted to his function by the laying on of the hands of the eldership only. The officers of a Church are chiefly three—ministers or pastors, elders, and deacons. As for the elders, not only their office, but their very name has been removed out of the English Church, and in their stead we yet maintain the lordship of one man over many Churches, yea over sundry shires. If you would restore the Church to her ancient officers you must do this : instead of an Archbishop or Lord Bishop you must make equality of ministers. Instead of Chancellors, Archdeacons, officials,

proctors, summoners, churchwardens, and such-
like, you have to plant a lawful and godly eldership. To these three jointly—ministers, elders,
and deacons—is the whole government of the
Church to be committed."

This was a well-defined position. There was a
" crisis " in the Church. The authors were discovered in the persons of John Field and Thomas
Wilcox, and they were sent to prison, where they
acknowledged that they had written the book
" in time for Parliament." Here they remained
for four months uncondemned, when they were
sentenced to a year's imprisonment. Before long,
however, they were released and resumed their
propaganda. Their " sufferings," as they were
called, and the mitigation of them mattered little
compared with the public excitement, which rose
to fever heat when Cartwright once more appeared on the scene, and in *The Second Admonition to Parliament* proceeded to outline the
method in which the reforms of Field and Wilcox
could best be accomplished. Nor did Cartwright's work exhaust the literature. Pamphlet
followed pamphlet in quick succession, in which
the woes of the Puritan sufferers were skilfully set
off by the declaration that they had been justly
punished if their platform was false; but that the
onus lay on the Bishops, for the sake of the
ignorant and those unskilled in theology, to make
things clear. If *The Admonition* is untrue, then
prison is a fair penalty; if it is true, then in-
justice must not triumph. Let the Bishops come

into the open. The onus is on them, and their office is the *casus belli*. But the Bishops were already at work, and once more their champion was Whitgift, whose *Answer to the Admonition* appeared early in 1573. It was an elaborate reply, dealing in the minutest detail with the entire Puritan position. Cartwright followed in May with *A Reply to the Answer*, in which nothing was added. Indeed, little could be added, although reply and counter-reply appeared in *A Defence of the Answer* by Whitgift and *A Second Reply* by his opponent. The question was now as clear-cut as possible, and the early work of Wilcox and Field remained as the plain statement of the Puritan case. Indeed, previous to his imprisonment, Field had taken part in the famous meeting at Wandsworth which disclosed the Puritan policy of turning the government of the Established Church into a Presbyterian system. From this point to Parker's death in 1575 there remains little to detain us. Cecil was dabbling in measures for real reform. The Ecclesiastical Commission pursued its policy. The Council urged the Bishops on, with the Queen in the background as it were—*fons et origo* of repression. Finally she came into the open and urged Parker to suppress " prophesyings "—the meetings which had grown out of the Northampton model for mutual edification in Scripture. More interesting, however, is the Primate's last visitation of Winchester Diocese, which he carried out at the request of the Diocesan, because the visitation enquiries provide us with a clear illustration of what was going on in many parts of England. Parker enquired if any had intruded themselves into the ministry without valid orders, and if laymen had administered the Sacraments. The Puritan movement was growing in boldness. With Parker's death we enter on an obscurer history, but it is well finally to redeem his character from the abuse of historians. No man did more in a position of exceeding difficulty to understand the Puritan position, and to deal in some way more kindly with it than the current theories would allow. He understood piety, and consequently he understood the inner spirit of the great rank and file of the conscientious men who sought in an irreligious age to serve God. It was their misfortune that their method of service did not appeal to the Queen. But Elizabeth was not as cunning in piety as she was pious in cunning.

With the advent of Grindal as Primate, new strength came to the Puritan party. Grindal's outstanding weakness was a constitutional incapacity for administration. The public history of his primacy illustrates serious attempts at reform in directions where it was most needed, but a passage-at-arms with the Queen over " prophesyings " prevented his efforts from almost undoubted failure. His quarrel with Elizabeth, however, proves him to have been a man of stronger character than that with which he is usually credited. He hoped to make " pro-

phesying " an aid to spirituality and to curb its
revolutionary tendencies by episcopal oversight.
Such ideals, on the other hand, had no place in
Elizabethan religious policy. It was a bold thing
to tell the Queen that he trusted that the arrangements with regard to religion would be left in the
hands of the Episcopate, and that many of them
supported his plans for making the object of her
displeasure beneficial to the Church. Elizabeth
for the moment treated him with contempt by
sending her orders to the individual Bishops and
omitting the usual courtesy of transmitting them
to the Primate. As soon, however, as "prophesy-
ing " had received a nominal official quietus in
the various dioceses, Grindal was sequestered
for six months, and never actually restored to the
full duties of the primacy. Appeals made by his
brethren were useless, and only death saved him
from deprivation. The eight years of his primacy
illustrates the Royal supremacy in all its naked
reality. If Elizabeth did not say " Proud Prelate, I will unfrock you," she at least acted it in
Grindal's case. Meanwhile Puritanism gathered
strength, and its platform was strengthened by
an English translation—Cartwright's work—of
Travers's *Disciplina Ecclesiæ Sacra ex Dei Verbo
descripta*. This work at once attained wide
popularity as a recognized system of Church
government, and in many cases the clergy of the
National Church bound themselves by subscription to it. In answer to the growing force of the
movement there was much tightening of the

forces of compulsion. Thus the Council urged the Bishops to suppress the custom of preaching while Prayer Book services and celebrations of Communion were neglected. On the other hand, Puritanism weakened its position by attempting to place too strict safeguards round amusement, which was more religiously valued during Elizabeth's reign than religion itself. Parliament bore witness, however, to the real state of affairs when a series of twenty-six Puritan articles was presented, demanding ordination by a presbytery, and practically incorporating the entire position taken up by Cartwright and Travers. To such demands the Episcopate were naturally deaf, but they certainly made valiant efforts to bring up ecclesiastical affairs to a higher standard of honesty and common decency. It soon became clear that Puritanism was passing beyond the hope of reforming the Established Church. The first step in the direction of separation came from Robert Browne, a man of eminent piety and of fame as a preacher, who saw that the real place for Puritanism was outside the Elizabethan Settlement. Browne's ecclesiastical polity approximated to that of the Independents, and with a friend, Robert Harrison, he made efforts to widen the number of his adherents through East Anglia. In 1581 Harrison was silenced by inhibition, and influence at Court was brought to bear on Browne. He resisted all efforts at reconciliation, and finally led to Middelburg in Zealand with his fellow-champion and a body of sympathizers.

Life at Middelburg, where Cartwright acted as pastor, was not quite agreeable to the leaders of the new Puritanism, as the exiles from England at Middelburg had not passed into the separatism camp. But literary efforts took the sting out of the disappointment, and Browne wrote there the three books which clearly outlined his position— *A Treatise of Reformation without tarrying for any; The Life and Manner of all true Christians; A Treatise upon the xxiii. of Matthew.* These writings at once brought trouble to the Puritans, as they were circulated widely in the Eastern Counties in spite of a Royal Proclamation issued in the middle of 1583. Two martyrdoms for Browne's opinions—especially that of denying all religious supremacy to the Crown—took place at Bury St. Edmunds about the same time, while a holocaust of Brownist literature lighted the difficult path of conscience. Thus the year 1583 marks an important epoch in Elizabethan Puritanism. The logical position of separation from the National Church had at last been arrived at, and the first sufferers had died for it.

Archbishop Whitgift's dealing with Puritanism may be conveniently divided into two divisions. First, from his consecration to the Marprelate Tracts, and, secondly, to the close of the reign. Each division has its characteristics and its literature, which can be considered more effectively by a clear-marked line of division. Before, however, turning to the history, it is necessary to go back in order to gather up the scattered threads of the problem. From the beginning the Government failed to grasp the Puritan position. Catholicism it understood, and with Catholicism no conceivable compromise could be possible. But it had never learned that too much stress might be laid on things of little import by civil authority in a Protestant organization. The Catholic Church made demands on conscience and on obedience by her divine claim. The National Church made them in the name of the Royal Supremacy, and outside that supremacy they were not binding. When the Puritan found that " surplice and cap " were as severely enforced as the Prayer Book and in the Queen's name, it was no far step to say that he had just as much right to decide his religious beliefs as the Queen had to dictate them to him. No divinity hedged the throne in religious matters. He logically concluded that, as the whole Reformation movement was a protest against authority in matters of faith and practice, there ought to be no new authority erected in them. Of course, this conclusion was arrived at gradually, and, of course, in its historical working out it created a system as arbitrary and authoritative as the Royal Supremacy itself ; but its processes were the early seeds of religious toleration. Toleration, as we have seen, was unknown in the age, and the Government was not in advance of its age. For it the National Religion as maintained by Act of Parliament was binding, and it could not enter into a position which demanded any other form of

Protestantism than that established by authority. In addition, Puritan appeals for real religion were addressed to deaf ears. Queen and Government saw nothing else in the Puritan than they saw in the Catholic—flies in the ointment of the apothecary, rifts within the lute. There is something splendid, however, in many of the Puritan protests. Many of them are no mere blasts or counterblasts of controversy, but deep cries for the waters of religion in a dry-parched land. True, they are Tudor cries, and offend our modern ears, so sensitive to the details of form and style; but the language of deep piety is just as real in the mouth of a sincere Tudor Puritan as in that of the saintly Bunyan or the evangelic Wesley. True, too, Puritanism had many lessons to learn in the ages that lay before it—as every religious system has had—but it is idle to blame it in Elizabeth's age for refusing to be coerced by authority, and that an irreligious authority. Its place was outside the National Religion, and it found it in spite of all, as, too, it found its own limitations as a human system. For different reasons the National Church could not embrace Catholic and Puritan, and they both conscientiously refused it. The claim which it soon made to be divine they could only reject, though from different points of view. Religion was more real to both of them than the Queen and Government believed, and it will be difficult to eliminate the Elizabethan Catholic and the Elizabethan Puritan in the final winnowing of all history. The Puritans have suffered at the hands of their own historians, and been wounded in the house of their friends, but it would be foolhardy to deny their sincerity. Their secession helped to greet the far-off dawn of toleration—a dawn which their own dark night of intolerance made all the more rosy-red.

Whitgift was the natural champion of the National Church. He had in the past taken up the gauntlets of Puritanism that mattered, and if his armour had been pierced in the Cartwright duel, he was not unwilling to have it repaired in the royal armoury. Nor had his lance grown rusty. Since the days of the Cambridge affray he had learned something of diocesan rule in different parts of England, and behind his adherence to the National Religion lay a conviction that Episcopacy was not a detail but an essential of ecclesiastical government. Calvinistic in theology, he was dour in action. The half-sequestered staff of Grindal had scarcely touched his fingers when he advanced on the Puritan lines with his famous articles, which carried war into the enemy's camp. On October 19, 1583, he opened the campaign with a letter to his brethren, enclosing certain articles which had received the Queen's approval. His reference to Catholic Nonconformists need not detain us. In connection with Puritanism, he ordered that all private preaching, reading, and catechizing be abolished; that none be permitted to preach, read, or catechize in any place unless he ministers the sacraments publicly at least four times a year according to the Book of Com-

mon Prayer; that all the clergymen wear the
habits prescribed in *The Advertisements* of 1566
and the Royal Injunctions of 1559; that none be
permitted to exercise public ministry unless ordained according to the laws of the realm, and
only after subscription to the three articles declaring that he accepted the Royal Supremacy, the
Book of Common Prayer, the Ordinal, and the
Thirty-Nine Articles. These commands were
signed by himself and eight other Bishops. Each
order was aimed at a very definite Puritan position. Puritan organizations for worship had developed in many parts of the country. Some of
the East Anglian clergy had definitely renounced
the Prayer Book or used it in a mutilated manner.
The clergy had become organized in several districts under a system foreign to that of the
National Church, and the secret service of Whitgift's antagonists consisted of many of the nobility
and Court favourites. The issuing of an Ecclesiastical Commission was natural, as the previous
Commission had lapsed with Grindal's death. It
was only significant by the fact that it was issued
to Whitgift, and not by anything new either in its
scope or methods. Whitgift accepted the machinery at his disposal, and when Cecil tried to prevent the new Commission, he did so because he
knew that Whitgift was not Grindal. Whitgift's
justification to Cecil was strong and uncompro-
mising, and for the moment Cecil retired from
the contest. On all sides, however, the Archbishop found that he was dealing with no insignificant foe. Promised reforms in the Church no

longer furnished grounds even for an armistice.
Subscription to the Royal Supremacy, the Prayer
Book, and the Ordinal was the real issue, and this
was made all the more vital by the fact that Whitgift demanded a declaration that the Prayer Book
and Ordinal contained nothing contrary to the
Word of God. For the Puritan such a declaration was impossible, as his champions had distinctly said time and again that the Ordinal could
not stand Scriptural test. To crown all his
troubles the Council attempted to moderate his
zeal, but Whitgift turned their attempts into an
expression of surprise at their impudence. For
a moment he held his hand and did not resort
to extremities, as he was puzzled by the challenge
that the Bishops themselves did not carry out in
full the orders of the Prayer Book. The Ecclesiastical Commission, however, continued its proceedings, and Cecil once more tried to influence
the Archbishop to moderate in some real manner
its procedure. He addressed a lengthy letter to
Whitgift urging several circumstances as an
excuse for his writing. Not only was he troubled
by many petitions from ministers who were recommended to him as peaceable men, but he was
also charged with neglect in his duty by not attempting to restrain the Archbishop's procedure.
In addition, he had himself carefully read the
articles which had been issued, and he felt a personal obligation to protest against them, " so
curiously penned, so full of branches and circumstances, as I think the Inquisitors of Spain use
not so many questions to entrap their prey . . .

this kind of proceeding is too much savouring of the Romish Inquisition, and is rather a device to seek for offenders than to reform any." Whitgift defended himself by an appeal to the customary methods of procedure in other courts, and while he acknowledged Cecil's public desire to maintain ecclesiastical peace, yet he wondered at his appeal when only those who had broken that peace had been dealt with, and that in the usual way. The real crux was the Puritan protest against the *ex officio* oath, and that oath had behind it some valuable weight in custom since the beginning of the reign. The matter did not get any further, but when Parliament assembled in November, 1584, the Puritans were prepared for a contest which, as of old, turned round the Queen's Supremacy in matters of religion and the palpable desire of the Commons to debate them. A characteristic petition of sixteen articles from the House of Commons deserves attention. Reforms were called for in various directions, which, however, were but the prelude to the significant request that adherence to the Prayer Book should not be enforced. Of course, the petition failed, as the House of Lords did not desire to court a royal reprimand. Outside Parliament the organization of Puritanism kept up a siege of members in almost modern style, while the Puritan Press urged the cause in no unmistakable terms. Meantime an answer had been prepared to those divisions of the petition which affected real abuses. Convocation had drawn up a series of reforms, and these were presented as a reply to

the Puritan demands in that connection by Whitgift himself, with his own original articles, however, appended to the scheme. The document
illustrates two points. It shows that the Episcopate was united on one issue at least. There
would be no concessions to Puritanism as a religious system. For a considerable time they had
been levelling up their administration, urged on
doubtlessly, among other things, by Puritan com-
plaints which were more than justified by the
existing state of affairs; but the days were past
when the Puritan cause could hope for any kind
of concession from the Episcopate, because Elizabeth herself was behind all. She supported the
action of the Bishops. Their scheme of reform
passed into Canons with her signature, and while
she soundly rated them for their slack administration—a somewhat exaggerated charge at this time
—she made it clear that they were her servants,
whom she could depose at will. As for the Commons, she pointed out that the religious affairs of
the nation were entirely in her hands. Out of the
chaos of debate and repression there emerge here
and there glimmers of gentler dealings, but these
were insignificant. The Ecclesiastical Commission pursued its course, and a Special Commission
in the north rivalled its southern model, while the
Assizes saw Puritans arraigned for drastic dealings with the Prayer Book. Vigorous attempts
to control the Press proved futile. The Temple
Church witnessed for a time the extraordinary
situation of two forms of worship every Sunday,
until Whitgift removed Travers from his position

as preacher there. Hooker, the new master, had, however, learned something for his great Apologia for the National Church, which was issued in the closing decade of the reign. The next Parliament disclosed further Puritan aggression. Puritan petitions and attempts to legislate in a Puritan direction followed on the old lines, until Knox's *Form of Common Prayer* was presented for approval as a substitute for the Prayer Book. It was evident that this meant a royal closure. Debate and appeals to sympathy for the repressed ministers only made the Queen more determined, and although the Puritan party in Convocation raised their voices against the Bishops, yet Parliament was in future, to a large degree, a closed field for Puritan demands. This fact did much to extend the influence of Puritanism. It began to widen its organization until it spread into many counties, while it stirred up the disappointed spirits of its adherents by a fresh and vigorous pamphlet entitled *A Learned Discourse of Ecclesiastical Government*. This pamphlet opened with the old appeal to Scripture, and in this appeal we find an early example of the claims made by later Puritanism that ecclesiastical government had moved along wrong lines from the earliest times. The author not only advances the old claim that Scripture did not warrant an Episcopate in the Church, but he goes further and argues that even if his system is completely new it ought to be brought in. He then proceeds to details. The first two of his Scriptural ministry—doctors and pastors—must regulate the doctrine imposed on the people; the second two—governors and deacons—must manage the disciplinary side. The placing of preaching, doctrine, and sacraments in the hands of doctors and pastors necessitated a wide development of clerical learning, leading up to a reform of University education. As the care of souls is the pastor's immediate duty, there must in future be no pluralities, and the ministry can be better supported by a return of all the money and lands taken from the old religion. In parochial life elders will assist the pastor in the care of the congregation, and the deacons will follow their prototype Stephen. A synod will gather up the broken units of parish administration. The Royal Supremacy in religion will be tolerated— in so far as Scriptural. The whole tone of the book is essentially moderate, but it was the precursor of the worst storm which broke round the National Church in Elizabeth's reign. Following the usual custom, a reply was prepared, which, if volume counted for anything, must have crushed the little Puritan olive-branch into dust. The Dean of Salisbury, John Bridges, got to work and produced a tome of almost fifteen hundred quarto pages in answer to the *Learned Discourse*. It was not so much a reply as an avalanche, intended to sweep the very name of Puritanism from the steep ascent of national religious unity. Counter-replies followed as restrained and as short as the *Discourse* of the present debate, and the whole episode might have passed into history without much further notice had not a new Puritan cham-

pion appeared on the scene and made an un-
puritanical charge *in medias res*, sweeping hierarchy and dour friend off their feet in the mad
onslaught of its satire—" M. Marprelate, gentle-
man."

Marprelate's identity must remain a mystery,
though recent research has added weight to the
old tradition which identifies him with Job
Throckmorton.   The matter is immaterial, but
there can be no doubt that up to this time neither
controversy nor literature in England knew anything to equal the unmerciful satire of this new
method in religious struggle.   Facts and fictions
trip one another in the fevered rush of barefaced
and merciless invective.   Never had real anger at
a foe been better presented in controversial literature.   The very pages writhe and laugh in their
only too earnest words.   The sentences caper in
indignant, vitriolic grotesques.   Every conceivable charge is brought against the Bishops from
the Primate down.   All is fair in love and war,
and Marprelate was in love with war.   If Elizabethan Puritanism had no other triumph, Marprelate's *Epistle* would be triumph enough.
Hardly had the ranks reformed, and the com-
batants shaken themselves to count their bruises,
when Marprelate charged again — a heavier
brigade—with *The Epitome*, which rode home to
the old battle cry of Scripture.   The plight of the
National Church was woeful, but it was eminently
laughable.   While Cecil and the Episcopate
searched for the printing presses, Cooper, Bishop
of Winchester, attempted to rally his episcopal

ranks with *An Admonition to the People of England*, which is historically valuable for its sketch of Elizabethan Puritanism as well as for its explanation of the appeal to Scripture as understood by the National Church. Undeterred by Cooper's really dignified defence, Marprelate brought him into the triumphant ridicule with an answer, *Ha y'any Work for Cooper?* and promised further fun in *More Work for Cooper*. The stage and opponents of his own stamp tried to laugh him out of the field, but Marprelate rode his warriors off because his drill-sergeant—Waldegrave the printer—refused to work in future, as Puritanism resented the low vices of its new auxiliary forces.

At this point the history of Elizabethan Puritanism is complicated by internal dissensions. Robert Browne, after unhappy experiences in the Low Countries and in Scotland, returned to England and resumed his ministry in the National Church, finding the paths of Separatism not by any means paths of peace. His defection did not, however, impede the progress of the ideas which he had sown, and the Separatist party which he originated soon found itself in difficulties, not only with Puritanism, but with the Government. The two most prominent Brownists were John Greenwood and Henry Barrow. Greenwood had a varied career of religious experience. He had been a parish clergyman of the Church of England, private chaplain to a nobleman of Puritan tendencies, and finally he emerged as a Separatist. Barrow was a lawyer of Gray's Inn, a connection of Bacon's, who had been turned from a life "vain and libertine to a preciseness of the highest degree." Early in October, 1586, a conventicle was broken up in London by order of the Diocesan Bishop, and Greenwood, who had been reading the Scriptures aloud, with several of the congregation, were taken prisoners. He had formed a friendship at Cambridge with Barrow, who in due course came to visit him in the Clink prison. This visit was the occasion of his arrest, and he was sent to Lambeth for examination before the Ecclesiastical Commissioners. He refused to give evidence, and was lodged in the Gatehouse. A week later another attempt was made by the officials, with a like result, and he, with Greenwood, lay in prison for five months, when he was indicted before a Commission drawn from the Episcopate and civil judges. Much of their history is derived from their own account. Whitgift examined Barrow, who declared in reply that all set forms of prayer were not only Popish, but bordering on idolatry, that the polity of the Established Church was not Christian in its origin, and that the Royal Supremacy could be admitted if it made no laws for religion additional to those provided in Scripture. He refused the oath of Supremacy, but professed his entire loyalty to the Queen ; and he emphasized the reality of the Puritan difficulty as seen in the Parliamentary struggle with Elizabeth by declaring that the Church ought to reform abuses apart from the Crown, and that with it lay the power to excommunicate the Sovereign. Greenwood took up a similar position. They were both condemned at the Newgate Sessions in the following May under an Act of Parliament passed in 1581 against those who withdrew from the Established Religion. This Act was in reality passed against Catholics, and the section under which they were condemned provided only for " withdrawal to the Romish religion." Failing to find securities, they were thrown into the Fleet, but obscurity hangs round their history at this point. It would appear that some mitigation was granted, but for some reason or other they were both soon back in prison. The next six years were largely spent there, with periods of liberty for Greenwood. Barrow's confinement was varied between compulsory examinations and the composition of pamphlets, which covered not only their religious position, but accounts of their questioning before the Special Commissioners appointed to deal with them. Some of Barrow's prison work reaches an almost sublime style, in which he set forth that will-o'-the-wisp of Christian history—a pure Church separate from unbelievers. Meanwhile their imprisonment was embittered by an attack on their tenets from those Puritans who refused to take up the Separatist position, while a plot to kill the Queen, though futile to the verge of madness, did not help to make prison life and prison hopes brighter. On all sides there was evidence of an official tightening up against all kinds of Nonconformity. Cartwright was already in confinement. Prisoners connected with the Marprelate Tracts were being examined, and Parliament was planning severe

legislation against all opponents of the National
Religion. Barrow and Greenwood had little to
hope for. On March 23, 1593, they were condemned to death for seditious libel. Twice they
were reprieved, but on April 6 they were conveyed
in the early morning along Holborn and executed
at Tyburn. Six weeks later the Puritan cause
claimed another martyr in John Penry, who
passed through Presbyterianism and Separatism
to death.

In Parliament the debates over Nonconformity
culminated in a penal statute which touched the
Puritan party in a manner which must have
surprised them, considering their old hopes for
reform through Parliamentary action. The Act
declared that if anyone above the age of sixteen
should refuse to come to church or persuade any
one from coming to church, or attend conventicles
or meetings for religion, he should be committed
to prison, without bail, until he should conform
to the National Religion. If he remained obsti-
nate and refused to be reconciled, he should be
banished the realm for ever unless licensed to
return. If he returned without licence he should
be treated as a felon without benefit of clergy.
Thus for the Separatists, at any rate, there was
in future only conformity or exile. Many of
them preferred the latter course. They collected
in Holland, where they gradually increased in
numbers till 1620, when they sailed for New England, there to pass through some necessary lessons
in their development towards religious liberty.

The closing scenes of Elizabethan Puritanism

date from Bancroft's sermon at St. Paul's Cross
on February 9, 1589. Bancroft had already dis-
tinguished himself as the champion of the State
Religion, and in his sermon he now advanced its
claims against the Puritan party by declaring
that Bishops were *jure divino* superior to other
clergy. This was at once a challenge and a
strength to Puritanism. The struggle passed
now quite outside the mere details of worship and
vestments—quite beyond the question of a Church
polity supported by the State; it became a clear-
cut issue between Episcopacy as a divine institution and a Presbyterian system. Thus the Episcopate shifted from the protecting wings of Queen
Elizabeth and prepared to weather the storm of a
claim of divine origin. The result was ominous.
There were not a few Puritans who had accepted
Episcopacy as long as it claimed only civil sanction. Indeed, the whole idea of the National
Church being governed by anything else except
civil officials was, as we shall see, foreign to the
age. These men had been prepared to tolerate
the new hierarchy, as they might have been prepared to tolerate any other Government officials
with whom they did not agree. When, however,
Bancroft made the far-reaching claim that they
held office by virtue of a divine right, the matter
assumed quite another aspect. Many were prepared to tolerate, and even to accept, an hier-
archical form of Church government as a convenient civil arrangement, who could not accept
it or even tolerate it when it lifted itself up into
such a sphere as the purposes of God. Thus Ban-

croft's sermon opened up a period of heart-search-ing, and many who had previously accepted the Established Religion stepped into the public ranks of Puritanism. For the religious peace of Eng-land Bancroft had therefore not done much good, and the matter was further complicated when it became known that many of the nobility resented the novel claim, and some of the lawyers declared that, if the Queen had decided to have had no Bishops, the Church would not be defective in any way. In addition, Bancroft's sermon raised the National Church to a position which in the eyes of the Puritans seemed almost blasphemous. As they surveyed the religious and moral condition of the country and contrasted it with the high hopes of the Reformation, and the fair promises of better living, higher morality, and nobler ideals, they instinctively felt that little divinity could exist in an institution which had singularly failed. From the bench of Bishops down to the ordinary everyday life of the villages and country parishes, corruption, vice, dishonesty, and a general care-lessness for higher things were evident. The Puritan argued in his dour logic that the National Religion, with its *jure divino* Bishops, had failed more signally than the Catholic Church with its *jure divino* Pope. It is in this connection that the pathos of the Elizabethan Settlement is deepest. Earnest Catholics and earnest Puritans could not but despise a system which had done nothing which it is the duty of religion to do— which is the very *raison d'être* of all religion. The Puritan hated the Catholic Church with all the prejudice of his upbringing. He hated the National Church with all the conviction derived from its failure. At the very best it was to him but statecraft in a religious setting, and, he argued, how can it be in government *jure divino* when it has spent its energies in repressing his own desire to serve God? He once again appealed to Scripture : " By their fruits ye shall know them."

From this point little more remains to be said. An analysis of the works of Hooker and Bancroft would not help our study much, and, in addition, they are more widely known to students of Elizabethan history than the tracts and pamphlets which have been followed here in somewhat close detail. Attempts were made in the concluding Parliaments of the reign by Puritan leaders, but they lacked the old persistence, and the Queen remained true to her original attitude. On the other hand, if Puritanism was a dead letter in Parliament, it suffered much in the Law Courts. It soon became clear that the Presbyterian system was in full working order in a wider area than the Government conceived. Many who had used it turned Queen's evidence, and the revelations widened out the controversy, not only over the form of Church government, but against the oath *ex officio*. An appeal to the judges led to a decision in its favour, but, after a term of severity, Whitgift for once at least did something to soften the harshness of the Queen's proceedings.

It may seem hard to find any clear line of history through the maze of the controversies with Eliza-

bethan Puritanism.   My aim in this study has to
a large extent been twofold. Firstly, to make
clear that the Catholic was not the only Elizabethan to refuse the Settlement, and that it is
only the wide sweeping pen of a partisan which
could tell us that, broadly speaking, that Settlement was acceptable to the nation.   Secondly, I
have tried to do justice to the Elizabethan Puritan.
Granted all his shortcomings, and they were many ;
granted the narrowness of his outlook, which
darkened for him and others future centuries, I
think he has been unfairly treated in this reign
at least.   If the position be conceded that religion
is more than obedience to a civil magistrate, that
it has a real relation to life and conduct, then it
seems uncontrovertible that he must stand with his
fellow-recusant as the best type of his age.   Doubtless both Catholic and Puritan recusants had
many extremists in their ranks, and many with
keen pens and captious wit, but when compared
with their opponents on the broad principle of a
living religion, I think there can be no doubt
where the victory lies.   It may be that I see too
much good in Elizabethan Puritanism, but I think
it can be said historically that it can lay claim to
not only an unconscious challenge to intolerance,
but to a spirit of piety unknown to the Elizabethan Church as far as history has disclosed its
inner life.   Divest the Puritan of the almost
necessary limitations of life in Elizabethan England, and he is not unworthy to stand in some
degree at least with some of those who for the
Old Religion were martyrs and confessors.

X

RESERVATION IN THE ANGLICAN
CHURCH, 1547—1661

THE question of Reservation has become prominent in Anglican circles within recent years,
and no very serious effort has been made to face
the question historically or to judge it from the
point of view of the practices which at least had
the countenance of the Reformers. We are solely
concerned with the facts of history, and not with
any question of doctrine. It has already been
pointed out how Reservation was dealt with up to
the issuing of *The First Prayer Book* in 1549, and
the period from that date up to the year which
gave the Prayer Book its present form will form
the subject of this study.

During the process of formulating the new
Liturgy it became evident that the Catholic
custom of Reservation, quite apart from the early
proceedings of the reign in this respect, was
doomed. At the close of 1548 a tract of Martyr's
was presented to Somerset which advised that
" The residue of this Sacrament, after the Communion is done, ought not to be kept as we see it
now in Popish churches," and in the great Parlia-

mentary debate on the Sacrament, the Bishop of Bath and Wells endeavoured, on December 14, 1548, to turn the real question at issue into a discussion about the rights and wrongs of reserving the Sacrament to the next day after a celebration. When we come to the study of the Prayer Books we are face to face with rubrics of very difficult interpretation. *The First Prayer Book* provided two alternatives :

" But if the sick person be not able to come to the church, and yet is desirous to receive the Communion in his house, then he must give knowledge over night, or else early in the morning to the curate, signifying also how many be appointed to communicate with him. And if the same day there be a celebration of the Holy Communion in the church, then shall the priest reserve (at the open Communion) so much of the Sacrament of the Body and Blood as shall serve the sick person and so many as shall communicate with him (if there be any); and so soon as he conveniently may, after the open Communion ended in the church, shall go and minister the same, first to those that are appointed to communicate with the sick (if there be any), and last of all to the sick person himself. But before the curate distribute the Holy Communion, the appointed *General Confession* must be made in the name of the communicants, the curate adding *the absolution with the comfortable sentences of Scripture* following in the open Communion. . . . But if the day be not appointed for the open Communion in the church, then (upon convenient warning given) the curate shall come and visit the sick person afore noon. And having a convenient place in the sick man's house (where he may reverently celebrate) with all things necessary for the same, and not being otherwise letted with the public service or any other just impediment, he shall there celebrate the Holy Communion after such form and sort as hereafter is appointed."

A form of service was prescribed " unto the end of the Canon." These provisions were generally disliked. To " celebrate " in the house of a sick person was an innovation which did not appeal either to Catholics or Protestants. To the former it naturally was distasteful, and many of the latter objected to it because they considered that it bore too pronounced a likeness to the " private Mass," while the extreme members of the party disliked any kind of Communion of the Sick. For example, Bullinger expressed this opinion in his *Fifth Decade* in 1551. The Lord's Supper, he maintains, is purely a public holy feast, and that, therefore, it should be given to no man privately. Bullinger even opposes those who wished to retain the " celebration " in private houses, but at the same time to introduce a strict rule that there should be others to communicate with the sick in order that all relationship to the " private Mass " might be abolished : "Forasmuch as that assembly is not public or general when four or five do communicate with the sick, their saying is nothing which say that the Supper may be ordained for the sick if so be that others do sup with them." Finally, he denies that there is any necessity for the sick to receive the Lord's Supper : " Neither is there any necessity to constrain us to minister the Sacrament to the sick," thus condemning both methods provided for in *The First Prayer Book*.

Many of the English Reformers held the same opinion, and their views were disseminated and gained ground in England just as Bullinger's opinions had considerable influence. Coverdale, in his preface to Calvin's *Treatise on the Sacrament*, says : " All they therefore do privately

receive the Sacrament either to merit themselves . . . or other do receive it to their damnation," and in another of his translations, *The
Treatise on Death,* it is expressly said that the
sick man " must satisfy himself with the general
breaking of bread whereof he was partaker with
the whole congregation." Many other opinions
of a similar tone might be quoted from the English
writers of the period, and Becon spends a hundred
large pages round the death-bed of a sick person
in his *Sick Man's Salve* without coming any nearer
the crucial point of giving him Communion than
pious reminiscences.

The provisions for Communion of the Sick were
once again in debate in the years 1551 and 1552.
Bucer made no objection to them, but Martyr, in
consistency with his tract already referred to,
quarrelled with the carrying of the Sacrament to
the sick : " Coram ægroto et simul cum eo com-
municantibus omnia quæ ad cœnam Domini neces-
sario requiruntur et dicantur et agantur," he
said, thus appearing to throw his weight on the
side of the private celebration rather than on that
of the alternative method provided in 1549. While
many of the English Reformers thus followed Bullinger, others did not, and Cox in particular pro-
tested against the sentence of his already quoted :
if a few persons, three or four or five, are allowed
to receive out of some hundreds who are or have
been present, why, he argues, should a sick person
be deprived of this benefit? This passage is an
important commentary upon the provisions of *The*

Second Prayer Book of 1552, in which extensive changes were made :

"... if the sick person be not able to come to church, and yet is desirous to receive the Communion in his house, then he must give knowledge over night, or else early in the morning to the curate, signifying also how many be appointed to communicate with him. And having a convenient place in the sick man's house, where the curate may reverently minister, and a good number to receive the Communion with the sick person, with all things necessary for the same, he shall there minister the Holy Communion."

" In the time of plague, sweat, or such other like contagious times of sicknesses or diseases, when none of the parish or neighbours can be gotten to communicate with the sick in their houses, for fear of infection, upon special request of the diseased, the minister may alone communicate with him."

Important innovations were thus made; the Communion with the reserved Sacrament was no longer ordered or provided for; the alternative method was much altered and curtailed; no liturgical forms were prescribed except the Collect, Epistle, and Gospel, and the stipulation already alluded to was introduced as a normal necessity for a sick Communion—that there should be " a good number to receive the Communion with the sick person "; and, most significant of all, the curate was now directed throughout to " minister," not to " celebrate," the Holy Communion. No order is given as to the service beyond the fact that the Collect, Epistle, and Gospel stand as in *The First Prayer Book*. The order of 1549 directing—

" *The Preface*. The Lord be with you.
" *Answer*. And with thy spirit.
" Lift up your hearts," etc. (unto the end of the Canon)—

disappears, but the rubric remains ordering the
priest to communicate himself first and " after
minister unto them that be appointed to communicate with the sick." The service thus becomes an administration, not a celebration; but
it seems to be a problem how to carry it out, and
no directions for this purpose are provided to
guide the curate.

When we turn to the Communion of the sick in
actual practice, we are equally at a loss to find
out what was done. Since private Communion
was so largely discouraged by the Reformers, and
the people were in all respects slow to communicate, it is most probable that very few sick Communions were ever made. We are thus thrown
back on treatises and writings highly controversial for evidence as to what was intended.

In a literature of almost overwhelming propor-
tions it is easy to find plenty of passages on the
subject of Reservation. Jewel's challenge produced a great mass of controversy on this subject,
and in other respects the reservation of the Sacrament was a commonplace of contemporary debate.
However, when each passage has been carefully
examined and scrutinized, it is abundantly clear
that in all of them, with, at the most, one or two
exceptions, what is in question is only the practice
of continual reservation apart from the question
of Communion. The carrying of the Sacrament
direct from a celebration in the church to the
home of a sick person is rarely mentioned; and
when it is, the Reformers leave aside the violent

language of attack which they regularly used against the Catholic practice of hanging up the Blessed Sacrament in a pyx, reserving it in a tabernacle, and carrying it with due pomp, devotion, honour, and reverence in processions; or that in which they defend themselves for having abolished these ancient customs. It is important to notice in the light of present-day Anglican controversy that the arguments which they use are constantly arguments which do not go against the method of Reservation provided by *The First Prayer Book*—*e.g.*, that the Sacrament is meant for Communion, and that whatever is over should not be kept " till the next day." Even the view that the Sacrament *extra usum* ceases to be the Sacrament is not supposed to militate against such a practice. Thus while the Reformers condemn root and branch the ancient customs of the Catholic Church, even the rough-tongued Becon says cautiously : " The Church of Christ when it was most pure . . . knew of no reservation of the Lord's Bread as it is now used in the Pope's Church." The point of discussion which brings up the question of Communion of the sick is not so much the challenge about reservation as the challenge about the " private Mass," or sometimes that about Communion in one kind, both of which were part of the stock-in-trade of the Reformers in their attack upon the Church. Frequently the defence was deceived into attempting to justify the Church's discipline on false lines, and we find Harding and others, in order to justify these customs, quoting instances of sick or private Communion. Thus the Christian woman mentioned by Tertullian or St. Cyprian's irreverent woman became the stock instances of the latter, and the Twelfth Nicene Canon and Serapion the favourite examples of the former. It was a tactical error to introduce such examples or to accept any challenge to the Primitive Church in such connections, but the answer which the English Reformers made to these pleas must be considered as well as the pleas themselves. They argued that these instances were exceptions and were not normal, and could not be quoted to justify the private Mass or Communion in one kind, as, indeed, no clear-minded Catholic would attempt to do. That is, however, their direct answer to the points at issue; but for the present purpose it is not so much this that is to be noted as their attitude to the instances cited by Catholics, which involved Reservation for the purposes of Communion in primitive times. The discussion of this appeal to primitive times does not come within the objects of this essay, but historically it must be noted that while the Reformers poured out horrible and violent condemnation on later matters of Catholic discipline, they walked respectfully (at least where it suited them) in the early ages. They speak with approval under the circumstances of the sending of the Sacrament to the absent as witnessed by Justin Martyr : " That which these sons received at home was part of that which was distributed in the common celebration where company were : and upon case of necessity sent to them being absent." " That may be granted to a lay person receiving which may not to a priest ministering; that some-time in necessity which may not be always at pleasure; that at home where none is that may not in the church where many be." This is the attitude of Bishop Cooper, and later on, when he deals directly with Reservation and condemns the practice, it is not the 1549 method which he has in view, but the Catholic custom. He admits that in primitive times " divers used Reservation," but says that there is no testimony in the Word of God to justify it, nor sign that all the Holy Fathers did approve of it The objections which he raises are largely those which would not apply to the method suggested in the Prayer Book of 1549. His first point is " recipitur non includitur "; his second and third the well-known passages of Hesychius and Pseudo-Clement, forbidding that the Sacrament should be kept " till the next day." Next, in answer to the case of Serapion, he says this is no proof of Communion in one kind without any condemnation expressed of the sick Communion. Two points are clear : he had the sanction of the Reformers for a certain method, and the Catholic custom was anathema, and wherever he found a position to attack he, like his fellows, lost no time in doing so.

The question comes up again in Jewel's *Reply to Harding*, and is dragged out in wearisome detail. Once again the " private Mass " and

Communion in one kind are in debate, and, indeed, raise it. Jewel recalls without comment that in early times the sick had the Sacrament ordinarily sent home to them. Harding had put the case very naturally of a demand for the viaticum from four or five houses in a parish at once : " The priest after that he hath received the Sacrament in the church taketh his natural sustenance and dineth, and then being called upon, carrieth the rest a mile or two to the sick in each house. None being disposed to receive with the sick, he doth that is required ; doth he not in this case communicate with them? and do they not communicate one with another?" Will Jewel call this a " private Mass "? Jewel replies : " Let us grant M. Harding his whole request ; let his priest come and minister to the sick. What maketh all this for his private Mass?" Now, we notice here that Jewel had an opportunity for attacking the Edwardine method, and that for some reason or other he did not do so, and he adds : " Again, grant we this action of the priest not only to be a private Mass, but also, the necessity of the sick considered, to be lawful ; yet could not this precedent make it lawful to be done openly in the church whereas is no such case of necessity." Then follow, as usual, Justin Martyr, Tertullian, and Cyprian, with Serapion and the accustomed examples. Jewel sticks to the Reformation attack against " the sole receiving in private houses " as elsewhere, but I have failed to find him condemning some kind of Reservation for

the sick.   Indeed, Harding complained against
him that he will not " in plain terms deny the
reservation and keeping of the Blessed Sacrament," but only deny " that it was in primitive
times or ought now to be hanged up under a
canopy." Harding saw clearly that Jewel was
content to be with all his brethren in the condemnation of the Church's present custom, and
that he would not condemn her custom in another
age, because some of the chief Reformers did not
do so.   Besides, Jewel had taken his stand, quite
arbitrarily it must be said, on a certain period in
the history of the Church, and he saw that he had
everything to lose if he abandoned that position.
He therefore stuck to his challenge, wisely for
himself, and defended it by arguments which,
if not inconsistent with the 1549 position, could not
in case of some national caprice be used against
it.   " Recipitur non includitur " is once more in
the forefront, and there follow the old rules prohibiting that the Sacrament should be kept to the
next day, or prescribing that it should be consumed by fire, by children, and so on.   He then
speaks of the ancient precedents of Reservation
in chests, baskets, napkins, and private houses as
being " abuses of the holy mysteries." Harding,
no doubt seeing that Jewel had conceded his position when he allowed that there was justifiable
Reservation in the early times, asks if he will
" agree to the keeping of the Sacrament " in some
better way, if the canopy and pyx is a bad way,
and doubtless anxious to press home that the

custom Jewel defended was not uniform from the beginning, but that the Church, as she had power to ordain, had power to change. Jewel, however, was too shrewd to give his opponent the necessary opening for a decisive blow, and answered that the only ancient way is that mentioned by St. Chrysostom, according to which "the Sacrament was to be received of the people at the Communion the next day, or in a very short time after," and in both kinds. " The manner in Græcia was during the time of Lent to consecrate only upon the Saturdays and Sundays, and yet, nevertheless, to communicate the same upon the other weekdays. For the end of this reservation in old times was not that the Sacrament should be adored, but that it should be received of the people; and specially that persons excommunicate, for whose sake it was reserved, being suddenly called out of this life, upon their repentance at all times might receive the Communion and depart with comport as the members of the Church of God." He goes on to declare that the pyx and canopy were more objectionable than the baskets and chests of early times because of the " danger of adoration " and of abuses which loomed so large in the imagination of the Reformers. It is the canopy, he says, "wherein all the question standeth, and to which his challenge is confined. The hanging of the Sacrament and the canopy, wherein the greatest danger stood, being removed, somewhat may be considered touching Reservation when it shall be thought necessary."

Now we are not concerned with Jewel's argument as such. His position was conceded by the Thirty-Nine Articles of his own Communion, which acknowledged that the Church had power to change her customs, and, indeed, Anglicanism made an appeal to " primitive times " on at least practice and custom, not to speak of matters of faith, only when this appeal fitted in with some preconceived notion of faith and practice which was neither primitive nor Catholic. The reason why we have entered into the unedifying literature of the period is to see what the Reformers' position was with regard to Communion of the sick quite apart from their attack on Catholicism, and it may thus be summed up—on all sides at least to quite recent times it has been much misunderstood and misrepresented because the literature has not been accurately studied. Prominent Reformers such as Cooper and Jewel have logically enough, considering the Edwardine and Elizabethan proceedings to which they owed their position, much to say about the Catholic practice of Reservation. At this we are not surprised, considering the extremely low notions of the Blessed Sacrament held by them, and the uniform attack made on Catholic teaching. On the other hand, it must be said historically that they say nothing against a Reservation for the purpose of Communion of the sick which does not extend over one day, and they look askance at any Reservation, even though they considered it an abuse, provided it was only for Communion of the sick. This is the position which must be conceded fairly to them, and a careful study of a wearisome literature confirms this conclusion. Illogical as their real attack was, it must not blind us historically to what they would allow, and with that alone we are at present concerned.

Passing, then, from the literature of controversy, it is necessary to return for a moment to *The Second Prayer Book*. We are struck not only by the omission of all directions about Reservation, but also by the omission of the direction to " celebrate," or rather by the substitution of the word " minister " for " celebrate." These are two technical Latin terms which somewhat naturally, owing to the recent dismissal of the old service books, passed into the Prayer Book in clear and definite distinction, and they are usually employed with accuracy by contemporary writers. To " celebrate " is the equivalent of to " consecrate," and to " minister " is the same as to " administer "—that is, to distribute Communion to those who receive. Thus Jewel, speaking of the Aquarii, says that they " did consecrate water and minister it to the people," while the adversaries " consecrate and minister unto the people no cup at all." Now, this is a typical passage. The term " minister " is also that regularly employed in all the discussion about Communion in one kind where there is no question of consecration. The change made therefore in 1552 cannot be passed over as unimportant and insignificant in dealing with the Anglican customs

of the period. The curate is directed not to consecrate any more than he is to reserve—he is to
minister. Elsewhere the term " celebration " is
not avoided in the Prayer Book of 1552, as " And
there shall be no celebration of the Lord's Supper,
except there be a good number to communicate
with the priest . . ." ; but it is cast out in the office
for " The Communion of the Sick." It would
seem an obvious deduction if we are to accept
consistency of usage to say that the curate is to
minister the Sacrament brought to the sick person
from some celebration ; but this view is full of
obvious difficulties. It might be contended, as
Sparrow did later, that the curate was thrown
back on the rubrics of the Prayer Book of 1549, but
there is the significant provision retained that the
curate, who now is told to " minister " instead of
to " celebrate," is still told to receive in the sick
man's house. This direction certainly seems contrary to the idea of a ministration of the reserved
Sacrament. It is possible that, along with the
growing ambiguity of the movement, " minister "
was chosen as an ambiguous term, and, indeed, it
is not too much to say that there seems to be a
studied ambiguity about all the directions for the
Communion of the sick, and the word "minister"
was beginning to be ambiguous. Thus Jewel,
whom we have quoted above as a user of accurate
and technical terms, also uses the word loosely
upon occasions as equivalent to *offerre, celebrare*—
to celebrate, consecrate—and in a passage already
quoted Cooper seems to be doing the same. It

may be said with confidence that the circumstances of Anglicanism about 1552 make it most
likely that such an ambiguous position about Communion of the sick was not only desirable but
almost necessary, and that the matter was left
thus after some serious debate which has not survived, if ever it were committed to paper. Some
were for no Communion at all, some for a celebration, some for a ministration, while even those who
most detested the Catholic custom were not in a
position, either in 1552 or 1559, to condemn the
method of 1549, though glad to see it quietly disappear. There is a note of comprehensiveness
for everything that was not definitely a Catholic
practice, and when the latter was eradicated completely from the new system, there seems to have
been a width and laxity characteristic of it. Such
arguments, however, prove no actual reservation
to have taken place; but they show that the Reformers left a loophole for it, with what intention it is at this distance impossible to decide.
Instances or more positive statements are needed
of actual reservation of the Sacrament for the
sick before the custom can be said to be established, or the rubrics interpreted to admit it, or
the practice of it justifiable in some form of which
we shall speak later in the Church of England.
Such evidence appears forthcoming.

First, we shall consider the *Reformatio
Legum*. When Parker revised the draft in 1561,
he found himself face to face with a statement

which seemed to close up the loophole left by the Prayer Book :

"Itaque nec in altum tolli sacramentum nec circumferri patimur, nec conservari, nec adorari."

Parker, knowing the Elizabeth policy was to comprehend as many non-Catholics within the Anglican Church as possible, added two phrases, so that it ran thus :

"Nec circumferri per agros patimur, nec conservari in crastinum, nec adorari."

The import of these changes is obvious : they make room for such a carrying of the Sacrament to the sick as had been allowed by the Prayer Book of 1549, and perhaps glanced at by that of 1552.

The Marian exiles, who returned to England under Elizabeth, hoping, as we have seen, that their influence would carry the English Reformers over to the side of their recent hosts, carried on a voluminous correspondence with those who had received them in Mary's reign, and in the same year, 1561, one of those numerous transactions took place by which they consulted the leaders of reform on the Continent as to the things that they, on their return to England, found open to question in the Anglican services and rules. Among these was Communion of the sick, and a question was forthwith propounded to Calvin by some unknown correspondent. His reply, dated August 12, 1561, runs thus :

"Cur cœnam ægrotis negandam esse non arbitrer multæ et graves causæ me impellunt. Video interea quam proclivis

in multos abusus sit lapsus quibus prudenter seduloque occur-
rendum esset. Nisi enim sit communicatio perperam deflec-
titur a sacra institutione Christi. Conveniat ergo aliquis
cœtus oportet ex cognitis familiaribus et vicinis ut fiat dis-
tributio ex mandato Christi. Deinde conjuncta sit actio cum
mysterii explicatione nec quicquam a communi ecclesiæ
ratione diversum.

"Promiscue etiam huc et illuc deferre valde pericolusum
est: atque hic difficillimum est cavere ne alios superstitio,
alios, ambitio et vana ostentatio ad petendum sollicitet,
Itaque judicio opus esset ac delectu ne quibus daretur nisi in
magno vitæ discrimine. Panem tanquam sacrum e templo
afferri præposterum est, gestari vero in pompa nullo modo
tolerabile."

In this letter there appears no question of a
celebration; granted that the sick are to be communicated, they must not receive alone, but the
distribution must be made to a company, with
some action and instruction agreeable to the
public service in a church. It would be dangerous
to carry the Sacrament to anyone indiscriminately
who for any reason asked for it; preposterous
to bring it from church as a sacred thing, and intolerable to carry it with any pomp. These
caveats of Calvin became apparently a source of
tradition, at least among a section of Anglicans.
They appear, for example, in an interesting
dialogue of 1617, which affords evidence that
Reservation, according to the method prescribed
in 1549, was still held not illegal. The book is
Hill's *Pathway to Prayer and Piety,* a celebrated
manual in several parts, written in 1613-1615,
which attained its eighth edition in 1629. The
author married Saravia's widow, and was himself Lecturer at St. Martin's-in-the-Fields, and

finally Rector of St. Bartholomew the Great. He died in 1623, and was buried in the latter church.

" *Q*. Is it lawful to prevent (*sic*) it privately? The answerer recalls how it was delivered privately to penitents on their death-bed in early days.

Q.   Did there any hurt come of this order?

A.   Very much. First, that if any were deadly sick the Eucharist must needs be administered to him. Secondly, that in Popery every parish priest must bring to every one of years, ready to die, this breaden god in a box with bell, book and cross ; and if any departed without receiving this journal he was not to be interred in Christian burial : if he did receive it he must needs in the end go to heaven.

Q.   Do all reformed Churches use this order privately to administer the Holy Communion?

A.   Some do not, and that for these reasons. [Then there follow ten reasons, five of which are connected with the fact of the administration being private ; three with abuses that come with the custom—' it caused public assemblies to be neglected,' ' it brought in a necessity of this Sacrament,' ' it caused some to neglect it in health because they were sure to have it in sickness.' The ninth refers to other means of comfort ; the tenth says that some of the Fathers objected to deferred Communion as they did to deferred Baptism.]

Q.   Do you well think that a minister may not administer this Sacrament to a sick or condemned man privately if he desire it?

A.   I dare not think it, and that for three reasons. [These may be shortly summarized : (*a*) I dare not deprive a man, (*b*) much less a faithful man, if those excommunicated have had the privilege ; (*c*) such a private Communion is a testimony of the receiver's conjunction with the whole Church.]

Q.   Are there no *caveats* to be given about this doctrine?

A.   Yes. 1. That it be sparingly used. 2. To such only as desire it. 3. That they be taught that it is not of necessity. 4. That some words of exhortation go with it. 5. That no pomp be used in carrying the Communion. 6. That the minister know it is not desired in superstition. 7. That it be done to such as cannot come. 8. That the party have a convenient company with him. 9. That if it may be done, the party then receive it privately when others so do in the congregation.   10. That in the administration the institution of Christ be observed, and all be done in remembrance of Christ's death.''

The procedure is outlined very clearly, and the connection with Calvin's *caveats* is obvious.   It has been impossible to trace the manner in which they exercised their influence, as Calvin's influence cannot have been wide at this period in England; all that can be said definitely is that his letter created a certain authority on the subject, which passed by some means into currency, and thus found its way into books of devotion or instruction.

We next turn to the Latin Prayer Book of 1560. I am conscious that everything connected with this book is thick with difficulties, and no solution to them seems probable at present.   The question of translation is perhaps one of the most difficult, as it was translated by Haddon, one of the most brilliant Latin scholars of the age.   It was prepared in the summer of 1559 and issued in 1560. It is a most difficult witness for our purpose.   It is clear that the grossest carelessness spoilt its preparation; the inaccuracies and misrepresentations of Aless's translation of *The First Prayer Book* of 1549 were retained, as well as sentences which had been correct enough as a translation of that book, but were entirely unlike the book of 1559.   On the other hand, there are places where a discrepancy exists between the English and Latin of 1559-1560 which cannot be the result of carelessness, but must have been made after due thought and deliberation. Thus the rubric before the Epistle agrees neither with the English of 1559 nor with the version by Aless, but a new translation of the rubric of 1549 is inserted in 1560. It can only be suggested that Haddon "was acting under the pressure of royal directions with some other purpose in view than accuracy of translation." And it is interesting, on the other hand, to note that the discrepancies between it and the authorized English Book of 1559 caused Anglicanism some anxious moments later in Elizabeth's reign at Cambridge. With regard to the Communion of the sick, the Latin Book of 1560 retains the rubrics of the previous Latin Book—that is, the rubrics of *The First Book of Common Prayer* of 1549 in a modified form, and thus countenances the administration of the reserved Sacrament. The question arises whether Haddon did this through carelessness or through pressure from above, or deliberately to fit in with prevailing custom. It is noticeable that the Edwardine Latin Book did not agree with the English Book of which it purported to be a translation. This is clear from the following parallel table :

And if the same day there be a celebration of the Holy Communion in the church, then shall the priest reserve at the open Communion so much of the Sacrament of the Body and Blood as shall serve the sick person, and so many	Quodsi contingat eodem die cœnam domini in ecclesia celebrari tunc sacerdos in cœna tantum Sacramenti servabit quantum sufficit ægroto.

as shall communicate with him, if there be any.

And so soon as he conveniently may, after the open Communion ended in the church, shall go and minister the same, first to those that are appointed to communicate with the sick (if there be any).

And last of all to the sick person himself.

But before the curate distribute . . . the appointed general confession must be made in the name of the communicants, the curate adding the absolution with the comfortable sentences of Scripture following in the open Communion. And after the Communion ended the Collect *Almighty and everlasting God, we most heartily thank Thee, etc.*

Et mox finita cœna (missa 1549) una cum aliquot ex his qui intersunt, ibit ad ægrotum et primo communicabit cum illis (eos 1549) qui assistunt ægroto (ægro 1549) et interfuerunt cœnæ.

Et postremo cum infirmo (infirmum 1549).

Sed primo fiat generalis confessio.

et absolutio

cum collecta ut supra est præscriptum.

The difference is that the sick man's friends are to be both at the church and sick-room, and thus furnish a link between the open and private Communion. Now, all this is reproduced in 1560, but with four minute alterations noted above, which certainly show that the passage was scrutinized and corrected. There was, then, some care taken, and the reproduction of the Reservation as defined in the Latin Book of 1549 was not altogether unnoticed. On the other hand, three of the four are mere corrections of grammar ; the fourth is the substitution of *cœna* for *missa,* and these are no proof that the intention and effect of the provisions were recognized. They seem more the corrections of a schoolmaster than of a liturgist.

If other signs of Reservation at this period were wanting, the evidence of such a dubious and unsatisfactory document as the Latin Book of 1560 would not go for much, but I think the evidence for such reservation in Elizabeth's time is stronger when we take it fully into account. It would seem to be evident that the retention of the rubrics of 1549 in 1560 may have been intentional, as being in accord with the doings of the day. It also must be remembered that Haddon's version had behind it royal authority, that Parker was ordered to regulate its use in the Province of Canterbury, and that there was issued a letter suggesting its employment in private and in the Universities. While it is impossible to explain the extraordinary divergencies between it and any English original, it cannot be said that it left the press without supervision and notice. It may be —and this is quite likely—that it was originally intended for the Pope's inspection.

It is not till later in Elizabeth's reign that the confusion between the words " minister " and " celebrate," of which we have noticed the beginning in Jewel and Cooper, was so well established that the order of the Elizabethan Book to minister the Communion was taken as an order to celebrate. This point is reached in Whitgift's controversy with Cartwright over *An Admonition to the Parliament*, which appeared in the middle of 1572. That celebrated Puritan manifesto objected

to private Communion as unscriptural. The
Answer pointed out that " it is ministered sometimes in private houses to sick persons " after
" the example of Christ, who ministered the
Supper in a private house." Throughout the
argument which follows, " to minister " is the
equivalent of " to celebrate," and the point at
issue is the private celebration. It is noticeable
that later on, when Cartwright spoke of the custom
of Justin Martyr's day as an abuse, Whitgift
objected to his dealing so cavalierly with ancient
authority; but yet he says : " Our Sacraments
now be more sincerely ministered than they were
in Justin's . . . time," and he is no doubt
speaking of the private celebration as being better
than the private administration, but the distinction is nowhere drawn, the two methods of
communicating the sick are given a common
defence, and Bucer's approval of Reservation for
the purpose is combined in the same plea as
Martyr's disapproval of that method and ad-
vocacy of the private celebration instead. Thence-
forth the direction " to minister " was taken as
a direction " to celebrate." The change was in
keeping with the general Reformation customs.
With very few Communions provided in the year—
three or four, or twelve at the most—the opportunities for " carrying the Communion " to the
sick were very few, and Communion of the Sick by
means of a private celebration became the regular
method in the somewhat rare cases where sick
Communion was demanded. Thus Andrewes, in

his *Answer* to Du Perron in 1629, says that no doubt the Sacrament was sent to the sick in primitive times, and " it is sure they made far greater account of the receiving it as their *viaticum* than some do now. But neither does this touch us who, at the desire of any that is in this case, may not refuse but go to him and minister it to him. So that Reservation needeth not; the intent is had without it." L'Estrange, in his *Alliance of Divine Offices,* first published in 1659, treats the existing direction to " minister " as being equivalent of the direction " to celebrate " in 1549, and brings the later provisions into line with the earlier ones, combining them without noting the alteration of terms.

It would appear also that the custom of Reservation had to a large extent become a dead letter in the Anglican Church when Hooker wrote the fifth book of his *Ecclesiastical Polity*. He deals at length on " the Eucharist seasonable on a deathbed," and, although the passage is of considerable length, it affords an illustration of theological opinion and Anglican custom towards the close of Elizabeth's reign. After referring to the fewness of communicants, he says : " There is in all the Scripture of God no one syllable which doth condemn communicating amongst the few, when the rest are departed from them. As for the last thing, which is our imparting this Sacrament privately to the sick, whereas there have been of old (they grant) two kinds of necessity wherein this Sacrament might be privately administered ;

of which two, the one being erroneously imagined, and the other (they say) continuing no longer in use, there remaineth unto us no necessity at all for which that custom should be retained. The falsely surmised necessity is that whereby some have thought all such excluded from possibility of salvation as did depart this life and never were made partakers of the Holy Eucharist. The other cause of necessity was, when men had fallen in time of persecution, and had afterwards repented them, but were not as yet received again unto the fellowship of this Communion, did at the hour of their death request it, that so they might rest with greater quietness and comfort of mind, being thereby assured of departure in unity of Christ's Church; which virtuous desire the Fathers did think it great impiety not to satisfy. This was Serapion's case of necessity. Serapion, a faithful aged person, and always of very upright life till fear of persecution in the end caused him to shrink back, after long sorrow for his scandalous offence and suit oftentimes made to be pardoned of the Church, fell at length into grievous sickness, and being ready to yield up the ghost was then more instant than ever before to receive the Sacrament. Which Sacrament was necessary in this case, not that Serapion had been deprived of everlasting life without it, but that his end was thereby to him made the more comfortable. And do we think that all cases of such necessity are clean vanished? Suppose that some have by mispersuasion lived in schism, withdrawn themselves from holy and public assemblies, hated the prayers and loathed the Sacraments of the Church, falsely presuming them to be fraught with impious and anti-Christian corruptions, which error the God of mercy and truth opening at length their eyes to see, they do not only repent them of the evil which they have done, but also in token thereof desire to receive comfort by that whereunto they have offered disgrace (which may be the case of many poor seduced souls even at this day); God forbid we should think that the Church doth sin in permitting the wounds of such to be supplied with that oil which this gracious Sacrament doth yield, and their bruised minds not only need but beg. There is nothing which the soul of man doth desire in that last hour so much as comfort against the natural terrors of death, and other scruples of conscience which commonly do then most trouble and perplex the weak; towards whom the very law of God doth exact at our hands all the helps that Christian lenity and indulgence can afford. Our general consolation departing this life is the hope of that glorious and blessed resurrection which the Apostle St. Paul nameth ἐξανάστασιν, to note that as all men should have their ἀνάστασιν and be raised again from the dead, so the just shall be taken up and exalted above the rest, whom the power of God doth raise but not exalt. This life and this resurrection of our Lord Jesus Christ is, for all men, as touching the sufficiency of that He hath done; but that which maketh us partakers thereof is our particular Communion with Christ; and this Sacrament a principal mean, as well to strengthen the bond, as to multiply in us the fruits of the same Communion. For which cause St. Cyprian termeth it ' a joyful solemnity of expedite and speedy resurrection '; Ignatius, ' a medicine which procureth immortality and preventeth death '; Irenæus, ' the nourishment of our bodies to eternal life, and their preservative from corruption.' Now, because that Sacrament, which all times we may receive unto this effect, is then most acceptable and most fruitful, when any special extraordinary occasion, nearly and presently urging, kindleth our desires towards it, their severity, who cleave unto that alone which is generally fit to be done, and so make all men's conditions alike, may add much affliction to divers and troubled and grieved minds, of whose particular estate particular respect being had, according to the charitable order of the Church wherein we live, there ensueth unto God that glory which His righteous saints, comforted in their great distresses, do yield, and unto them which have their reasonable petitions satisfied, the same contentment, tranquillity, and joy that others before them, by means of like satisfaction, have reaped, and wherein we all are or should be desirous finally to take our leave of the world, whensoever our own uncertain time of most assured departure shall come. Concerning therefore both prayers and Sacraments, together with our usual and received form of administering the same in the Church of England, let this much suffice."

Hooker uses the terms "imparting" and "privately administered," which, I think, are synonymous. He has been discussing the question of administering the Sacrament to few persons in public, and passes on to the question of Communion of the Sick, using the same term, so that we may conclude he intends a celebration, and in no way does he seem to imply that the Reservation of 1549 could be held to be part of the Anglican discipline. His reference to Serapion is not a reference to Reservation, but is brought forward as a support for the Communion of those who would return from error on their death-beds or in illness. Indeed, Hooker's whole dealings with the subject are taken up with the general usefulness of Communion in sickness, and not with methods of administering it, as there seems to have been a laxness about it in his day. It may, however, be justly concluded that, had he known that the method of Reservation allowed in 1549 was still legal (if not in actual use), he would have referred to it and defended it as he does " private administration." All along he has dealt with points of Puritan attack, and this would undoubtedly have been one had there been any recent tradition in its favour. But, as we have seen, the custom was dying out, and the terms " to celebrate " and "to minister " were becoming interchangeable. The nearest tradition would be some thirty years before, with which the malcontents among

Anglicans were not probably familiar. Indeed, it would seem from Hooker, that a tradition had grown up of the sick not being communicated at all, and he shelves the question of method, if ever he considered it apart from interpreting the words " to minister " as equivalent " to cele- brate " in the sick person's house, and turns to the much more prominent question before him. Finally, there remains the very troublesome task of reckoning with the well-known passage in Sparrow's *Rationale,* first published in 1655 or 1657. Its bearing on the Prayer Book of 1662 need not for the present purpose be taken into account; the only question is the evidence which it gives as to the previous Book. The following is the main passage as it was meant to stand in the first edition :

" The Rubric of the Communion of the Sick directs the priest to deliver the Communion to the sick, but does not there set down how much of the Communion Service shall be used at the delivery of the Communion to the sick ; and therefore it seems to me to refer to the former directions in time past. Now the direction formerly was this : *If the same day* (that the sick is to receive the Communion) *there be a celebration of the Holy Communion in the Church then shall the priest reserve . . . shall go and minister . . .* ; *but before the curate distribute the Holy Communion, the appointed General Con- fession . . . Absolution, with the comfortable sentences of Scripture following in the open Communion.* And after the Communion ended, *the Collect* is to be used which begins ' Almighty and everlasting God, we most heartily thank Thee,' etc. *But if the day* wherein the sick person is to receive the Communion *be not appointed for the open Communion in the Church, then upon convenient warning given, the curate shall go and visit the sick person afore noon.* And cutting off the form of the visitation at the Psalm 'In Thee, O Lord,' shall go straight to the Communion, *Rubr.* 3, *Com. of Sick ;*

that is, after he hath said the Collect, Epistle, and Gospel there
directed, he shall go to the Communion Service *K. Edw. VI.* 1."

Earlier in the section there is the statement :

" If the sick person desires it, the priest may communicate
him in his private house, if there be *a convenient place where*
the curate *may reverently minister.*"

Here there is no interpretation of the term
" minister." It is merely quoted from the rubric.
It is the other passage which must determine
Sparrow's view. As quoted above, it is little more
than a rehearsal, with unimportant additions and
omissions, of the rubrics of the Prayer Book of
1549. It is certainly noticeable that he quotes
the rubrics of *both* the Edwardine methods—the
Reservation as well as the celebration—when the
second would have been enough if he was con-
templating a celebration as the only method, and
the first he would more naturally have omitted
had he had any strong view that the method of
Reservation which he cited was no longer available. It is possible to say in reply, and to say
with some truth, that Sparrow had not the question of Reservation before him—he is only dealing
with the service to be used, and he quotes the two
precedents. But the answer is obvious and conclusive—that such a service as that prescribed in
the case of Reservation is quite inapplicable in
the other case, and, therefore, this could only
have been cited in view of Reservation.

But this passage has a history, and that history
is significant. The text of it as it actually stands
on the page of Sparrow's first edition is not as it

is above quoted, but contains an additional phrase which was there by mistake, and was noted for omission in the table of *errata*. The passage in its mistaken form had the following addition at the point marked in the quotation, already given, by an asterisk :

"and so proceeding in the Communion Service to the end . . . the end of the consecration and distribution."

It is not clear by what process this interpolation became inserted in the middle of the quotation of the rubric in the text of the first edition ; probably Sparrow wrote it because he had in his mind only the method of celebration for the sick. On reflection, however, he deleted the passage, and instead of trying illogically and unrubrically to force the Edwardine provision for Reservation into becoming a provision for celebration, he corrected himself and made it stand there in its proper colours as a rubric directing Reservation. The mistake and correction make it clear that the rubric was not carelessly but deliberately cited, and that Sparrow, with his eyes open, referred to both of the Edwardine alternatives as guides for want of better and more definite guidance. This being so, I think we must maintain that the citations have some bearing on the question of Reservation, and that Sparrow had the point in his mind when he referred to them. He may doubtless have begun with only the one of the alternative methods in his mind—a celebration in the sick person's house ; but by the time when he had

finished correcting the proofs and had made the
table at the end of the book,* and at the time when
he had sent his book forth to the world, he must
have been conscious that he was recommending
the possibility of Reservation as well by the correction which he had made. The strength of this
recommendation is not perhaps very great. To
Sparrow it was more than likely an abstract question, not a practical one ; a possibility under the
existing rubric and on previous precedent, rather
than a thing desirable at the time. But it comes
at the end of an historical enquiry as to the interpretation of the Elizabethan rubric as one last
evidence that, to say the least, Sparrow did not
consider it inconsistent with some sort of Reservation.

In 1661 came the last revision of the Prayer
Book and the alteration of the rubric at this point.
The curate was definitely directed "to celebrate,"
and so Sparrow's mistaken passage was allowed
to stand when the other *errata* were corrected, no
doubt on the ground that the new rubric justified
the interpolation. In the second and subsequent
editions the passage then stood substantially as
it had before. This was a very clumsy way of
dealing with the case. The whole line of comment
was out of date when the new book came out, and
any author seriously revising his book must have

* This has "How much of the Communion Service shall be
used at the delivery of the Communion to the sick in case
there had been that day a Communion (p. 304)." This entry
stands alone, as there is no corresponding one with regard to
the alternative method. This is significant.

rewritten the whole section.   But Sparrow never
did seriously revise the book in view of the new
Prayer Book, either in this respect or in others;
someone went through the *errata*, corrected the
rest, and refused to correct this passage, leaving
it a bungle (made worse by a gratuitous mistake
of the corrector, who slipped into the text the
word " immediately," which really formed part
of the *directions* in the table of *errata*, not part of
the correction to be made), but a bungle which no
doubt he thought more consonant with the new
rubrics than the amended passage would have
been.   It is, therefore, valueless as a commentary
on the rubric of 1662, but it must at least appear
in any historical survey of the previous rubrics
and their interpretation.

Having now surveyed the period from 1549 to
1661-62, is it possible to arrive at any conclusion
as to what the Reformers meant to be done in the
Anglican Church with regard to Communion of
the sick, and what were the customs prevailing
during this period ?   The years between the first
two books are clear enough—there were two
methods, both novel, but one at least bearing a
dim resemblance to the custom prevalent in England under the Catholic Church.   From 1552 on
there seems to have been a loophole for communicating the sick with the Sacrament reserved
from a public celebration, and this was perhaps
glanced at as having the authority of the 1549
book and Calvin behind it.   On the other hand,
it has been impossible after diligent search to

locate an actual instance of the custom. It is
difficult to say where such a record would be kept,
and it is also very unlikely that any written
account of it would be made. At the same time,
no mention of it takes place in the Visitation documents of the period, where we should expect to
find it were it in use, either admitting it as legal
or ordering it to be discontinued as inadmissible.
In "The Order of the Articles prescribed to
Ministers," however, which the new bench of
Bishops drew up as a temporary expedient in
1560-61, it is to be noted that the following article
was included :

"Sacramentum Eucharistiæ neque ex usu primitivæ
ecclesiæ aut servabatur, aut circumferebatur, vel elevabatur
ut adoraretur."

All idea of reserving the Sacrament regularly
for the sick is historically untrue to the Anglican
position. As we have seen, a case can be made
out for taking it straight from church to the house
of the sick person, but Reservation (however carefully guarded and hidden away), in order that
at any moment the Sacrament might be carried
to the sick, cannot claim from history to have any
place in the Anglican Church. We have no concern with the question of the *jus liturgicum* in the
Anglican episcopate, and, indeed, it is a point on
which they are largely disagreed among themselves.
How far they are justified in allowing continual
Reservation for the sick—quite apart, as they insist,
from adoration—is a matter for the Anglican
Communion at large to determine. But it may

be said that any notion of a " Sacrament chapel," or "tabernacle," or "receptacle shut off from the people," is quite contrary to the history of the Reformation in England, and that this is clear among countless conflicting practices and inconsistencies in other respects is one of the commonplaces of history. The normal method of communicating the sick from the time of Whitgift on was to celebrate in the sick person's house, and while it seems evident that there was a tradition in favour of the method of Reservation as allowed in 1549, it is almost certain that no instance is on record, and that, had it been done, it would have been denounced as contrary, not perhaps to a traditional legality, but certainly to the spirit of the Anglican Church.

INDEX

Acts of Parliament: Annates, 42, 44; Appeals, 45; Six Articles, 46, 65, 86; on Sacrament of Altar, 52; Chantries, 55; First Uniformity, 63, 88; Second Uniformity, 81, 116; Fasting and Abstinence, 103; Tithes, 115; annulling Catherine's divorce, declaring Mary legitimate, 126; Elizabethan Uniformity and Supremacy, 143; to secure Elizabeth on throne, 189, 190; against Catholics, 189; against Jesuits, etc., 191; against Non-Conformity, 192.

Admonition to Parliament, 256, 258, 259, 304.

Admonition to the People of England, Bishop Cooper's, 274.

Advertisements, The, issued by Parker, 241; scope of, *ibid.;* enforced, 244, 255, 267.

Aless, Latin translator of *The First Prayer Book,* 301.

Alexander VI. dies, 23.

Allen, Cardinal Wm.: Catholic champion, 184; placed in his historical setting, 186, 194; compared with English Cardinals of sixteenth century, 195; birth and education, 196; exile from England, 197; writes *Certain Brief Reasons,* *ibid.;* visits England and again goes into exile, *ibid.;* writes *Purgatory,* *ibid.;* visits Rome, 198; founds Douay, *ibid.;* writes *A Brief History,* etc., *ibid.;* moves college to Rheims, *ibid.;* character of his college, 199; connection with treasonable schemes, *ibid.;* influenced by Parsons, 200; created Cardinal, *ibid.;* continues to hope in political schemes, 201; writes *Life of Ed. Campion,* *ibid.;* writes *An Apology, Instructions Concerning Government of Seminaries, Defence of English Catholics,* 202; superintends translation of Scriptures, *ibid.;* Analyses of his *Defence,* 203, 212; *Defence* answered by Bilson, 221.

Alley, Bishop, 136.

Alliance of Divine Offices, L'Estrange's, 306.

All Souls' College, Oxford, organs removed in 1549 from, 93.

Altars, history of, under Edward VI., 94-95.

Alva, Duke of, 210, 219.

Andrewes, Bishop, *Answer* of 306.

Angelus Bell, history of, 97.

Answer for the Times to the Examination, etc., 247.

Answer to du Perron, of Bishop Andrewes, 306.

318

DATE DUE